W[
Autobiogr

MW00951586

By Judy Apicella
Copyright 2018

Table of Contents

CHAPTER ONE

ARE YOU A GOOD WITCH OR A BAD WITCH?

I love those books where the writer creates vibrant images that fill your mind through the exquisite use of language. Where they speak of sunlight flowing through the trees as it's shining rays gently reflect off of the morning dew, creating rainbows which say good morning to the world, and you truly feel it. Sadly though, I am not that kind of writer. I actually have never thought of myself as a writer, although I would have loved to because I love to read. I am a mom, a wife, an herbalist, Reiki Master, Healer, Yoga Teacher, Alpaca Farmer and in the Strega Nonna sense, a witch. I have a wonderful son, Nico and a husband named Salvatore and many beautiful people and animals in my life. I have been blessed to gain other loving beings through my life, one being Diana who became like a daughter to me and Jen Jen who also became a like another daughter and part of our family. I am writing this book for them so that someday when I transcend to another realm, they will know my mind. Perhaps it will help them to realize my eternal presence with them. Perhaps it will help them understand my daily thoughts, in this realm, about life, the earth, the universe, herbs, religion, the Divine One. All I know is that I must write it for them. I must write it for me, from my heart and just let it pour out, all the crazy stuff, the sane stuff and everything in between.

I grew up in a family where love was always in abundance. It was not something I even thought about, I just always knew that I was loved dearly by my mom and dad. My mother, Rachel was Catholic and my father, Jordan was Jewish, and we celebrated all of the holidays of both faiths. My mom feared that in that my dad was not Catholic he would not be in the same afterlife as she would be, which lead me on my path, in so many ways. What is the afterlife, what is reality?

I was a happy child, really happy. I loved life, animals, and the earth. My mom once worried that I was too happy. What happens when she gets older and "life" happens, things that are not so happy, will it crush her, she pondered. Well, a lot of those "life moments" did happen but I did not let them get me, for life is to get, to live and dive into not to be gotten by. I wanted to see what was beyond matter. What was my spirit? What was this energy that connects us all? I wanted to find the magic in life. I wanted to discover what was beneath all this "stuff." Throughout my life there were magical moments, angelic moments, earthly moments, and sometimes even scary moments but it wasn't until I was in college that I was first called a Witch.

Now I have grown to embrace the term but then it was new to me, although not in an offensive way. I will never forget, Kitty, who lived two doors down from me in my college dorm, looking at me with her head slightly tilted downward and her large, brown eyes piercing through me as she calmly said, "Do you know you are a witch?" I remember my mouth dropping open and I felt that the moment seemed to last for an eternity as I, in turn, stared back, getting sucked into those big brown orbs and feeling like I was shot out of reality. "Oh yes, you have powers," she continued. What kind of powers was she talking about? I wondered. Then I thought, we all have powers, we are all as powerful as we want to be, but I said nothing. As much as I thought she was nuts I was also intrigued, I mean wouldn't you be if someone told you that you were a witch? Weren't witches bad and scary? I walked away from Kitty feeling strange.

I didn't tell anyone except my boyfriend, at the time, Bobby Katsch who had a way of finding humor in everything. He thought this was the funniest thing on the planet and ran around for five minutes laughing and making flicking gestures in the air with his fingers repeating, "are you a good witch or a bad witch," like in the Wizard of Oz. But I jump ahead. Back to my childhood.

CHAPTER 2

ANGELS AND GUIDES

My mom would often tell me the story about her guardian angel. It was an important part of her life and her energy, and she wanted me to understand it and remember it. Sometimes, when we are young, we think our moms are telling "that story again" or "that" idea again, not fully understanding that they are trying to imprint something on us in hopes of giving us a foundation that is strong and, in this case, soulful. Her "guardian angel" came to her right after my sister was born in 1960. It was the first time my mom went out with her newborn child, and she was nervous. There is no school for how to be a mom, no guidebook. Some books may proclaim they do so, but I don't think most people feel "I got this, no problem." You have a new life for which you are responsible, a life that is part of you. It is no small responsibility, but you try your best and know that your love will guide the way.

My mom was feeling all of these things as she headed to Howard Johnson's, a little local restaurant, with my dad. She said she kept praying for guidance. It was a sunny winter day in March. The snow had been accumulating over the week and was piled high. Another reason she wanted to go out. The restaurant was on, what you would call, a busy street, for a little town like Poughkeepsie, New York. My mom looked at my dad as he parked the car and smiled at her. My dad had a great smile, it made you feel warm and loved. He really looked at you and made you feel you were being looked at and cared about. My mom felt love pour over her, she felt the light become a little brighter. She wrapped my sister tighter in the blanket and got out of the car. Her gaze fixed immediately on an old man that was walking down the street. He drew her attention, like a magnet. He had a very long white beard and long white hair. He wore a brown leather jacket and carried a wooden cane, but he did not use it for he walked perfectly upright. He was mesmerizing. By now my dad had walked around the car to meet her. She looked at my dad and then they both looked down because right at their feet was a pure white dove staring up at them. The dove was as white as the snow. White doves were not common in Poughkeepsie and my mom wondered where she came from and why she was hanging out in a Howard Johnson's parking lot on a cold winter day. She looked back up at the road and the man had disappeared, but there was nowhere he could have gone. It was an open road, and you could see about a mile ahead. Perplexed she looked back down, and the dove was gone. She turned to my dad and felt an overwhelming peace. A secure sense that everything was going to be alright.

That story had a big imprint on me, for I never doubted the presence of angels or spirit guides. I always carried that story with me and still do. My mom and I were very close, and my dad and I were very close. We shared our thoughts, our love, and our lives. Many years later when I was in my first year of college I went home for Thanksgiving and my dad sat me down and told me that my mom had cancer and was in the hospital. I remember the look on his face, I will never forget it as he told me she did not have long. Despair does not even begin to convey how I felt. We sat in silence not knowing how to prepare for what was ahead. My thoughts of angels and spirit guides temporarily disappeared as did her story. I just felt lost.

The next month I spent most of my time, in the hospital room with her, only popping back to school for a necessary spurt. I wanted to be there with her, for her. I remember when I got to the hospital, she was very calm, very serene and I wondered what kind of state she was in. How could she be so calm? Was it the drugs? It was not. It was something else. I spent day after day with her so I could grasp as many moments as possible. I felt I could not even attempt to repay an ounce of all she had given to me, of all the times she had been there for me, and I knew she did not want me to repay anything. She was an amazing mom.

When I was around five years old, I asked my mom why people were afraid of death if they were going to "heaven?" Why be sad if you were going somewhere better than this and you would be with Jesus? Now I was sure about Jesus because I saw him in my room, a lot, when I was young. He just stood there, peaceful, calm, and glowing. It kind of freaked my mom out, especially the time we went to light a candle in church and no one else was there and I started answering someone. She asked who I was talking to. "Jesus!" I said, matter of factly. My mom was a little stunned. She told me that we fear death because we are human and humans often forget what is deeper, what is of the spirit, where we came from and where we are to return to. Well, when my mom was in the hospital, I forgot too. All I saw was my mom dying and I was scared, but why wasn't she? What was she feeling and touching?

One day she did indeed get scared, and she became very agitated. She wanted to leave the hospital, she didn't want "this", couldn't take it. As she got more and more upset my dad and I were feeling her fear and trying to calm her, as well as keep calm ourselves. I wanted to scream and get her out of the hospital. In addition to the hospital care, my dad had hired a 24-hour nurse to always be with her. He was telling the nurse that it might be best to take my mom home. She said she would see what she could do. Then suddenly time seemed to pause. We all stopped and turned to the window. It was a cold and blustery winter day in December. The sky was dark. We looked out at nine doves in a perfect V formation. They flew up to her window, turned and flew away. They were all silver-grey except for the lead dove who was pure white. Something happened at that moment. Something shifted. The fear and anxiety melted away. We all felt it, we were calm. My mom decided to stay in the hospital because she felt she needed the care they were giving her and since my dad and I were there most of the time, anyway, it was a place she felt comfortable. The whole world seemed to change after that.

My dad went home to get some much-needed rest and I sat down next to the nurse who had a calm, peaceful energy. She looked at me and nodded. After a while she asked me what I thought about what had just occurred, but I could not put my feelings into words. How do you describe an experience you can't even comprehend? She told me she had been a nurse for many years, caring for those who were passing on. "Passing on" were the words she used, for she said life was a passage. She had experienced many amazing stories where the patient truly felt and saw their loved ones, who had gone before, and she also felt their presence. One time she was with a man who told her he was afraid to die but was in extreme pain and didn't want to live either. He was conflicted and scared. She told him to open up to what was around him. To breath and find peace and see what others had seen. She advised him to keep his mind opened to who was coming to help him along the next part of his path. He took a deep breath and paused, he then stared into space and smiled. He told her that his brother was there, he knew he had come to get him, and he was now ready to go and with a whoosh was gone. She told me to be aware, aware of more than what I would normally see, to also open to those who would come to help. I told her I would try and thought of the doves.

A few nights later, my mom was talking to someone. She was clearly, having a back-and-forth conversation. It was not me or the nurse that she spoke to, so when she was done, I asked who she was speaking with. She told me it was her mom and dad, both of whom had died before I ever met them. I tried to feel them but could not connect, although I knew she truly did. That night I woke up with a jolt, in the middle of the night. I was in the hospital bed next to her. The nurse had stepped out and my mom was asleep. I smelled a strange but wonderful old-fashioned perfume and pipe smoke. I ran out into the hall to see who was there but there was no one. I ran around the circular hallway, and all was quiet. The next morning, I told my mom and she said it was her parents, her dad Corinto and her mom Marianna. She then told me that we had to talk. She began saying, what I thought were, strange things at the time. She told me that I would be the only one in the room when she "went" and wanted me to know that she would always be with me, that this (she pointed to her body) was matter but her soul would always be present and always be there. She told me that my Great Aunt Palma would start screaming over the body but that I should tell her that the body was a shell. That I should remind her that the soul was free and forever present. I thought maybe she was a little delirious from the pain medication, but I listened because somehow, deep inside, this was making sense. She told me one of my aunts would come to our house with lots of food and try to "take me" but that I needed to be strong and say no. I thought, I am 19 years old, who would try to take me. She told me to remember the story of THE

LITTLE PRINCE and again stressed that she would always be with me and that I needed to remember her when I looked at the stars.

My mom's dad Corinto had died on December 29th in 1963 and my dad told me that my mom was waiting to go on that day. I don't know if he felt it or if she had told him. When the morning of December 28th arrived, I awoke, in the hospital bed next to hers to a huge snowstorm with blustering winds and a lot of beautiful snow falling in giant flakes. The nurse said she was worried about the roads and wanted to get home and asked if I minded her leaving a few minutes early, in that the other nurse would arrive any minute. I told her to go. Just after she exited, the phone rang, and it was the other nurse. She was caught in the snow and would be late. I turned to my mom with a Humphrey Bogart smile and said "it's just you and me kid..." but then I stopped myself short. I was the only one in the room with her, no 24-hour nurse. She looked at me with the purest most serene expression and said, "they told me I had to go a day early." I did not question who "they" were, for more pressing things took over. I knew it was time. She asked me to sing the Beatles song that she liked so I started singing "LET IT BE."

I was holding her hand, sitting next to her and she just stopped breathing. I looked at her and I cannot explain why, at this time in my life, I was COMPELLED to go to the picture window, but I didn't question that either, I just went. I looked down and walking below her window was an old man with a long white beard, long white hair and a brown leather jacket. He had a wooden cane but was not using it for he was walking upright. I felt like I was in a dream. I felt a sense of peace.

She had sent me her angel.

Sure enough, at the wake my Aunt Palma walked over to the casket and started screaming "OH DIO! Dio, Rachel! "I did as my mom requested and told her to stop yelling, that my mom wanted her to know that the body was a shell, and she knew that my mom was still with us in spirit. It was like a switch went on in her brain and she snapped her head and said "ok" and calmly knelt. Then my other aunt came to the house. She had been at her vacation home and had a lot of food. She was stuffing it in the freezer and turned to me and said, "I know you and your sister are older but if you want, we could adopt you and take care of you." She was being nice, but she was the last person I would want to "take care" of me and I found it insulting to me and my dad. Then I remembered what my mom said, and I calmly told her that we were fine, but thank you.

A few nights later I awoke and felt my mom in the room with me. I knew if I opened my eyes, I would see her. At this point in my journey, I was not ready for that, so I thanked her for coming but asked her to not be materially visible to me. I felt, almost a change in channels and then opened my eyes. I knew she was there but did not actually see her. At the time, that was what I was comfortable with. I did and still do always feel my mom.

CHAPTER 3

FIRE

Once back at Manhattanville College, I must say it was difficult, I was trying to feel her but was also overwhelmed with grief. I had a friend who told me to meditate by looking into a candle flame. She talked me through the meditation, and I got lost, at some point, in the depth of the flame and no longer heard what she was saying. It was like I was one with the fire and it was speaking to me. I was surely no longer in the same reality. Fire had always been a powerful energy for me. I loved to watch the fire in the fireplace at my dad's house and could sit there for hours. In this flame I began to feel my mom's presence and it was strong, comforting and very real. I was with her. When I came back, I looked out the window and saw the most beautiful sunset I had ever seen in my life. It was red and orange like the candle flame and it filled the sky. Glorious does not describe it. I told my friend my mom had sent the sunset for I knew she had.

The next day I was walking down the hall and ran into Kitty, who once again stared at me with those big brown eyes and asked me if anything was happening, not like "what's up" but really asking if anything was happened. I felt like she was staring right through me. I was not unnerved but it did make me pause. I told her nothing was happening. She humphed like, yeah, and invited me into her room. Whenever I was in Kitty's room we never sat, we always stood. I don't know why but in hindsight maybe it was because I was preparing to run if I felt the need, even though I began to really like Kitty, in a not totally comfortable sort of way. She was intriguing and a little crazy. She told me that she was a witch. So I asked "aren't witches bad?" "Not all of them," was her reply. She told me there were dark witches and white witches and she, of course, was a white witch. I was still intrigued. I remember she showed me a black book that had symbols in it that were foreign to me at the time. In hindsight perhaps they were alchemical symbols but I cannot be sure. I remember she read me a kind of spell. I have to admit, I thought all this was pretty cool but having been raised by a mother who was very Catholic and a father who was Jewish I felt that this was somehow forbidden, but I stayed, none the less. Kitty said she would teach me things, so I listened to the words she read. There was nothing bad in what she was telling me, so I was not sure if I thought Kitty was scary because of my fears or because there was something darker there. I cannot even tell you to this day. In my third year of college some strange things began to occur. I moved into a suite with 4 other girls, 3 of which were good friends of mine. I had my own small bedroom, and we had a common living room and bathroom. In the winter I got Mononucleosis and was feeling really tired and wanted to stay in bed a lot. I did not have the positive energy of my mom; I was feeling sick and sad. I was an art and dance major and was asked by one of my painting teachers to do a self-portrait. I often wore these big blue sunglasses, that were my moms, and I decided to keep them on as I stared in the mirror and painted my image. Upon completion I showed it to my teacher for review. He looked at it and did not speak for a full minute, then I got a "WOW," but not wow like you are so awesome, more like "Wow, are you sure you are ok?" I did not understand. I looked at my painting and thought, what's the big deal, it's me. It's how I feel. I wondered why was he looking at me like that? I brought the painting back to my friend Denise and asked her if she liked it. She told me it was pretty scary and asked if I needed to talk. I looked at my portrait and loved the colors, dark purple and blue with a hint of light blue and purple for highlights. I had done a good job on the face and even the hair looked real. Denise said she was not talking about technique.

I moved on in my art class to begin making masks for my senior project which was to combine art and dance. I chose to choreograph a dance and make masks for the other performers. I loved masks and wrote a paper about the use of them in Kabuki and the great German choreographer, Mary Wigman. I used plaster gauze as a base, then I used wire and beads as extensions and later painted them and attached some material. To make the base I needed a face and did not want to use my own so one of my art teachers gave me a bust of Caesar. I worked in the art studio until they locked it up for the night, then I would bring Caesar back to my room to work more. I carried the bust around with me to dinner and plopped it on the table and ate with Caesar.

One night I went back to my dorm suite, and everyone was asleep, I had been walking in the starlight, gazing, thinking for longer than I realized. When I entered the living room of my suite, I felt a strange energy and I froze. All was dark and quiet. I heard a ratting noise and looked over to see the doorknob of my roommate's door shaking and jiggling. I knew my roommate was sleeping and would not do something like that. I felt a fear surge through me, and I did not know what was happening. I just stared and it seemed to shake all the more, I almost felt like I was being pulled down. Then I started to pray. The next morning, I asked my roommate if she had woken up in the night to jiggle her doorknob. She laughed and then realized I was serious and said "no." I did not feel like sharing what had happened for I did not even know what happened myself. I made sure I got back to my suite when everyone was still awake after that.

A couple of weeks later, I was still trying to forget what had happened. I had a friend who did something that really annoyed me, but I was not the type to get angry or yell, so I decided a prank would be in line. That was weird because I was not into pranks, at all, though I proceeded. I got a couple of friends together and we taped newspaper all over his door. He was inside sleeping, so the joke was, when he woke up, he would open the door to see the newspaper and have to rip through it to get out. Not really funny, not really me, but common at college in those days. It was not a mean joke for it was just newspaper, easy to push through. My friends and I got done taping the door and as we were walking away, we paused to see if he might come out soon. We waited 5 minutes and talked, and I finally admitted that I was, indeed, angry. As I felt the anger move through me one of my friends turned and screamed. As I looked up, I saw that the newspaper, which was about 20 feet from us, was now ablaze in fire. I don't even remember how we put it out, I think someone ran and got towels to hit it with. There was a lot of commotion. We got my friend safely out of his room, but he was freaking out. I asked him why he had lit the paper on fire. "ME!" He exclaimed. "Well, how did it start then?" Everyone looked at me and told me that it was me. I was totally shocked. "I didn't start the fire,' I said, "you were there, I wasn't even near the door." "I know," said one of my friends, "but you got angry." "How can you start a fire 20 feet away with anger?" I asked but no one replied.

Later Kitty came to fetch me and bring me to her room. After she closed the door, she stared at me with the head tilt and the big eyes and said "I heard you started a fire." I said, "I did not start a fire, where did you hear that?" She said, "Everyone knows you started it." "EVERYONE?!" I exclaimed, "I wasn't even near the door, I didn't even have a match…." "I know," she said. "I told you, you have powers. Were you angry?"

Well, at that point Kitty went from being amusing to very upsetting. Now she was really annoying me, and I had enough. I started to get angry with her and the next thing I knew the garbage can that was 5 feet away from us went up in flames. I screamed and Kitty jumped back and then ran for some water. She was not so calm at this point and asked why I did that to her, she said she was trying to help. I had fallen through the wormhole. "What!?" I yelled. Kitty said that I had better learn about my powers, my emotions right now were "Firing up," Ha, ha, Kitty. I wanted to run from her room but also knew now that there was some truth to what she was trying to convey to me and I needed to know more. Was she causing this, I thought, had Kitty somehow unleashed an energy in me? She told me that I had to first realize and acknowledge what was happening, face it and control it. I did not even think this was real, how could I control it? I ran to the great lawn and sat under the statue of the Sacred Heart of Jesus and prayed for a very long while.

I started to go to church every day after that, but I felt a darkness around me. A darkness that I couldn't understand. I was later told that when you open to the spirit world, to other realms, you have to be really careful and only open to good, to the light. When I opened with my mom it was all good, but after when I let sorrow take over, I allowed another energy to enter. I know now that when you open without protecting yourself, that is what you are doing, opening to whatever is out there and trust me, there is good and light and love in abundance but there is also darkness and things that are definitely not of the light. But, as I said, I did not know this at the time. I had to learn how to protect myself and I did it the hard way.

As I sat, I tried to think about things in my life that perhaps I had not faced before. Did I ever start a fire before? I did not recall ever doing so but then again, I did not think I had done so this time either. Other strange memories did come back to me though. Witchy memories? I remembered a time when I was very young and there was this book that was my sisters. It was about this little ballerina and had beautiful illustrations. My sister and I loved ballet which we studied with Mrs. Esser on the next street over. My sister began going through some "stuff" and stopped dancing. The next year I got the part of Snow White in the ballet.

My sister seemed angry with me and with my mom and I was young and did not understand what was happening to her. My mom said that it would be best to pack the book away and put it in the attic. We put it in a box with some other books we had grown out of and forgot about it. Later that year my mom and I were up talking, in the playroom, until the wee hours of the morning. We talked of many things, one of them was about my cat Rufus Butterworth.

He was a beautiful red tabby cat who had died about a month before and I was still having a tough time dealing with it. He and I were very connected, and he had died in my arms with a scream. It was tearing at me. My mom told me that I had been there for him and had given him love. Why did he scream like that, I wondered? She did not know. She did tell me that she had to admit that Rufus was a very "different" kind of cat. That he had a kind of human quality or perhaps otherworldly quality about him. We finally fell asleep on our prospective couches, and both awoke at 3 am. I told her that I had just had a terrible nightmare. "I saw a witch-like, old haggard woman standing…., " I began…."on the rug," my mom finished. "Yes," I said. I did not have to ask for I knew she saw her too. "Then there was this cat, that was grey and was ……., I said…. "Sitting right there," my mom once again finished, as she pointed to the exact spot, I had seen the cat. She said it was hissing and I nodded yes. We talked ourselves into believing that we had the same dream but neither of us were convinced. We said some prayers and when we could not keep our eyes open any longer, we fell asleep. They next morning there were paw prints all over the mirror. I, myself had cleaned it with Windex every week and they had not been there. What was happening!?

The next day my mom felt that we should throw out the ballet book, although I did not know why. We went upstairs and opened the box. When I opened the book, all of the pages were scratched and ripped like a cat had shredded them. The other books were fine. We took the box and brought it to the garbage can which was on the street, for it was garbage pick-up day, and threw it in. The next morning when my dad went to bring the garbage cans back down the driveway, he told us the book was on the street. I was scared.

I remember after that I was often in a half wake, half sleep state and felt something or someone walking their hands up my body. I could not pull myself out of this state. We did a lot of praying and healing and I think it went away for a while. A few years later, the family stayed up late to watch the Oscars. Rocky had won for best picture. I went to bed at midnight and a minute after I closed my eyes I felt hands walking up my legs, up my body, but I was wide awake, I only had my eyes closed now. I screamed so loud and pulled my head under the pillow, when I heard my sister cry. I opened my eyes to see her over me. Then I understood it was her, I did not think it had been her the other nights, but it was her that night. Why was she walking her hands up me like that? Something broke between us that evening although it was not great prior to that.

As I sat on the quad, staring at the statue of Jesus, pondering my past, I knew something dark had entered. My friend Carol came by, and I told her I wanted to go home to see my dad for the weekend and asked if she wanted to come. She said yes and off we went. We had a nice meal with my dad and then went to sleep in my bedroom. I slept in my single bed and Carol slept happily on the floor on a small foam mattress my dad had set out. In the morning she looked at me with an odd expression. She then asked why Bobby, my boyfriend, had come over during the night. "BOBBY!?" I asked. No he was not there, why did she think that? She said that someone big and muscular, like Bobby, had stepped over her during the night and was leaning over me, staring at me. She said it was not my dad and she assumed it was Bobby. She felt a little weird, so she rolled over and went back to sleep. I felt thrown into the wormhole again. What was she talking about? I asked her over and over if she was sure! Was she really awake? She seemed very sure.

CHAPTER 4

STYGIAN BATTLE

We headed back to school, and I started work again on my senior project which would culminate in a concert. I decided my piece would be called Stygian Battle, (which means very dark or relating to the River Styx). It was a battle of good against evil. I had 6 dancers that were dressed in black and were wearing the masks that I had now completed. I took slide photos of them and would flash the images on the wall throughout the performance.

The dancers held painted hula-hoops which they used as magical tools to entice me. I was dressed in white and had no mask. The piece started with me on stage and them at the back of the theater, creeping through the audience. This was pre-Phantom of the Opera. I was unaware of their presence at first but as they drew closer, I became drawn to them, and they came to the stage and surrounded me. At times they would pull me with the hoops and almost cast a spell on me, capturing me. I began to crawl through their hoops, quite literally. At other times I would get away. I had slides of the various masks flashing on the back wall of the stage, giving an eerie feel. One day at rehearsal I was crawling through the hoops, and I heard a clunk. I looked down and the big gold crucifix that I wore around my neck, from my mom, was bent like a cursive t and was laying on the ground. We all stared at the impossible bend in the strong metal which had moved with no impact whatsoever. My friend Denise, remarked "this is not good!" I ended rehearsal holding the cross and pushing it with my fingers to try to reshape it but the metal was too strong.

I did a preview of my project for a local corporation who was hosting an event with some Japanese partners. After the show we had a gathering so I could hear their comments. They all said they loved it, it was very creative and inventive but sad that evil got me in the end. "No," I said, "evil did not get me, I got away." All the businessmen looked at me and said, "NO YOU DIDN'T." What reality was I in? Definitely my own. I really thought my story was a fight between good and evil in which I had won. Apparently, I was the only one who did not think that evil had conquered. I had to fix this, I had to re-choreograph and I also had to fix my life.

As I entered my senior year, I requested a single room. Everyone said that would not happen, there were very few single rooms in the senior dorm. I got a letter in August stating that I had been approved for a single, but it was in the Freshman dorm. There were only two Singles available there and one was mine if I wanted it. I was happy about this. I thought I needed some time alone to soul search. It was a small room. As I was moving my things in, I saw Kitty. She told me that she was in the room down the hall that was the exact mirror of mine. I was happy to have her nearby. I went to visit her, and she had her room decorated with a crystal ball on her desk and beautiful scarves everywhere. She had a lamp with beads on it that was covered with material. I guess I had avoided her for a while, so I sat with her to catch up. She told me she was practicing magic and felt strong. We talked for a while, and I went back to my room. Later that night someone knocked on my door, I opened it to see a young man that I did not know. He said "Oh, hi, I did not want to disturb you. I just wanted to see who got the room. Are you going to stay here or are you going to move?" I told him I would stay and did not know why he was asking me this. He said, "this is the room with the Devil." "The Devil!" I exclaimed. He then pointed to a high closet. I needed to stand on a chair to open it and when I did, I almost fell off the chair. There, on the inside of the cabinet door was the head of the devil, painted in white. He raised his eyebrow and again asked if I was going to stay and then left.

I ran to my dear friend and savior, Totsy. She took me to the hardware store, and we got some paint thinner. I went back to my room, but it would not come off. I took one of my mom's rosary beads and strung it over the top of the door of the cabinet, over the face of the devil and went to sit down on my bed. A few minutes later the rosary shattered, and beads flew all over the place. I don't know if you ever saw rosary beads but that is close to impossible. They are not strung together on one cord; each bead is separated by metal links. I ran to Totsy. I told her that I didn't feel right. She said she was really worried about me. I told her I wanted to meditate. She said she didn't think that was a very good idea at that moment in time. I got angry and insisted, again, angry and insisting is showing up here but was not really me. I was more hippy calm, but there it was again. She acquiesced and we began to meditate with a candle. We were staring into the flame, but it was not like the time after my mom died. Things got dark, really dark, and I heard Totsy yell "STOP!" I felt like I heard her from far away. We had to pray, she demanded. I felt confused and started to say the OUR FATHER with her, which I said every day in church, but a couple of lines in, I could not remember the words. She got very upset and kept telling me that I knew this prayer and helped me say it, forced me to say it. I felt something break as I did. She then called her sister who was a psychic and worked for the psychic phone network. I thought, you have got to be kidding me. She said her sister could, hopefully, give us some guidance. She said that although I may think of the psychic network as silly her sister really knew things that other people did not and could tell people things about their lives and future which were all true. I agreed to the call. Her sister did wind up helping me and really did know things. She said that I had to watch what I opened to and only open to the light and be very conscious of what I was doing. I can't say it was an easy or short journey. I spent a lot of time with Jesus and the Sacred Heart statue. I had to start a new journey, a different one. Opening to - only the Divine.

I let a lot of these energies and feelings come through in my art. I did a pen and ink drawing of fairies in a tree which I washed with watercolors after. I felt I had to paint something fun, fantasy filled, light, not knowing in my later years I would really believe that fairies exist. I felt happy when I looked at the painting and showed my art teacher, who threw it on the table and said he did not like it. He said that life was not all happy, fairies and fantasy.

I did not even reply for if I had shared what life was at that point, it would have been too much to bear, so I said, "ok" and I painted another painting. In this one there was a background of dark green leaves with beautiful masks coming through the leaves, they were not even really masks for they were faces that had pointed heads. I painted them in metallic colors, beautiful colors, copper, gold, deep ruby. I thought it was magnificent, everyone agreed yet it was still scary. I felt that the painting was getting rid of something, healing it. Little by little, step by step I was learning how to break away from the darkness and reunite with the light.

My dad was my strongest supporter, patiently dealing with all I was going through and standing firm, like a rock, in my life. His father had been an artist. He watched the change in my work, quietly. I felt his strength and love and it helped me to step into the light. When I did the final presentation of my senior project it was clear that I got away from evil, good had overcome.

I began to feel like everything was breaking apart, in order to rebuild. Totsy told me it was like the Tower in the Tarot Cards. The tower represents the energy of a time when we need to go into, what we think is our structure, our foundation, and let it go, let it explode so we can let in new energies and start another path. I did a pen and ink of that feeling.

My paintings and my life began to shift. They also seemed to take on a life of their own that was more elemental. I painted earth people who seemed to flow out of the earth, fire people who were coming out of the flames and dancing and an elemental flowing dancer. I was mastering the elemental energies and my fire-starting capabilities. I decided to paint water people who were part of a wave. It was funny because I did not really complete this or feel the same about it as I did the earth and fire people. I slowly began to feel the water energy helping me to flow and I needed to embrace that and flow with positive change and I felt one with the earth. I was given an assignment to take a Master Artist and place something of my own in it. I chose a crystal ball, which seemed to open up seeing into my future.

When I began my next piece, I felt like I had drifted somewhere else, perhaps into another reality. I did not even remember drawing it. It was like I woke up in front of a giant pad with a pencil in hand and there was this image in front of me. It was of a woman with an ankh around her neck. She was wearing a robe and a headdress. Her arm was stretched up to the sky and she was standing in front of the Sphinx.

I found an Ankh necklace which I bought for myself and wore it every day along with my feather earrings. When my drawing was complete, I hung it on the wall in my room, right next to my favorite poster of Jesus telling the children to come to him and a Rolling Stones poster. Totsy said my drawing looked like The Magician from the Tarot. Every time I would look at her, I felt like it was me. I felt strong. I could feel the magic of EGYPT and all her mysteries around me. It was a powerful feeling. I loved that picture, and I loved my ankh. I thought it was the Magician guiding me. I would not know how very significant that image would be to me until many years later.

CHAPTER 5

A GIANT LEAP

The next part of my journey would be to step out into the working world, for it was almost time for graduation. I had been through so much but felt I had climbed a mountain peak of life and was, for now, at the summit. What the next climb would hold, I did not know. I had some people comment that it would be difficult for me to find a good job since I had focused on art and dance but I never worried because I loved what I did so very much, that I knew and trusted that I would create my own future. This I learned from my dad.

I knew he was very smart and worked for IBM, but I didn't know he was truly brilliant. He never talked much about himself, and I remember when I was 16, I asked him why there was a picture of a strange man, that I didn't know, leaning over a giant computer in our hallway. He laughed and said it was Werner Von Braun and he was leaning over the 7090 computers (pronounced seven oh ninety), which he, my dad, designed. I asked him who Werner Von Braun was and what the 7090 did. In case you don't know Werner Von Braun was a German Scientist who was brought to America after World War II. His dream was to build a rocket and go to the moon, "Impossible" most thought, but of course he did.

Von Braun began under Hitler and built rockets as weapons, but his true goal was brought to fruition in America with the space program, but to do this he needed a computer for ground control. That is where my dad came in. My dad smiled at me and went into his office and returned with a one-inch-thick notebook. We sat down and he showed me. It was all handwritten in pencil and filled with mathematical calculations and symbols. He explained that it was his work for creating the 7090 computer, he showed me the patent he received. I was so impressed and proud, although I could not understand any of the mathematical equations that filled the pages. I thought, my dad was amazing. He told me that when he was in high school (in the 50's) there were no jobs in the computer industry because there were really no computers, for the most part. Engineering was not something they considered a "good choice" for college. He disregarded their warnings and always told me, "You must do what you love, you will create something out of that." Well, he certainly did and gave me the support to do what I loved and taught me to trust in my future and follow my heart. I am very blessed for his guidance.

After my dad passed, I went to the Smithsonian Air and Space Museum with my husband, Salvatore and my son, Nico, who was 3 at the time. I found a tribute to the 7090 there. They could not put the whole computer in because it was so massive, not like computers these days. The 7090 could fill a room. Salvatore took a picture of Nico and I in front of it.

I knew that because my dad worked for IBM, he did not get public credit, although he got awards through IBM. The plaque at the museum spoke of Werner Von Braun and IBM but not my dad. I wrote a letter to inquire if the museum would be willing to put up a plaque that honored my father. I asked if they would place it with the exhibit. (I included my dad's patent on the project). I got a response from Paul Ceruzzi who was the Curator of The Division of Space. He said that, in his opinion, the 7090 was one of the most important computers in the history of all computers. He sent me a book he wrote entitled A HISTORY OF MODERN COMPUTING, in which he discussed the 7090 and its great value. He said that although they would soon rotate the exhibit and it would come down soon, he would like to keep my dad's work and information in their archives, so I sent him my dad's workbook. Mr. Ceruzzi later said that he had to admit that my dad's work was so advanced that even he could not understand a lot of it. He was very grateful to have it in their collection.

My dad created his dream, beyond what most people would

imagine. He loved engineering and made a path, a big one, for himself. I lived and still live by that spirit. Do what you love, work hard, love what you do and trust! Many years later when I was watching the movie HIDDEN FIGURES, I was brought to tears. It is an amazing and beautiful story about the women of color who were the human computers for the first space flights. Central to the movie was the arrival, at NASA, of my dad's computer, the 7090. Although they did not mention him by name, it was him, it was his tribute. I love that movie and quickly got the book.

I followed my dad's advice and always chose happiness. While I was in college, I did not stress about what job I would get after, I just worked as hard as I could, taking the required courses and the ones that I really loved. Isn't that the way it is supposed to be? Aren't you supposed to enjoy college, to learn and absorb all you can and then see where it leads you? Although my college years sounded creepy there were many wonderful times. I loved learning about Art, Art History, Religions, Astronomy, Archeology and more. I filled myself with as much knowledge as I could get. I thought it sad that some students regarded education as something they were forced to do or wanted to cheat and get out of things. I thought that so odd because they were cheating themselves. Education is a gift. In our history there were many who craved an education, craved to learn to read and write and sought out knowledge. Today we are handed this gift on a silver platter, so I found it sad to see students not caring.

I had two jobs at college. I was very close to my dance teacher, Greta LeVart. She was a small woman of stature but large in energy and heart. She loved dance, as did I and shared that gift with great exuberance and love. I loved her dearly and spent much time with her and with dance. Her husband Herb was a corporate photographer, and I became his assistant. It was a great job. He was a wonderful man, and I learned a lot about portrait photography and got paid very well. I also ran the Manhattanville photo lab/darkroom. At work I was allowed to spend time on my own projects, developing film and photos. Film is a whole different world from digital photography (which did not exist way back when) and I loved it and miss it to this day. The Dark Room has the really dark, developing room where there cannot even be a speck of light. You have to feel the camera and pull out the film and put it into a container with chemicals and seal it tightly. This is a really wonderful exercise in using your other senses. You cannot use your eyes; it is all about touch. It makes you experience that sense in a more magnified way. It is also very calming, being in total darkness. Little did I know how healing this was. It would be many years before I would fully get this concept.

After you develop the film, you go into the "Dark Room" where there is a little bit of red light (the blue spectrum would expose your print). There were big machines called Enlargers. You put your negative in and the enlarger finely controls the focus and exposes the negative to the photo paper below. You can add more light in areas and make them brighter and play around with the photo. Then you put them into a developer bath, then a fixer bath. I think this is a lost art. Digital photography is much simpler and I love it, but there is something to be said for being at peace, in the dark, for seeing your photo go through the stages of development and choosing lights and darks and actually printing it out yourself. I felt I had a wonderful foundation that would help me with future job options.

When I was nearing graduation, I went to the career center to learn how to write a resume, on a typewriter, of course. As I was leaving there was a little note on the "JOB OPENINGS BOARD." It said, "Public Relations person needed for dance company. Contact American Ballet Company..." and gave the number. I asked if I could have a copy. I ran to Greta. She said she had never heard of American Ballet Company. She thought perhaps, they were trying to imitate, the very famous, American Ballet Theatre which was run by Mikhail Baryshnikov. She said it was probably a small NY company and would be a good start and I should call. I did and got a scheduled interview for the following week. Greta wished me luck and told me to wear a suit! I went to the local thrift shop and got myself a rose colored one that had a modern flair. I was ready.

I showed up at the address given, 890 Broadway in New York City and after I got buzzed in the front door, I went straight to the reception desk. A lovely young woman smiled and told me to have a seat. When I sat down, I took a deep breath and was able to take note of my surroundings. There was a large poster of the ballet FANCY FREE in front of me and it said AMERICAN BALLET THEATRE. I turned and there was another poster that also said AMERICAN BALLET THEATRE. American Ballet Theatre?! That is one of the most famous companies in the world, I thought. I had applied to American Ballet Company. This could not be possible. To be sure, I took a deep breath and walked back up to the desk and said "umm, excuse me.... is this American Ballet Company or American Ballet Theatre?" She smiled again and said it was American Ballet Theatre. I showed her my paper and she suggested that they may have written that because they did not want to be inundated by fans. I tried not to fall on the floor and quietly returned to my seat. This would be a dream. American Ballet Theatre was one of the most famous companies in all the world. Mikhail Baryshnikov the most famous dancer in the world, someone I was in awe of. I had seen him/them in films and read about them but to be here now was amazing. I suddenly got nervous, very nervous and that was the moment I was called in for my interview. I felt a lump in my throat. Would I be able to speak? As I entered the office, I was greeted by Elena Gordon who told me she had attended Manhattanville College also. She introduced me to Bob Pontarelli who was sitting at a desk. He went to greet me, and a little Shih Tzu puppy jumped off of his lap onto the desk. I think I squealed in delight and all my fears were gone. I played with the puppy for a bit and then talked to them about my life, Manhattanville and dancing. Over a half hour went by and it seemed like 5 minutes. When I got back to school, I ran to Greta to tell her. She could not believe it. One week later I got a call from Elena telling me there had been about 500 applicants and I got the job. I called my dad immediately and thanked him for his wise guidance. One day at work I was walking down the corridor and almost ran right into Baryshnikov, Misha, as I learned to call him. He smiled and said "hello," I almost burst apart with excitement. My dad was right, believe and miracles will happen.

My job was a PR (Public Relations) assistant, in the office and on tour with the company. On the road I would set up interviews, oversee them, help write press releases, watch rehearsals, and attend performances. I had to be available during intermission to answer any questions the press may have and make sure they were attended to. Most of the questions were ones that I had no answer for, since I just started, so I did a lot of running backstage to find Flo who knew EVERYTHING. I watched Swan Lake, Giselle, Don Quixote, and Cinderella. I even got to take company class some mornings next to Misha, who would smile and look at me from time to time, at which point I wanted to crawl out of the room. Misha embraced dance in a way that made you feel his passion. I will never forget a performance of Les Sylphides that he was in. There was one part of the ballet where he was off to the side, standing still, the beautiful ballerinas where dancing and dancing while he stood. He then slowly began to raise his arm gesturing towards them. I can still feel that energy to this day, it radiated from him. He did not dance with his body. He danced with his soul. I often use him as an example when I teach Shakespeare and acting classes to kids, and when I teach yoga. I tell them, dancing, acting, singing, yoga, must come from deep inside. Don't just move your body or speak, feel it, and let the audience feel it too. The energy should emit from every part of your being. Don't just lift your arm, send sparks out of your fingers.

My favorite ballet, of all, was Romeo and Juliet by Sir Kenneth Mac Millan, Sir Kenneth was an amazing choreographer and I loved watching him work and seeing how his guidance would transform the dancers. The sets were by Nicholas Georgiadis and they were amazing. There were angels in the tomb scene that hung from the ceiling. They weighed 2 tons each. They had their own truck to transport them and were gorgeous. Every time I saw that ballet, I felt like I was seeing it for the first time. It sent my spirit soaring.

At one point Antony Tudor came to set one of his ballets on the company. I loved him. Every time he was at the studio I would run down and ask him if he wanted coffee so, I could spend a moment with him. He finally figured out that, getting coffee was not my job and that I was just trying to be with him, so he finally told me to just sit near him and watch him work. It was an amazing experience.

I got to experience and know some of the greatest dancers in the world, like Cynthia Gregory and Fernando Bujones who would often state "I am Fernando Bujones, the greatest dancer in the world." There were fabulous galas with flowing Dom Perignon, champagne. My first gala was in Washington D.C and it was my job to stand near Misha and make sure the press didn't bother him. I was supposed to be acting really cool and mingling nearby, at the ready to stop any "would be" interviewer, but I think I just stood there smiling and staring at him. A few weeks later I was attending an opening party in Los Angeles and stood near the entrance to greet Gene Kelly, Goldie Hawn and many more.

It was a beautiful life, and my dad would often join me on tour to hang out and watch the ballet. It was wonderful and difficult at the same time. Wonderful for obvious reasons and difficult because, on the road, which was most of the year, I worked about 12-15 hours a day, seven days a week and went from city to city. It was also hard because I wanted to dance, although I appreciated my opportunity. One day I was sitting outside the theatre in San Francisco talking to a few of the corps de ballet. They had begun to complain about how they did not have big enough roles, how the principal dancers got all the good parts and the soloists next. As they went on, I thought about perspective, which, to me, is a very important thing to think about in life. It helps solve a lot of problems. I looked at them and told them they should look at their lives from my perspective. How lucky they were to be dancing with one of the most famous companies in the world. Performing the most beautiful ballets with amazing choreographers on the best stages in the country. I told them, if I could be on stage and just do the ballroom dance from Romeo and Juliet once in my life, I would be so happy. They all stared at me and thought. They finally nodded in agreement and walked away much happier. We must learn to enjoy our lives, to be happy with what we have. There is certainly nothing wrong with wanting more but we must see the gifts that are present in our daily lives or move on, which I finally did after about 14 months of beautiful work. I was pretty tired from all the hours, exhausted was more like it and I also wanted to pursue my own dance career which is not an easy thing to do in NYC. Or I should say, easy to pursue it, but not so easy to get jobs. I loved dance class and voice lessons, but auditions were abundant, and jobs were few. At any given audition you would encounter 500 people or more. It made me appreciate the odds I had overcome in getting my job with ABT. I did a few great shows and one Off Broadway original called A Spinning Tale.

I loved this mountain but also knew that I had again reached the top and had to climb another.

CHAPTER 6

ENERGY HEALING

My next path turned into a magical healing one where I was presented with teachers who would help to guide my way. My first was my friend Katiti's father, who was teaching an energy healing class, which she, I and a couple of others attended. It was amazing. It was mysterious and mystical, and I dove in, feeling this was a positive experience and would be nothing like the way I opened in college. I learned how to begin to manipulate energy and re-create it. Although this was all pre–Saucer's Apprentice- the one with Nicolas Cage, not Mickey, it felt like that scene where he was taught to create a ball of energy and utilize it. I was amazed to learn that with concentration you could send energy to someone with the intention to heal them or find out what was wrong with them. We learned how to scan the body to feel energy blocks so we could focus on working on those spots. We were not touching the other person, but rather our hands were inches away from their bodies. We would ask if they felt anything. Heat was often the answer. We experimented with sending healing from farther away and noticed that in time we could actually make each other rock back and forth. To test that it was really us, we would have the person close their eyes and stand about 6 feet away. We would send and see if they rocked, stop, and see if they stopped. It was amazing to see that as soon as we stopped sending the energy and healing, they would stop rocking. When I would do healing work I felt like I was uniting with something greater than myself. It was not really ME sending healing, I was opening to something greater than me to let the healing flow through me. I was tapping into the Divine Energy, where we are all one and all part of the ONE. I believe this is something we can all learn to do.

I soon realized that I was putting this teacher on a high pedestal, forgetting that it is where many fall from. I put some others on pedestals after that too, until I got stronger with myself and became cautious of who I was learning from and what their sources of energy and healing were. My first lesson in this was when my friend's father started to fall into the darkness. Instead of feeling Divine energy was guiding him, he began to say that he was the greatest healer, and we did not have to tap into the Divine, we had to tap into him. He did healing and massage for a living so one day I went for a private session. He asked me if I thought I could try to channel as he worked, for he wanted to experiment with that. I trusted him, at that point, so I said I would try. He guided me through a meditation, and I opened to what he was saying. The next thing I knew, I could hear my voice from far away but could not control it. Someone was talking through me, it was not something evil or negative, by any means, but it was not me. I recall it was something about cats and how they were from another "realm" (for lack of a better word). How they had a beautiful strength and energy and we had to honor that and how they were much more intelligent than most people thought (although I knew that). I know many people channel amazing information, but I was not ready for this, not then anyway. I finally pushed it away. My teacher thought this was great and wanted to work with me more on this but as I said it was not something that I wanted to personally do.

I soon began to hear "I" way too many times, coming from my teacher's mouth. "I" can be a very bad word when used in a self-centered, powerful way. I knew I had to move on. I have learned that when you hear a lot of I's and me's it is best to step away or run. I decided to study on my own for a while and once again reminded myself to be more careful and only work with the light. I know many people believe that science and magic are very different but to me they are very much the same. They say magic is undiscovered science but to me there is so much more to magic than that. I spent my time exploring this idea. It helped me clarify what healing was to me. I thought of how everything vibrates, we know that through our basic study of science. If molecules heat up, they vibrate faster, cool down and they vibrate slower. I thought about the heat that is sent during a healing and how the molecules must be moving faster, working to heal. I then thought about the concept of matching vibrations to destroy something in the same manner that an opera singer can break a crystal glass by hitting a high note and matching the vibration of the glass, thus shattering it. Here I ask you to think of Nicola Tesla. I hope you all know Tesla, for sadly many don't. Nicola

Tesla was born in 1856, in Serbia at midnight during a fierce lightning storm. His Midwife took this as a bad omen and said he would be a child of darkness, but his mother said that he would be a child of light. His mother was correct. Tesla is the creator of our electric AC current, the Tesla Coil and many other amazing inventions, including the basis of smart phones. When Tesla first arrived in America, he worked for Thomas Alva Edison and got screwed over by him. Tesla had told Edison that he could create a better dynamo and in essence AC current, whereas Edison was working on DC current which is used in batteries. Edison told Tesla if he could create this "better dynamo," that he would give him $50,000. When Tesla, indeed accomplish this task, Edison asked him why he had not understood a joke when he heard one. That is when Tesla left. He found his own "lab" in lower Manhattan and began working on his ideas. In one of his experiments he, kind-of, destroyed a big part of downtown New York City because he was experimenting in his lab with vibration.

He found that if he matched a vibration, just as the Opera Singer breaking a glass, that he could break or destroy things. Unfortunately, the vibration he matched was structural and it got very earthquakey, (I know that's not a word). So now let's put that into healing. If you use your vibration to connect to a higher vibration, you could destroy pain in someone, or disease, in essence, heal them. Always and only through the light, of course.

There was another man named Royal Rife. Rife claimed to have documented a "Mortal Oscillatory Rate" (or frequency) for various pathogenic (capable of producing disease) organisms and was able to destroy the organisms by vibrating them at this particular rate. In other words, he would match the vibration and destroy disease with his machine. His approach was scientific and involved blood tests. Many did not believe his work possible, but others said that he scared the medical world and got "shut down". Funny how both Rife and Tesla were pushed aside because no one could make money off of them and others feared them. Tesla was trying to give free electricity to the world and Rife was trying to heal people. I have found this theme has often been repeated in our culture. It is more about money than health and happiness and I discovered how deep that idea is imbedded in our society.

But back to energy. Vibrations that match vibrations can counteract one another. So, we can see some science in the magic. To do these practices we must indeed, practice. I think that was one of the big messages that Jesus told us. I don't think he incarnated to show us what he could do, and we should just watch, he was showing us what WE could do. He said if you have the faith of a mustard seed, you can move a mountain. I believe this, so I practiced, and practiced and practiced, on myself, on my animals, on anyone who would let me. One day I went to visit my dad and he had a stone that had built up internally, near his throat. The Doctor wanted him to return the next day to talk about possible surgery. I did a healing on him and at the end he said he felt much better (he was always very honest and would have told me if he did not). The next day the Doctor told him the stone was gone.

If you would like to begin a healing practice, start by finding a comfortable seated position, preferably cross legged on the floor but a chair will do, if that is better for you. State either out loud or strongly in your mind that you are opening to the Divine Light ONLY, through love and through light, through ONLY the highest and the best. Rub your hands together, really hard, back and forth so you create friction. As your hands begin to feel hot, close your eyes and let your mind clear. Thoughts may come and go and that is ok but try to let the thoughts go more than come. Focus on the heat you feel in your hands. Then slowly start to separate them until they are about three inches apart, palms facing in, like you are holding a ball between them. Focus your mind on the warmth you are creating and picture the molecules moving. Feel that energy build up and trust that it is truly present. Then move your hands to either side of your head and continue to create the energy and heat and see it flowing into your brain. Let your breath become more relaxed and sit with this flow for a few minutes. If you need to rub your hands together again, do so. After a few minutes put your right hand about one inch above your head and your left hand in front of the center of your forehead. Once again feel the energy flow into you and breathe deeply. Hold this for a couple of minutes. Then move your right hand to the center of your throat and your left to the center of your chest, once again feeling the energy flow into you. Then put your hands on either side of your lower abdomen and repeat. Trust. Just trust and let it flow. You have just given yourself a healing. Now all you need to do is practice, practice, practice. Practice on yourself, your friends, your dog, your cat, a tree. Animals are the best to work on, they are very sensitive to the vibration and will often move the part of their body that they want healed toward your hands and when they are done, they will walk away. If you, do it from a distance, they will often look at your hands, because they know. They feel you. The laying on of hands is an ancient practice, that should indeed be practiced. Just think, you would not want a doctor doing surgery on you if they did not practice, so practice and wonders will happen.

A few years into my healing practice I was given a challenge. A woman had come into town for 8 days. She said she had Lyme Disease and it had been with her for 5 years. She was constantly in pain and had tried everything, medically and naturally, and nothing was working. She asked if I would do healing work with her. I told her we should do three sessions and that I could not guarantee anything. She said she understood. To start the first session, I called upon the Divine Light through the Highest and the Best. I knew I had to step out of the way so the higher energy could move through me without being blocked. I was only a small part of this, more of an observer. As I let my mind go, I felt a peace pour over me and began to feel removed from my body. First, I saw white light begin to swirl through her, it then turned into beautiful colors and lights that expanded and then began to form geometric shapes like a kaleidoscope. I watched it as if I were watching a movie and went farther and farther "out" or "in." The colors were intense, and I saw the spectacular sacred geometry filling her. It coursed through her blood, her body, her very cells and I was moving with it. I finally came back to my body and an hour had gone by. It felt like 10 minutes. I was still a little out of it and so was she, but she got up and said she felt better. We did three of those sessions and at the end of the week she told me she was free of her pain. She could now move her neck and arms which had been stiff and sore, and she felt great. She said she had not had that experience in five years. I will stress here that I did not heal her. I was the tool that the Divine worked through. Does it always work? Yes and No. I think when you are sending healing through love and light, whoever you are sending to will get what they need. Sometimes that is not what they want or think. The person who you are working on has their choices also, not a choice physically but spiritually, karmically. Believe it or not some people choose illness for whatever reason and some even choose death. I have been ill, at times, myself and I surely don't feel I am choosing it but I feel there are lessons to be learned, often hard ones. As a healer this is difficult to understand at first, and difficult to not get into "I helped, I failed" mode. You must make peace with the reality of our human condition and be okay with it and your role in it. We must open up to a higher guidance that is also a light within us.

CHAPTER 7

THE DOVE

Along my path I was shown yet another beautiful mountain. I had become friends with a Hollywood Casting Director named Joy Todd. She was a wonderful woman. One day we were talking about my dad and how I wished he could meet someone to keep him company, although he was very happy. She told me that she was friends with Sylvester Stallone's aunt and asked if we should set them up. We did and they met in the city and had a wonderful time and chatted on the phone after that but lived too far away from each other to have it progress. As I told Joy about my mom, I shared with her the story of the Dove. She loved it and said it gave her hope. She suggested that I write it as an episode for the show Quantum Leap, for she knew the Producer. I had never really written anything except in school, where I was surely not considered a good writing student, but I started to write. I found it very healing. The more I wrote the better I felt. Emotions were pouring out of me. I was seeing the spiritual side of my mom's passing again. I went back and told Joy that I was feeling this healing and needed to just write it down, not as an episode but just write, I called it *THE DOVE*. She told me I should keep writing and maybe it would turn into a movie script. By the time I was done Joy had moved to LA and we had lost touch. I decided to take some screenwriting classes and learn the art of writing a film. It was a wonderful journey, and I grew to love writing. Years passed and one afternoon when I was in my apartment in Manhattan, sitting on my bed, with my two pugs Jimmie and Lucy and my two cats. I began thinking about my mom, but I couldn't feel her, I felt out of touch. I told her I didn't know what to do with the script, I had completed it but what now? Movies were not an easy thing to get produced. I asked her for a sign, a clear sign. I sat and sat and suddenly my mom's Daily Missile - Prayer Book, which she used to read every day, fell. It was across the room. No one was there, the animals were all with me. There was no reason for it to have fallen. I went to pick it up and told my mom that was indeed a very clear sign and thanked her but was not sure what it meant. I then saw that a little white card had fallen out. I had read that book many times and had never seen this little card, EVER. I read it-

I'd like to be with you today
If only for awhile
I'd like to share your company
and see your cheery smile
but since that seems impossible
I'll do the next best thing
and be with you in heart and mind
by just remembering.

I felt my mom right there with me. I felt her presence and her comfort. I know she was there. Miracles are all around us, every day, and if we choose to, we will see them. If not, if we are so busy, or so involved in the material world, then we will miss them. We need to stop to see the wonder that presents itself.

A couple of years went by and I would pick up the script and rewrite it or just let it be. I thought that maybe that was all I was supposed to do, just write it. At that point I owned a Coffee Bar called THE COFFEE POT, in midtown Manhattan. One day, a lovely woman came in and asked if she could do Tarot Card Readings at my place. I had so much work to do and not much time, but there was something about her, so I stopped everything and we sat. One hour later we were still talking, she told me I had written something and had to make a film about it. I was shocked, I told her about my script and that I named it THE DOVE. She smiled and told me that was her name, Dove, Lilith Dove. Ah, another sign.

I learned that my destiny was not to be a famous film maker but to do the task of writing and making the film. It was a healing journey for me and would one day be for my family, when I had one. That was around the time that I met Salvatore and decided to attend a small film school in NYC and made the movie myself, with a lot of support from Lilith, Salvatore, my friend Joyce (who I met in film school) and others. I made it on a very low budget, or no budget and it looked it, but again the journey was in the doing and the spiritual energy of the story. In the middle of filming, I became pregnant with Nico. I knew then the film was about ancestry and sharing our stories.

The first screening of the movie was a gift from Lilith. She set up the whole night. A couple of days prior I was sitting in the bedroom with Salvatore. There had been a problem with the air conditioner and whenever it rained it leaked and was damaging the wall. Salvatore said "LOOK!" I turned to see that the water spot had turned into a DOVE. Ok, at this point you might be saying, she is crazy, or this is not true, she is making this stuff up, but I swear it is all true. I had a couple of screenings of the movie, and many responded that the story gave them hope. I won "THE DOVE AWARD" (ironically) for family films. I had such peace with my mom now and her passing. I know it was hard for my dad to watch because it showed her death, as spiritual as it was, but I think it also gave him peace. He said it was important for him to see how I viewed her passing and life after this incarnation. Salvatore designed the DVD cover, using the image of the actual stain.

The Dove still appears to me, often, as a sign. Before Lucy, my sweet little pug passed, a dove walked right into our apartment in NYC and just stood there, in the living room, staring at us. Another time, at our farm, Nico and Salvatore had just come home and got out of the car and a dove walked right up to Nico and stood at his feet. Salvatore went around the car and the dove just stood there. We had an alpaca named Maggie who had been ill for a very long time. They thought it was stomach cancer. I had kept her somewhat healthy and happy for 3 years more than she probably should have lived, with daily doses of Frankincense, probiotics and special food, herbs, and healings. When we went up to the field that night, she had passed to the next realm. Salvatore said that was why the dove came and of course I knew it was so. When we finally returned to the house with tears in our eyes, I saw the dove standing at our front door. I knew it was my mom. I walked up to her, and she just walked around my feet, Salvatore and Nico were a couple of minutes behind me. I sat and she stood in front of me, staring at me. I knew she was telling me that she was still there, and Maggie was with her now. I heard Maggie say, "thank you, thank you for all of your love and care." It was a good 5 minutes that the dove stayed there. I said thank you, mom, for coming. Nico and Salvatore were standing behind me at this point and she looked at us and flew into a nearby tree. We all felt her peace and looked above at her watching over us. After a couple more minutes she flew away. She even came back to remind me to write this story.

Another part of my healing journey was through the Aquarian Foundation, where I learned how to protect myself, totally, how to set up healing transmutations and many more wonderful things. It was run by Keith Milton Rhinehart- KMR, who discovered at a young age that he had the gift of mediumship. He could go into a trance and beings would communicate through him. He believed in proof and evidence and all those who went to observe him would leave saying they truly believed he could indeed communicate with these beings. He did something called Billets which is when you hold a piece of paper that has a number on it or you write your initials on it and place it close to your heart for a few minutes, you then place it back into a pile. Keith would take one of the papers and hold it to his head and would then be able to read information that the person needed. He would make people gasp; his information was totally accurate. He even once wrote a response to a billet in Arabic, which he did not even know. He later went on to verbally speak the information from those he channeled. There was one time when New York City was about to be hit by a hurricane, it was going to be devastating. KMR gathered people from all over the world to pray and send thoughts of pushing the storm out to sea at precisely the same time. Just as this was happening, the storm, for no reason whatsoever, turned away from the shore and into the middle of the ocean.

It was at the Aquarian Foundation in NY where some gifted individuals did billets like KMR. It was amazing to me because I would get the same exact reading until I changed what was needed. I mean literally the same, word for word reading time after time. One time it was "do not cast your pearls before swine," over and over until I stopped hanging out with those who were not appreciating me. Another time I was told that I was in the history books. Not one of the most famous, but I was known in history, and it was affecting this lifetime. I thought about it but could not come up with anyone who I felt. There were other nights that were "healing nights" where you could go to the front of the room and place a chair before you, if people wanted a healing from you, they would sit in your chair. It took me awhile before I got the courage to head up to the front of the room with a chair. I placed the chair in front of me and waited. Eventually a young woman, who I had seen there a few times, but did not know, quietly walked up and sat in my chair. I began the healing and started to get images in my head. I saw her surrounded by a golden-yellow light, then she entered a golden chariot with a Pegasus type horse that flew her high into the sky and up into the light. She disappeared into this magnificent golden-yellow fire. It was so beautiful. When the healing ended, I told her what I saw. Her eyes lit up and filled with tears and she smiled and hugged me. What I did not know was that she was very ill and died 2 weeks later. I hope my vision gave her some comfort.

The more I learned about healing the more amazing it all became, and all made sense because it is essentially Quantum Physics. I learned how to release stress by actually moving it out of your heart chakra and letting it float away. It is amazing how many ways are available for us to change our lives. I got certified in Inter-Dimensional Healing and became a Reiki Master. When the day came that I was told that Lucy, my sweet pug had cancer I felt my heart break, Salvatore did too. She was part of our family and we loved her so much. I tried everything I could do to heal her, but she was not getting better. The Vet talked us into Chemotherapy, and I wish I had known what I know now, because I did that for us not for her. She was suffering but it was too hard to part with her. As I said before, it is not always up to us to decide if a person or animal lives or dies but this was extremely difficult. We tend to think of our human existence as the best thing in the world. Well, maybe in this world it is the best because it is what we know but when we truly connect to our soul, our spirit, and realize we are all one with the Divine then maybe saving everyone and every animal is not the true healing path. That is one very hard step to learn. When you begin healing work you want to heal everyone, and you feel responsible. You feel guilty if that being does not get better and you feel terrible if they die. That is a difficult healing lesson and one I still am learning more about. A very wise woman once told me that it was a very heavy burden to think I was "responsible" for the life or death of any being. Well, put that way I saw it differently. No, I am not responsible, no I cannot feel guilty. I believe I can raise vibrations and change energy, I believe that it is a gift that we all have if we choose to do it and our greatest teacher was Jesus, but we are not him, so it is too much to feel guilt and feel that we are solely responsible.

Salvatore and I were planning our wedding in Italy, he was born in Modena and his mom still lived there. His dad was born on the Amalfi Coast where he still had a family home. It was a very special place to Salvatore. We planned our wedding in Ravello. After Lucy got ill, we decided that we did not want to leave her and changed our wedding to our apartment in New York City. Our apartment was Mickey Roarke's apartment from the movie, 9 1/2 WEEKS. It was beautiful with a big greenhouse living room and 2 huge outdoor decks that overlooked the whole city and could fit a nice little crowd. The decks totaled 3,000 square feet. We set tables outside and had a small band with a harpist. It was a beautiful wedding. Jimmie and Lucy walked down the aisle, Lucy with a ribbon around her neck filled with flowers and Jimmie with a little bow tie. One cat just hung out, and the other had since passed on.

On the day of our wedding things kept happening, my sister called to say she would be late (she was my maid of honor). Diana, who was my flower girl did not come, until the reception, because her mom was getting her hair done and it took too long. I sat on the bed with Lucy on my lap and Jimmie at my side. One of the Spiritual Officiates who was performing part of the ceremony came in and asked if I was alright. She then asked how I could be so calm with all the craziness. I told her the only thing that mattered was that I was marrying Salvatore, it was not about how perfect the ceremony was but that I would commit my love to him and to me that made the day perfect. I had Salvatore, my dad, my dogs, cat, and great friends around. I then showed her the water stain and she said, "it looks like a dove, did you paint that?" I told her the story. We had an amazing day.

The day before Lucy died, I conceived Nico. I literally felt his spirit enter my body with a Whoosh that filled my whole body, and I knew that instant that I was pregnant. That's Nico, making his wonderful energy and presence known even to this day. I felt part of

Lucy's energy bond with his and I felt peace. The beginning of a life. Creation.

CHAPTER 8

SALVATORE

The Dove helped lead me to Salvatore, I know this because what we share is a connection that is complete. We may not always believe the same exact thing, but we can relate to each other on all levels, physical, spiritual, emotional. It is a relationship of giving on both sides, of supporting through all of our ups and downs and knowing that we will always be there for each other.

We met at his dad's restaurant, Amarone, on 9th Ave, in NYC, it was near my apartment, and I enjoyed eating there. One day one of the waiters introduced me to Salvatore. He seemed shy and had an energy that made me feel peaceful and I felt connected to him. After that he asked me to come to the restaurant on New Year's Eve to celebrate with him, for he had to work. I told him I was going out with my friend Arthur, but I would see if he wanted to come there to eat. I saw Salvatore's face tilt down, so I quickly told him that, my dear friend Arthur Matera, was 70 years old and very gay, so there was no worry. He cheered up. I did go to see him after I hung out with Arthur, and we had a great night. The next night it was so cold in NYC, no one wanted to go out, but I put my pugs, Jimmie and Lucy in their coats and walked to the restaurant to see him. He came outside and told me how much he loved Jimmie and Lucy. That meant the world to me. After that thing happened quite quickly. He told me he had never been to Disney World and since I work for Disney and love Disney, I decided to take him there. We felt like kids and had a great time. He asked me to marry him in at the Animal Kingdom Lodge and then formally in the restaurant in Mexico at Epcot. I then got a Mickey Mouse ring to seal the deal. He later got me another one, but I cherish Mickey.

When I got home, I told my cousins that I was engaged but every family event that occurred was a day that Salvatore was working. At one point my cousin asked if Salvatore was real because they never saw him, and I had a Mickey Mouse ring.

On our wedding day, my dad walked me down the red carpet, Salvatore's mom had come from Italy as well as his Aunt Rosaria and his dad from New Jersey. I was sad to find out later that Arthur Matera had come to the bottom of the stairs that lead to our Penthouse but was too ill to make it up. I later told him that Salvatore and I would have carried him. Arthur, my New Year's Eve date was married to Barbara Matera. They owned Barbara Matera Limited and made many of the costumes for Broadway shows including, THE LION KING and AIDA. Barbara's intricate bead work and selection of beads from around the world (Africa for The Lion King) made each piece a work of art. I have a scarf that she hands beading that is so detailed and exquisite. Salvatore loved the priests robe in Aida and loved the show.

As a wedding gift, Arthur had made him the outfit. It was beautiful and Salvatore was radiant. I wore a vintage gown. I felt so much love and joy. I could not even image how much more joy and love this wonderful man would bring to me for all of my life.

I was pregnant with Nico a couple of months later and our lives have evolved so much since those early days. We have each grown in our own right, but the most important thing is that we grow together. We support each other and we do it all with love. Nico and Salvatore are my love, my life, my heart. The pride and joy they bring me every day cannot possibly be expressed. They are a part of me. I know that Nico does not always understand my role as a parent, which is to guide and teach, but that is ok. I will always do my job, to love him, guide him, protect him, and teach him. He has created such magic in his life from Blacksmithing to Shakespeare and more. The magic is in him and he shines it with a light that is his own. I love these two so very much, words could never express how very much.

CHAPTER 9

IN THE BEGINNING?

I began to think about the creation of the earth, of mankind and an energy that we are all a part of. I believe that we all came from THE

DIVINE ONE and are still one with THE DIVINE. When I do healings I feel other dimensions, sometimes past lives, sometimes the future, a premonition, if you will. It is almost like words are pouring out of my mouth with advice and information that is from beyond me, although not like when I was told to channel before. This flowed from me, and I was comfortable with it. One premonition I had was before I was married. As I said, I had owned a Coffee Bar on 49th street and 9th Avenue in Manhattan, and around May of that year I got the feeling I needed to sell it. I talked with my friend Colette who owned a little clothing boutique and she said she felt the same thing. Ironically, or not, a couple of days later I received a call from a real estate broker who had contacted me years prior asking if I was interested in selling. At the time I told her no. This time she said she already had the buyer, and my answer was yes. Something was shifting, it was time. I felt that something was going to happen, something not good, something huge and I did not want to be in business in NYC at that point. The deal was final in August of 2001, and I decided to take a vacation. I was thinking about Europe or somewhere I would fly. Every night I had the same dream. I was in a plane and the plane was in NY headed for a high building and I was screaming "Doesn't anyone see this!? Doesn't anyone see that we are going to hit the building!?" Then I would do one of those moves where you try to guide the plane up by imagining you are steering and pulling the pretend wheel up. All the while I was scrunching up my face with effort, in fright. Then I would wake up. I had this same dream night after night. Finally, I decided I would drive to Fire Island instead of flying anywhere. I was going to leave Sept.11

but wound up leaving the 10th. I remember watching the smoke from the towers on the beach where I sat. I was glad I chose not to fly. It was a warning, maybe to me personally, maybe to the world.

Years later I had another dream, in this one Salvatore and I were standing in a glass room above the ocean and a huge tsunami came. It was wiping out everything beneath us. I knew we were safe but all those I watched were not. I woke up that morning shaking and told Salvatore about it, but what could I do, call the White House, and say "hey, I saw a tsunami in my dreams, it is going to be a bad one." One week later the tsunami hit Indonesia and it was terrible indeed. I had another dream like that before the earthquake and tsunami in Japan at Fukushima nuclear power plant which left a path of instant destruction and devastation for many years to come. I wondered why was I shown these things? I couldn't do anything. I couldn't help anyone. I didn't even know where it would hit in my dream or when it would hit. A healer friend told me she didn't think I was supposed to do anything about it. She thought I was just very connected to the Earth and the vibration, and I felt it coming. That made sense in a way but why was I given visions I could not do anything about.

My path lead me on an journey of healing through food and what we put in our bodies. From the time I was 8 years old I was a vegetarian, for the most part. I had a couple years here and there that I ate meat but very few. Later in life I embraced more of a vegan diet. I also began to study homeopathy and herbs. Little did I know how far I would go on this path later in life. When I was pregnant with Nico, I was eating healthy, organic, vegetarian food and planning a natural birth. I had a nutritional expert, Dr. Dulin who worked based on your blood work and a wonderful mid-wife and doula. Dr. Dulin told me that I had low adrenals and should eat meat, I chose not to, at the time, and took all the supplements he suggested and ate a lot of nut butters and beans (but did not keep up with this for as long as I should have, after years we tend to forget and slack but that is another book for another day).

I remember when Nico was 2, he got a high fever and was not feeling well. I gave him cold drinks and put him to bed, and he fell asleep. I called his doctor, freaking out, oh my God, my baby is sick, he has a high fever, what should I do? The Doctor asked, what was the fever, what were the symptoms. Then he asked if I had any wine in the house. Oh, yes, I said thinking he would tell me how to make some concoction to heal Nico. "Have a glass," he said. What? I thought. He then calmly told me, what everyone should know. Fever is the body's way of fighting infection, if the fever is not too high (over 102-103) then let it run its course. Let it do its job of FIGHTING the infection, that is how the body works. I sat there stunned and later pondered how we take medicine to bring down a fever and are stopping the body from fighting the infection. It really makes no sense. We want instant gratification in this world and often mistakenly stop symptoms QUICKLY and prolong or remove the healing process totally.

At this point in time, we had decided to move from NYC to Connecticut. At first it was hard for me, leaving behind the city and our awesome apartment. I was on top of the world there. Why would I want to move to Connecticut? But Salvatore had grown up in Modena,

Italy spending most of his time with his grandparents on their farm with grapes and potatoes growing and he did not like the energy of NYC, neither did Nico. When we would go to the country, they always seemed calmer and happier. We chose a new life. We bought a 50-acre property that was beautiful and, at first, lonely. Salvatore was still working in the city and Nico was 2 and I only knew my friend Beth, who lived close by, and my dad was 40 minutes away. I was at a store one day and saw this book THE MEDICINE WHEEL GARDEN by Barrie E. Kavasch. I loved the cover; it had a huge round garden surrounded by big stones. There was a row of stones that made a cross through the middle with herbs filling each quadrant. I read the bio and saw that Barrie was a descendant of Pocahontas and a Master herbalist. I bought the book and read through the wonderful stories of what a Medicine Wheel Garden was and the tradition of Native Americans who had them for health and ritual purposes. In the back Barrie had herbal recipes. I had to make a Medicine Wheel Garden. There was a way of incorporating the 4 cardinal directions, peace poles and plants. I flipped open the book again and saw that Barrie lived in the next town. I went back to the store and asked if they knew her. Of course, they did, was the reply. They gave me her phone number and I dialed, not knowing what to expect. I heard the sweetest voice that sent out loving vibrations, tell me she would come over and show me how to create one. WOW, I thought. I asked her how much it would cost, and she did not answer so I decided I would trust, and it would be affordable. Barrie came over and spent the day with Nico, Salvatore and I. We walked our property, identifying herbs. She showed us how to journal plants by placing a leaf under a page in your journal and on the previous page color over it with a pencil or crayon, so you have the imprint. After you would label them and write some of their healing properties. I felt something ancient inside of me had reawakened. It was otherworldly, other dimensional. It felt, as if, I had returned home, a home from a past life. Nico journaled and listened intently to every word she said, even though he was only 3 at the time. Barrie helped us choose a place for our garden and taught us how to do it. When the day's journey ended, I thought it was worth any amount of money. "What do I owe you?" I asked. "Oh, my dear," she sweetly said, "nothing." I was awash in peace and love. I hugged her and she told me that she could be found, very often, at her friend Barrie Sachs' store, called Happy Rainbows in the next town over, Sherman. In the years to come I would find an herb on my property that she hadn't identified for me (there were so many) and bring it to her and she would tell me all about. I also read book after book after book and did my own self-study on how to use herbs and how to make remedies. I was hooked.

A great blessing from this path is that I met one of my dearest friends in my life, Barrie Sachs, she is a beautiful, kind, loving and giving soul. Happy Rainbows is a magical little world that you enter through a rainbow arched door tucked back in the corner of a small parking lot. Inside there are crystals and teas, fairy dust, essential oils, incense and more. Nico and I would enter the portal and never leave. It is a tiny little place, but you can stay there for hours talking to Barrie and finding magical things.

One day Barrie invited me to her home to make dream catchers and be part of a drumming circle. I had never been to one before and did not know what to expect. As I entered, I felt like I knew many of the people there, although not in this lifetime. The first person I met was Lightning Heart who was a Native American Indian who had been struck by lightning 3 times and lived. Then I met Nancy and Patricia, Nancy was a naturopathic doctor and was writing a book entitled HEALING CANCER PEACEFULLY, a journey about her herbal path through cancer. The minute I saw her, and Patricia I felt a connection.

Barrie called everyone to the living room so she could teach us how to make a dream catcher, some already knew how to do this. If you don't know, a dream catcher is a Native American tool, if you will, for catching bad thoughts and negativity before it enters your room or your dream state. You hang it in your bedroom window or over your bed. It has a spider web pattern and for the outside we used grape vines that Barrie had harvested which we shaped into a circle. Beads and feathers are also used. We were all struggling a bit with the technique of the web, and I turned to Salvatore who was quietly almost done with the most beautiful dream catcher I had ever seen. Everyone stopped to look at this lovely sight. Barrie asked if he had ever made one before. No, he replied and kept working. "Past life, past life, past life" was mumbled through the group. We were then presented with a variety of Native American drums and told to drum in a big circle. Barrie said that the rhythm would naturally come together from the group's energy, and we would end when the energy motivated us all to stop. No voice command would be given. I began to drum, as did Nico, and I felt like I was transported to another time and place. I felt I was in an Indian village surrounded by teepees with a blazing fire. At one point I returned to the present and noticed Salvatore was not drumming, he was off to the side, watching as I faded back to wherever I was. Later I asked why he did not participate in the drumming. "I was observing" he said. What were you observing, I asked? "The biggest bunch of witches I ever saw in my life." AHHHH I was home. Now I do not mean an evil witch, I think that witches long ago were the wise woman, the herbalists, the healers and got an extremely bad deal in the inquisition and in Salem and maybe even with Kitty. I think we should be proud to return to that tradition, (although it seems to be a fad now to call yourself a Witch, I do so in a different sense, one of a lifetime or lifetimes). A whole new world was opening to me, a wonderful world that I had known before.

One of my yoga students went to Salem Mass., a place I visited as a kid and loved. She brought me back a book about witches. The real witches and the witch trials. I read it and as I got to a particular part, it felt strangely familiar to me. I felt I knew this woman. NO, actually I should say, I felt I was this woman. She was a strong, fiery individual who was an herbalist and would publicly yell at anyone who tried to put down what she was doing. She stood up for herself and her beliefs and was killed for it. I had dreams about being burned at the stake but read that she was hung. Why did I keep having this dream? I decided to meditate on this. I found my quiet space and no longer needed to look into a candle flame, I could reach this state in many ways at many times. I saw myself during the inquisition, it was another lifetime. I was being persecuted for my practice of herbal medicine and my beliefs. The mayor of the town was someone I knew now in this lifetime who was not a positive person in my life. The mayor was reading my crimes, out loud, as I was tied to the stake, surrounded by wood. He was happy to have power over me. I saw that he was angry because I had rejected his offer for romance in that life. A man was holding a torch and lit the fire. As I felt the heat, I looked at the man and the mayor and saw the faces of two people in my present lifetime (the torch holder being my sister). I knew that I had to get them out of my life. A week later the mayor/woman in this life came to my yoga class and I went to adjust her head as she was laying down. She gave me a strange smile and let out a soft sighing moan that was a little creepy. I saw the image rush back and knew it was her. When I got home, the lighter of the flame battered me with a nasty phone call. It took me a little time, but I stepped far away from both of them.

Instead of letting this past life get me down, it empowered me. I felt strong. I felt that I would never let anyone squash me for my beliefs, ever again. I felt more connected to myself, to nature and to my spirit guides, of which I have many. Salvatore was also connecting to his spirit guide but got a little stuck with the receiving of the message. This was a time before Lucy (our pug) had died and before Nico was conceived. He kept having this reoccurring dream in which a beautiful grey and white wolf would appear before him. He had the same dream every night and the wolf would stand in front of him. I asked him what he thought the wolf wanted. He said he did not know. I told him that dreams are very powerful and as much as they guide you, you must participate. I told him the next time the wolf came he should ask the wolf, in his dream, what the wolf wanted. Night after night the wolf came to Salvatore and morning after morning I asked if he had asked the wolf what he wanted. "I forgot," was the answer. Until one morning, I got a different answer. The wolf came to him and was staring at him, and Salvatore was staring back, finally, Lucy jumped into his dream and said, "ask the wolf, ask your wolf!" So, he did. The wolf walked him to a lake where there was a dock. I was sitting on the dock with a two-year-old child, whom he described as a young boy with blondish/brown hair and big eyes who was with Jimmie, my other pug. The wolf nodded to Salvatore and then walked away with Lucy. As the wolf walked toward the woods he turned into Salvatore's grandfather, a great and loving man who had passed when Salvatore was 16. Within the year Lucy died and I was pregnant with Nico who at the age of 2 looked exactly like the image the wolf showed Salvatore.

I began to have many experiences with past lives. When I would give someone a healing I would see images, almost like a movie, pass in front of my mind. I would tell my client what I saw, and they would always say that was what was occurring in this lifetime also. I began to discover that we repeat energies over and over again, until we heal them. Through my healing work I saw many people repeat mistakes from past lifetimes, life after life continuing until they took the time and energy to seek healing and actually change. Some lives were hard to share, they were brutal. I know many people are told, that in a past life, they were someone famous, but I mostly saw lives where people were poor, struggling, working hard. I saw stories, stories that related to their pattern that they were repeating now. If the person I was working with would accept the past life and LEARN FROM IT, they usually moved out of the cycle and onto something better. We repeat energies, from choosing a partner who is not positive in our lives to patterns of low self-worth and much more. We must change the energy and release it. Just as everything vibrates, and we can match vibration and heal we can also remove negative vibrations that are harming us. They stick to us and stay with us lifetime after lifetime until we work to let them loose, so we are free.

Barrie Sachs performs something called THE SINGING BOWLS. The singing bowls are a transcending experience that you should not miss in your lifetime. She has various sized quartz crystal bowls which she places on a blanket in the center of the room. Everyone lays around the room on blankets and yoga mats with their heads facing the bowls. Each bowl has its own musical note, and each relates to a different chakra. Chakras are energy centers in your body, and out of your body. We are made of energy; we are filled with energy and have places where that energy gathers. If you have ever had acupuncture or a massage you can feel where the energy is blocked when the practitioner presses on a particular spot or puts a needle there because it hurts. The practitioner will then release the energy with pressure or the needle. Once the energy begins to flow freely you can start the healing process and feel better. There are seven main chakras in your body. If your chakras are out of balance, so are you. Barrie's singing bowl ceremony is a great way to heal and balance your chakras through sound vibration. It usually lasts about one hour, and Barrie tells you to let the bowls take you where they will and if you fall asleep, try not to snore.

The first experience I had with this ceremony was at our yoga studio. I was lying in between Salvatore and Nico and Barrie was guiding us through sound. As the bowls rang, I felt my body melt away and a colorful cloud engulfed me. I was lifted above my body and was melting into something beyond the physical. The colors began to form a scene before me from a moment in time long ago. I saw two older women and a young boy walking on a path through the woods. I knew one woman was me, the other was Barrie and the boy was Nico, but we did not look the same as we do in this lifetime. We were harvesting herbs. The scene changed and I was lying on the ground. "Nico" and "Barrie" were comforting me and the boy, (Nico) looked devastated. I realized that I had gotten bit by a poisonous snake and was dying. I was trying to tell the boy that I would be with him in spirit always and the woman (Barrie) would take care of him and raise him. I felt the energy drain from that body and I came back to the present, to the singing bowl as Barrie was ending the session. I looked over at Nico and he was very upset. I ask what he saw. He almost started to cry and then described the exact same vision I had seen. Very often, after that, when Nico and I were at a singing bowl we would have the same past life experience. One time he was a young Indian warrior off to battle on his horse, I was old and staying behind. He did not want to leave me, but I told him he had to move on his path and live his life, with strength. He saw the same lifetime, the same story. Barrie was there for me and Nico in our past life and I would realize later that she was also there for me in this life, in so many wonderful ways, as a true and loving friend.

CHAPTER 10

EGYPT AND CHANTING

I wanted to know more about healing with sound, an ancient healing art that dates back to Ancient Egypt and probably even much earlier than that. There is a place called Abu Garab in Egypt. It is in the band of peace, where there are 6 plateaus. The northern most is Abu Rowash, then Giza, Abu Garab, Abusir, Saqqara and Dashour. You can see the next pyramid or group of pyramids from the previous one. At Abu Garab there is a very large quartz crystal altar. It is circular in the middle, carved flat on top with carvings that point to the four cardinal directions, north, south, east, and west. Adjacent are giant crystal bowls. There are holes on the sides. Many scholars will tell you that this is thought to be a sacrificial altar and the holes in the bowls, they thought, were to let the blood from the sacrifice pour out. Some very wise archeologists chose to open their eyes and began to ponder what this could really be. They presented their findings in a wonderful documentary series called THE PYRAMID CODE. They interviewed Hakim Awyan an Egyptian Egyptologist and archeologist. Hakim told his amazing story. He was an Indigenous Wisdom Keeper, yes, an

Indigenous Wisdom Keeper, great job title, isn't it? He grew up in the band of peace and his job was to learn, keep and hold the oral traditions of the Ancient Egyptians. Hakim said as a child he would play in the tunnels under the pyramids, which were filled with water. Water that leads to the ocean. As I watched the show I began to ponder, were these perhaps giant singing bowls?

Further down the band of peace is the step pyramid at Saqqara - the only real pyramid "TOMB." Saqqara has a courtyard which dates back before 2900 BC. Hakim tells us that in the courtyard were three chambers that were part of THE HOUSE OF SPIRIT, a healing sanctuary, where you can find an investigation table with steps leading up to it. Hakim said the patient chose where to stand and each point was connected to a chamber (there are 22). The healer would go inside the chamber, where there was running water underneath, and stick their head in a niche and listen. Through the vibration they could tell what was wrong with the patient. Did they heal them with vibration? Sound? The large singing bowls at Abu Garab?

In most cultures, music, sound, chant, is vital. During the time of slavery in America, some Africans were forced to leave their tribes and families to come here and to be slaves. They held on to their traditions and would drum. The slave owners feared the drums and the power of the beat. The Africans were actually communicating with the drums. The drums were expressing words, ideas and emotions. Many Indigenous Tribes call the drum the heartbeat of Mother Earth. The Aboriginal people from Australia began using sound over 40,000 years ago to heal diseases, broken bones and muscles using what is now the didgeridoo. Pythagorus believed that the proper use of sound was medicine. Singing bowls have been used for thousands of years in Tibet, China, and Japan. The sounds of bowls were also used throughout time and place. Chanting is such a vital part of Buddhist, Jewish, Christian, and Islamic Cultures. Chant is a form of prayer. Chanting mantras, the name of the Divine, of God are still used throughout the world.

From the first time I heard the deep voice of Krishna Das radiate through my being with an OM, I was hooked. Listening to him chant brought me deeper and deeper into a place of peace. Krishna Das was born in Brooklyn, NY and went to Stony Brook College. He was struggling with depression. His dream was to be a rock star and he had the voice for it. He was asked to be the lead singer in Blue Oyster Cult but at the time he was called to a place that was his true destiny, so he turned down the offer. Ram Das came into his life and told him that he needed to go to India where he met his Guru, Neem Karoli Baba or Maharishi. Krishna Das knew his current path was one of self-destruction and it was time to find a change. He said that when he met his guru he was overwhelmed with a feeling of LOVE, pure and unconditional LOVE, pouring so powerfully out of this being. In his book CHANTS OF A LIFETIME, which I recommend to you highly, he tells the story of his first experience with Chant. He was in India, for his first visit, to meet Neem Karoli Baba. He was bathing in his presence when "Baba" asked the Westerners to Chant Hare Krishna for hours, outside because the Kirtan Wallahs, as they were called, had been thrown out for doing stuff they should not have. Krishna Das was not happy about this. He wanted to be near Baba. He explains how he had to repeat Hare Krishna, Hare Krishna, Krishna, Krishna, Hare, Hare and he was bored out of his mind. He took a number of trips to the bathroom, he let his mind wander to the United States, people in his life until a moment when something happened. He says he got lost in the chant. He then wanted to change his life from suffering and addiction to spreading healing and love through chant, which he does so powerfully with his music. He explains that by chanting the Divine name you find the path, you find peace.

One day the "westerners" asked Neem Karoli Baba how to meditate. He thought for a long time and then told them to meditate like Christ. They thought about this and later pursued the question for they did not know what his answer meant. Baba sat silent for a very long time, until he said, "He lost himself in love." Wow, I thought, to lose yourself in love. That is true healing and light. I began to chant. I would put on Krishna Das and he would say a line and I would repeat it, which is what Kirtan singing is, call and response. It was like flushing all the junk out of my mind. All those thoughts, the mind chatter, Chitta Vritti, would fade away. I started playing Krishna Das for my students in my yoga classes that I taught at my studio and at Kent Prep School where I teach yoga four days a week to the high school students and one day to the administration and faculty. I have boys from the Football team take my class. Girls and boys on the basketball and Hockey teams, Pianists, Mathematicians and Robotics Team students. They are all wonderful and I feel great joy sharing yoga with them and seeing them find some peace in this crazy world. When they hear Krishna Das for the first time, I see them breath deeper. One by one, most ask, who is chanting. I share his own words through his book as they learn the asanas that are the gateway to health in body, soul, and mind. They download his music, and it helps them relieve stress in so many ways, helps them sleep, keeps them calm before exams, finding calm at take-off if they fear flying. One young man, who I think will change the world for the better, said to me one day before class, can you please play the Krishna Das CD that has the hands in prayer on the front. He had been through a traumatic experience for one of the students had committed suicide and he was the one who found him first. My heart felt warm as I put it on the CD knowing it would help him find some peace. Krishna Das heals through chant.

A Krishna Das concert is an experience that is enlightening. He chants and tells stories about his life while you float around and at some point, some of us, get up and start dancing, twirling, letting the music flow through every cell in our bodies. It is so freeing and wonderful. An outpouring of love. Chanting changes the brain, it increases the thickness of the hippocampus, which is the part of the brain that is memory and learning. It also reduces the amygdala (STRESS, fear). It all makes sense if you think about what I said earlier, everything vibrates, we all vibrate. Change the Vibration, raise the vibration and you are healthy and happy. It is magic.

Every summer I treat myself to a yoga retreat with my teachers Sharon Gannon and David Life at their Wild Woodstock Yoga Retreat. Sharon and David are wonderful beings who share yoga, teachings, healing, love, and light with many. They are definitely lights in this world. I love that they are seekers of knowledge, seekers of the light. I say seekers because although they have such wisdom they are always seeking more, always reading, learning, studying. That is what I do and live and feel and I think it is so important. If you could see their amazing library you would understand, it is filled with books, from great historical figures to various religions and so much more. To truly teach others, to heal and expand, you must first do it yourself. They are continually expanding so I continually learn from them. I love and thank them for this, and they have become dear friends and a special part of my life. I love them both with all my heart and cherish their friendship. They introduced me to the chants of Bhagavan Das, who was with Krishna Das in India with Neem Karoli Baba. He gave a concert at the retreat one night. Upon entering the studio, I saw a beautiful picture of Baba at the altar-stage, where Bhagavan Das and a woman with hair down to her waist sat. Both were dressed in white. There were candles burning in front of them and bowls filled with rose petals. They held large Indian instruments. As they began to chant, I truly went deeper and deeper into another dimension. I was conscious of the music and my body, but I was not in it. I was not above it; I was expanded beyond it. Three hours later, as the concert was ending, the beautiful lady was throwing rose petals at us and giving us cookies, I came back into my body, maybe that's why they give you cookies, to be more aware of the physical because it was not easy to get fully back in there. I was so expanded I didn't think I would fit in my car to drive home, nor did I think I could drive, but they brought us back enough to safely travel. The power of chant is amazing.

CHAPTER 11

HEALING ANIMALS and the REALM BEYOND

The more I shared chanting the more I saw people growing and healing with it. At our alpaca farm sanctuary, we have 29 alpacas 1 pig, 1 sheep, 11 cats, 2 dogs and chickens. They are all wonderful and it is, to me, another form of meditation, to spend time with them, to care for them, to feel their vibration. You can look at taking care of them two ways, one way is - I (quit literally) deal with a lot of shit, every day. There is so much to do. I have to clean poop piles, clean and change water buckets, lift heavy bales of hay etc, etc. or you can look at it the way I do, with joy. I get to spend time with the most beautiful and wonderful beings who are a part of my family. As I clean, they come up and sniff me and run around. Some of them play little games like taking my hat and pulling it off my head when I am not looking (Gypsy Rose). They almost smile at me as I turn around, only for them to do it again. One even puts his head on my chest so I can pet him, and they often won't let me do my work (D'Artagnan). It is wonderful and I love it. I sing and chant while I do my chores.

Some of the barn cats that live with us are what they call "shaky cats". They were born with a small cerebellum and have no coordination, so they tend to fall over a lot when they walk. They have to stay inside, and Nico put thick rubber mats down in the hay room so they can live there with their mom, brothers and sisters and not get hurt. Don't feel sorry for them, they live in their higher consciousness and are proud and happy cats. We used to have to hold them while they ate, or they would fall into each other and not get enough food. Then one day Nico found this large kitty condo shaped like a flower at Goodwill and we brought it home to them. Yoda, the tiniest kitty, who would often get pushed away at feeding time, found her way into the flower, and learned that she could happily eat in an upright position balancing against the sides of the "stem." We got another large cat scratcher that was shaped like a triangle and Velcro would then place himself in the center where he could eat upright. They were finding their way. Every morning Nico does "kitty therapy" with them, holding them as they walk around. They are getting steadier as time moves along because they are developing muscle and muscle memory. Now Salvatore was looking at farm life more in the first way. Work hard, get it done, ugggghhhh. Then one day I heard Krishna Das playing in the barn, and I walked in and he was happily cleaning the barn and listening to the chant. He smiled at me and said it changed the way he thought. He spent a long time up there that day. I have learned so much about healing and life through my animals. They are a gift of love.

How did the whole alpaca sanctuary begin? It started when Nico was three, I wanted to take him to the Sheep and Wool Festival. It is a wonderful festival held locally in October where there are sheep and alpacas and wonderful things made out of their fiber. I asked my dad to come with Nico and I, Salvatore was working, and off we all went. As we walked around, I saw my first alpaca ever. I looked into this wonderful beings' eyes, and I felt such love. They radiate a vibration that is so amazing. I stared into one particular alpaca's huge eyes for a very long time and then I turned to my dad and told him I wanted an alpaca. He said he thought they were very expensive, I agreed but I felt a connection that I could not explain. My dad bought Nico a little white fluffy alpaca toy and we had a great day. In December of that year my dad passed away, quit suddenly, after a heart attack. The night he died I cried and cried but then I heard his voice, loud and clear, as if he were in the room with me, saying "I am still here, I am still here, "then finally yelling "I AM STILL HERE!" I realized he was. I told him I knew he was there, and I knew he would show me a sign. About a month later we were renting out the gatehouse on our property and a woman called with some questions. She told me she had two alpacas and asked if she could bring them to live on the farm with her. I was overjoyed and told her so. She came to visit and told me this was the place for her alpacas. Later she phoned and said she could not rent the house; she was going through a divorce and things were getting difficult. She said she had to sell the alpacas, who were normally very expensive, but she would sell them to me at a low price. I accepted because I knew this was a sign from my dad and I wanted the alpacas. Cinnamon and Shakespeare arrived. Cinnamon was the color of cinnamon and wore a knit scarf of the same color. Shakespeare was pure white and donned a white scarf. I was so excited, and I raised my head to the sky and thanked my dad.

Our alpaca family has grown to 29 and we are now a rescue sanctuary where we have rescued and helped many alpacas. I was given some very ill alpacas and had to learn how to care for them. I would lay my hands on them and try to listen to what they needed. I often got answers, like a whisper in my brain, telling me herbs they needed, homeopathic remedies, guidance. I tried to listen and open, through the highest and the best. One of my alpacas, King Solomon, had mange, which is like an eczema for alpacas. He was in bad shape when he arrived on the farm. He had a terrible fungus on his feet that had never healed and there were raw, and he had dry/bloody patches all over his body. He had runny eyes that were sadly squinting. I called the vet who said there were some medicines we could do internally and externally, but they would not help much. I knew I could help him and I began to give him healings through which I would open to where I was guided and what I should do. I started mixing essential oils that I was shown in the meditations and finally had my potion ready. I sprayed it on him every morning and every night. Within 2 months he was back to his full fleece and no longer had fungus on his toes. I made a salve for his eyes, and they were getting better also (although sometimes I did need the medicine here for you don't want to put too much in the eyes). The vet came by one day and was standing near him looking around. She then asked in a compassionate voice, where the alpaca was. "Right there," I replied, pointing to Solomon. She did a double take and said, "no, the one with the severe mange." When she finally realized it was him, she could not believe it.

I gave the remedy to other friends whose animals, including

dogs, had skin problems and it worked beautifully. One day I was telling the story to one of Nico's friends and she told me that she had eczema for 3 years and had tried every medicine and natural remedy the doctors could think of, but nothing worked. She asked if she could try my spray. I gave her a bottle and three weeks later she came to me, pulled up her sleeves and said it was gone, all gone. I was so happy. I then started to sell the spray at farmers markets. At one market a man approached me with dry, scaly, red hands and said he would buy a bottle and would return next week to tell me if it worked. I told him, he would have to give it more than one week. The following week I was writing a receipt and felt a hand in front of my face. I looked at the hand, and up at the man, I looked back at the hand because the skin looked perfect and back at the man because he was the one from the week before. He smiled. I was happy I could help him. I cannot say that it works 100% of the time but most of the time people come back with a hug and a smile saying it worked. I started to use it on everything after that. Sofia, my pug had some lumps on her skin, I sprayed it, they were gone. She had some waxy buildup in her ears, spray and it was gone. Once Salvatore was at a Farmer's Market and a man had tried it weeks before, he hugged Salvatore and told him he was healed of terrible eczema and his life was now changed. He was so very grateful. I use therapeutic grade oils and my mix contains cedar, rosemary, and lavender.

One of the alpacas we took in was a famous alpaca named "Quick Silver." He was one of the first alpacas to come from Peru. He was very old, around 19, and we were told that he did not get up much anymore and they did not know if he would even make the van ride over to our farm, they doubted it. I talked to Nico and told him we needed to take this alpaca for as long as he would live and try to help him even though it would be sad when he died, which might be shortly after he got here. Nico agreed, he said we had to give him a good and happy home. When Quick Silver arrived, he came out of the van, and he could barely stand or barely walk. Salvatore and I decided he should live with the girls, for they were calmer. He was obviously not in any shape to mate with the girls, so we did not have to worry about him getting one of them pregnant. We parked the van near the girl's barn. Quick Silver stumbled out and we sadly and slowly walked him step by step to the girl's pasture and opened the gate. At times I did not think he would make it there. When he got into the girl's field, he looked up and saw he was surrounded by girls. In a matter of seconds he jumped, quite literally, into full life and started jumping on all of the girls. He lived a long and happy year and then died peacefully one day with his head on Salvatore's lap while I gave him a healing. Right before he passed the girl alpacas came in one by one and bowed to him, sniffed his head, and left. They knew it was his time to move on and came to send him off. It was very sad but also very peaceful and beautiful to see how they treated death. We would see his image, often after that, in the fields and felt his gratitude.

Our next challenge was a sick alpaca named Snow Queen. She was a beautiful, all white girl and she had become partially paralyzed after meningeal worm. She could move her legs and when we lifted her, she could stand and take some steps but could not do it on her own. We were growing exhausted after 2 months of lifting her 4 times a day. She was 150 pounds. Salvatore found a wonderful farmer, online, who had designed a kind of sling and pulley for alpacas. When it arrived we set it up outside. Once we lifted her, we could help her walk there and harness her. She could take little steps around by herself and stand and eat and be part of her herd and I could do physical therapy with her. Our Vet came to do acupuncture.

Everyday morning when I went to the girl's barn, I was greeted by a beautiful white turkey. She would follow me everywhere and loved to be around when we set up Snow Queen. She would sit with me as I did physical therapy and then walk away. Jen Jen, who started helping us with the animals and quickly became one of our family named her Regina. One day I looked at Jen Jen with horror. Regina was from the farm across the street. They are the most wonderful people you could meet but they are a "farm" and I thought of Regina's fate. It was almost my birthday and Salvatore asked me what I wanted. "Regina!" I said. Please go pay our neighbor whatever he would get for her to be a Thanksgiving Dinner and let her live. Our neighbor was happy to do so and continued to feed her when she wandered back to him. When the time came for Snow Queen to leave this form, Regina was right there. I thanked Snow Queen for her strength and all of the lessons she had taught me. I anointed her body with Frankincense Oil as Regina watched. I then thanked Regina for always being at my side. I felt she was there for me. What I quickly realized was that she had been there for Snow Queen, for shortly after Snow Queen passed Regina was gone. I feared something had gotten her and she was now in the realm with Snow Queen but one day, months later, Nico and I saw her walking towards us accompanied by a large grey turkey and a little baby turkey. She stood and stared at us, as if to say, this is my family now. They then turned and walked off, never to be seen again.

A few years later Maybelline, a beautiful brown alpaca with white spots and white stripes around her eyes had a baby who we named Hanuman (the monkey god who was filled with devotion). He was born on the 4th of July and weighed 14 pounds. He stood up right away, which they do, and began to sniff around. I have never seen an alpaca actually being born, although I really wanted to. I even attended classes to learn how to assist in the process if necessary. When an alpaca is due, I am up there all day long. They always wait until the minute you leave to give birth. When the baby is born you want to make sure that the baby nurses within the first half hour or so. Hanuman did not. We went through four long hours of calling the vet who did not come because it was the fourth of July, and he was away. He gave us instructions which we followed, squeeze some milk out and let the baby drink it then brings the baby to the mom. Nothing was working. Hours passed, which was not good, and I finally realized I was in farmer mode and stressing out and not in healer mode. I took a deep breath and decided to balance their chakras. I placed my hands first above Maybelline's Root Chakra. It took a while before I felt the energy of the fiery ball of red light. I was making clockwise circular motions with my hands following where the energy lead me. Then I moved up below the belly to the orange chakra, again, making the energetic hand circles and so on through each chakra up through the crown. The lower chakras seemed stuck but got moving after a while. I than started the same process with baby Hanuman. When I was done, he looked at me and walked straight to his mom and started nursing. It was midnight by them. Ahhhhhh, the power of healing and faith. Hanuman is a very healthy big boy who lives in the barn with his dad and his mom is great too.

CHAPTER 12

MAX

I have grown to view life and death, life, and past lives as part of the whole, part of the one vibration where the past, present and future are all one. When we are younger, we are not blocked by matter, we are still close to the divine realm. The more we attach to the material world the more difficult it is for us to see what is beyond it. People often forget the spirit they truly are or cover the spirit energy with material energy, so they lose contact with the SOURCE. We need to support our children's connection so they never lose it. When Nico was 3, we were in the car and he asked "Mommy, who is Max?" "Max? You mean our cat?" I asked. "No mommy, it is a man." I got a chill because I felt something. All I could think about was my dad's dad, Mac, or Max as they called him. I had never met him, he died before my mom and dad were married. I said "Do you mean grandpa's daddy? The picture in the hall of the man with the mustache and the uniform?" "Yes!" he said. "That's him." Another wave of knowing filled my body. "Why," I asked. "Oh, because he's right here, next to me." I felt it, I felt him. I told Nico to ask him why he was there, what he wanted, but he only told Nico he was there to say hi. That night I went into meditation/healing mode and asked why he came, what did he want, even though, deep inside, I knew. He told me to tell my dad to have ginger, it was important. Ginger helps increase circulation and prevent blood clots. I knew it was my dad's heart. He had a quadruple by-pass about 15 years earlier and felt great since, although he did not take care of himself in the way I would have wished.

That night, I had a very strange dream, I was passing by Stewart's, a shop near my dad's house, and I saw the sign for the store as a map, showing me direction, which I later realized was to my dad's house. I then entered a dark tunnel, it was a strange tunnel, it was a pinkish brown and soft. The walls were thick and inside it was very dark. The tunnel seemed to go on forever. There were parts that were so congested I could barely get through. I kept saying to myself, there is no way out of this, no way. I woke up and felt that it was hard to breath.

It was Thanksgiving Day and I had to work in the city at the Macy's Parade, which is fun. I work for Disney, special events and get to do a lot of cool stuff like that. Salvatore and Nico came with me, and we took the train to my dad's house afterwards. He came to pick us up so we could have Thanksgiving Dinner together, with lots of wonderful veggies and salad. He had gathered the whole family. On the way there

I told him about Max. He sat quietly for a moment and stared. He then looked up and took a deep breath and said he didn't like ginger. That was my dad, knowing the deeper meaning but making a little joke. I said he could get a natural ginger ale at the health food store. Then I looked at him and said, "you mean your dad came from the spirit world to give you a message and you're not going to do it?" He thought about it with a kind-of laugh and said he guessed I was right.

The day was wonderful, my dad's wife Lois' kids had all come with their children from Washington and Virginia, my sister was there. She had not visited for about 20 years. This was a gathering that had not happened before. My dad was so happy. After dinner I found him in the family room watching Disney movies with all the young children, on the couch. They were surrounding him. He had the most content look on his face. I sat with him, and we watched Fantasia. The next day after everyone left my dad had a heart attack. He was in the hospital, and they were doing a procedure and I was in the waiting room, the nurse came to get me when I was in the bathroom and told my dad I was not there. My dad said, he was sure I was, and she came back and there I was. Sadly, I was the only one there. My sister did not come for things like this, and Lois did not either. Within 2 weeks he died. I realized the tunnel that I had been in was one of his arteries. The doctor said they were so blocked and as he explained I went back to my dream and felt it. This was such a great loss. My father meant the world to me, to Nico, to Salvatore, to many. He had so much love and kindness in him, and he always had wise words and guidance. Although I had seen the signs from Max, through my dream, it still did not seem like it would have manifested. Even when I have premonitions, I still don't always understand how real they are, or maybe I don't want to.

I tried to reach through the sorrow so I could feel him and hear him. Nico was devastated. I asked him if he felt grandpa, he said, "no". I told him to try, and he said he could not. Now, Nico is a very "connected" child, this is the boy who, from the time he could talk, told me to balance his root chakra. I was surprised, "nothing?" I asked, "No," he said. I knew it was his grief that was stopping him. I sat with him on my bed one night and told him we were going to meditate. We started with a few deep breaths and then I told him to picture himself surrounded by a white fiery light and we did the white, violet and silver meditation. I told him to feel grandpa, to open his heart past the sadness. He took a deep breath and opened his eyes. His whole face changed, it lit up. He stared and smiled and said, "OH THERE YOU ARE!" He saw my dad clear as a bell. After that my dad would come to him all the time, especially at night. He was still guiding, teaching, loving. You see, it never goes away, it just changes form.

I remember on Star Trek, the original Star Trek, there was an episode where these beings turn into light at the end and they tell Captain Kirk that they can take on physical form but don't need it, they were much more evolved than humans. I believe it is like that. The more evolved we become spiritually the less we need matter.

As I went through my dad's things, I found some letters from Max which he had sent home from the army. He was stationed in France during WWII. I also found letters from my dad that he sent home to his parents when he was in the army stationed in Korea. I felt transported to a different place and time, as I read them. I felt like I was there and could see what they saw. I think letter writing, which is so sadly lost now, was another way we could time travel and see the past. Those letters helped me to find another part of my dad that I had not known. A way to connect to him and go beyond time. What is time travel, I pondered, for I felt as if I was on the edge of touching it.

Einstein says time is relative, he also said "...for us physicists believe the separation between past, present, and future is only an illusion, although a convincing one." I did not know how relevant this statement was. When I was going through my dad's things, I appreciated his filing system. The drawers were labeled, in a dad kind of way, I can't quit remember now but things like ridiculous, silly, illogical, and so on. When I opened the top drawer I laughed, there were bags of snickers bars that he had hidden for munching. That was my dad.

Animals also are closer to the spirit energy. Max the cat, that I thought Nico was referring to in the car that day, was a magical cat. He came to us in an interesting way. Nico and I were at Happy Rainbows talking to Barrie and there was a photo of a red tabby cat on the wall. Nico looked at it and said we had to get the cat. I told him that it was a picture of a cat not a cat that needed a home but then Barrie said that the cat, Max, did indeed need a home. She said they were friends of hers from New York and their dog had attacked the cat because they had moved and now lived on one floor whereas before they had two and the animals were separate. They were devastated to have Max leave their lives and Max needed a great home. Nico, of course, said the great home was ours and of course, I agreed.

On the day that Max arrived two old ladies came into the house with the carrier. The older one, Irene, the mom, asked me if I knew anything about homeopathy and handed me some information. I told her I practiced herbs and used some homeopathy. She was delighted. They told us Max was at least 12 years old, if not much older, they had rescued him many years earlier. She and her daughter Jeanette left telling Nico that he was their hero and a hero to Max. They came back once every year to visit Max and Nico and sent Nico and Max Christmas gifts every year. We became good friends. Nico bonded with Max immediately although Max took a little longer to adjust to the new environment he also bonded with Nico in a beautiful way, once he felt settled. Max would follow Nico and sleep on the bed with Jimmie and Sofia and Nico. He was so happy.

One night Nico and I were watching the movie Halloween Town. A great and fun Halloween film with Debbie Reynolds who plays the grandmother of Marney. Reynolds is a witch that comes from Halloween Town to visit her daughter, also a witch, who lives in the mortal realm and is trying to leave behind any thought of her magical past. Marney, the older daughter, loves Halloween but her mother will not let her partake in any celebrations. Marney is frustrated. When her grandmother arrives on Halloween night Marney overhears a conversation in which the grandmother is telling the mom that it is Marney's sixteenth birthday, and she must come back to Halloween Town with her to begin her magical witch training. It must be before midnight, or she will lose her powers. The mom says no for she does not want her children to know anything about their witchy and magical ancestry. At this point, my little Nico paused the movie and said, "Is there something you want to tell me?" I asked what he meant. He thought long and hard and mustered up his strength and said, "Am I a Witch? Or a Wizard?" I told him he was indeed but that it was different than in the movie. Magic, at least ours, was about healing and seeing. I also told him about my college fire lighting. He was content and so was Max. As I watched them, I stopped the film again and told him that Max was his familiar, Butterball was mine. He smiled and placed his hand on Max.

A few years later Max was beginning to get thinner and thinner, the Vet said that it was his thyroid and at the time I did not know as much about herbs as I do now and decided to do the advised medicine. Max was strong but I was concerned. One day Max was gone, we could not find him anywhere, we looked and looked but no Max. Did he get out, I thought? Nico was worried too, then a few days later, there was Max. Where did he go, I thought? This happened a few times over a period of about 5 weeks. Nico said that Max was really Puss In Boots and that he was the head of a Magical School for Wizards and would transport Nico there every night and they would have adventures. Nico said when Max was not here, he was there. One day Max went to the other realm and did not come back. We were all very sad, but Nico still saw him and went on nightly adventures with him.

As I write this story now it has been many years since I saw Max in physical form. One day I went to my old computer and found a picture of Max. That voice that I hear during healings came through and

I heard Max say, loud and clear," I'M COMING BACK! "What? I thought. "I'M COMING BACK!" "Oh, my dear Maxy," I said, we are not getting a kitten anytime soon. "NO," he said, "I am coming back just like this." I looked at the image of my skinny Max with his strange spine and remembered his odd walk. "Are you just going to appear in the middle of the living room?" I asked. "YES!" was the reply I heard. Two days later Salvatore called me and told me that he was at PETCO getting cat litter and that Max was there. "WHAT?!" I thought. He said the shelter had sent over some cats to try to get them adopted since Christmas was approaching. I thought, oh, that is nice, a cat that looks like Max and put it aside. Before Christmas Nico and I always buy food and litter and bring it to the shelter. This past year before we had even thought about this, Salvatore called and told me he was at the store and had bought all the food and litter and was heading to the shelter. "OK," I thought. That is odd because Nico and I always do that. He called an hour later and asked if I had seen the text he sent. "Of course, I did not," I responded. I never check my texts. I looked and almost dropped the phone. There was a picture of Max.

At this point in life Nico was 13 years old and I had been feeling my little wizard and all his magical beliefs fading away. Although he still did herbs with me and sometimes healings. Nico took the phone and looked and almost started to cry. "It's MAX! I don't understand! How can this be?" "I don't know either," I replied. "We have to go get him," he said. Salvatore came home and said that Max had followed him all around the shelter. He said, IT WAS MAX! That night Nico and I went to the shelter and sure enough, there was Max, they called him

COSMO. How old is COSMO? I asked. They said he was 9 at the oldest. (It had been years now that Max had gone to the other realm). He had Max' spine, Max' walk, Max' meow. He was Max reincarnated. He saw Nico and ran to him and butted his head against Nico's, he then waited until we filled out the adoption papers and got in the carrier all by himself.

When we got him home, we put him in the upstairs bedroom just so Ball, Penny and Sofia could adjust to him via smell. As you may know, bringing an older cat into a house with 2 older dogs and a cat could be difficult but since it was Max it was not. Two days after arrival, Max walked out of the room and Ball cat was overjoyed. He remembered Max and followed him everywhere and played with him. Max let Ball follow and they ran around all night playing, night after night.

I also knew it was Max because Max was used to all of my herbal remedies that I put in his food, which most cats will not tolerate. He was skinny and I was worried about his kidneys and thyroid. His fur was almost wiry and not smooth or soft. We fed him cooked chicken with zucchini, and I put dandelion root (which I had in the freezer for Sofia) in and a mix of other herbs and he ate it right away. Jen Jen came home for Christmas. By now she was in Veterinary school in Glasgow Scotland. She got into the room where Max was and froze. "It's MAX!" she said. Now being an almost VET, she had to be sure. She went and felt his spine, watched him walk, all the Max-isms. "THIS IS MAX!", she said. "I KNOW," was my reply. I did not know why he chose to come back as Max in the later stages of life. Why he chose to come back with thyroid issues and a crooked spine. Maybe he wanted us to understand that the material Max can pop in and out however he chooses. Perhaps he wanted us, or Nico and Salvatore to be 100 percent sure it was him. I would have believed no matter what form he chose. I don't know how long Max will choose to stay. I got a message/feeling that it would not be long, in this body, but that after he will return in another body that is much healthier and younger.

"The most beautiful experience we can have is the mysterious. It is the fundamental emotion that stands at the cradle of true art and true science.
Whoever does not know it and can no longer wonder, no longer marvel, is as
good as dead, and his eyes are dimmed." Another Einstein Quote

Max came back for Nico, to make him believe again.

My Mom and Dad

Me as Snow White

My Self Portrait

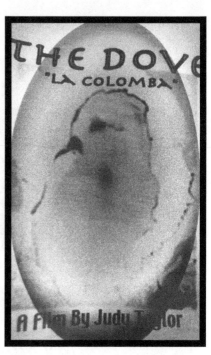

Water Stain of Dove

Salvatore and Nico

Drawing of Hatchepsut

My Paintings

CHAPTER 13

YOGA

I am a yoga teacher and believe in my yoga practice. I believe it helps me find peace, love, ME, and a realm that is beyond this physical one. I began doing yoga when I was about 5 years old. My mom would watch Lilias Folan on our little black and white TV and practice with her every morning. I remember she did the LION POSE. That is where you spread your fingers and stick out your tongue as far out and down as you can and bug out your eyes, while you look up. I loved that posture and I loved doing yoga with my mom in the morning. It gave me a great base and taught me how to breath and move. It taught me how to heal my body and meditate. Yoga has changed my life and when I teach my students at Kent Prep School, I see them change. They put down their phones, they breath, they move. By the end of the term most of them have transformed and are filled with questions and find some peace and joy.

In this day and age, everything is presented to us immediately via the internet, cell phones, pills, drugs, and most humans demand immediate results. Many say their internet is slow if it takes 30 seconds to load a page, 30 seconds! Yoga helps to teach us patience and calm our body and mind so we can get to a state of opening, a state where we can calm the mind with meditation, but it does not happen with one class or two. There is a reason that yoga is called a practice, as is meditation. You must actually practice it and do it every day or at least a couple of times a week. If you seek the magic pill, these days, the magic mushroom or the Ayahuasca, you are missing the practice and the journey. In your yoga and meditation **practice** you must go deeper each time to get to a higher state of consciousness. Some yoga practices do not do headstands, I do. I think they are vital in assisting you to find your higher self, which you just must take the time and look for because it is YOU. When you do a headstand, you are affecting your pineal gland, that little pinecone shaped gland in the center of your brain, your third eye, your higher consciousness. When you start to incorporate headstands into your life you actually can get high. I recommend starting little by little (at first do it against a wall with a good yoga teacher to guide you). Try to build up to 2 minutes a day. It truly connects you with YOU and brings you to another state of being. While in your headstand listen to some Krishna Das, Bhaghavan Das or other chanting and breathe deeply to help you transcend. If thoughts come up in your mind, go into your breath and let them go. See what the world looks like upside down. This is the time for you to connect, to yoke with the Divine, to see YOUR journey, where you are being guided spiritually. If you can advance to 5 minutes a day or at least a couple of times a week, it will help you see your life in a different way and you will also never need a face lift. We need to turn our material world upside down, quite literally to step out of stress and fear that has become ingrained in us and enter a higher state of being.

I tell all my students - you don't need alcohol or drugs, you have the best drug in the world right in your brain, you just need to activate it. Another plus, it doesn't mess with your physical body, it heals it. One of my students, Jamil, who was a basketball player, is a wonderful young man. He decided that he would build up to a 10-minute headstand during the term. The second to last day he accomplished his goal and did a full 10. He came out and had the most serene look on his face. He steadied himself against the wall and I told him to sit for a minute or 2 or 3, until he came back into his physical body. He sat through a long meditation. After class he floated off with his fellow teammates to attend a practice. The next day he came to class with the same serene look. I asked if he went to practice the previous day. He smiled and shook his head no. The other boys said "yes you did," so he smiled and shook his head yes. I asked how he did. They said it was one of his best practices to date. He then proceeded to have one of his best yoga classes also. The longest I ever held a headstand, to date, is 16 minutes. I floated around for 3 days after that; all was well in the world. Nothing bothered me. I seemed to be partially in this dimension while also being partially in another.

We have all the tools to be healthy, to be happy and to find what is real, but we must work to get there. Through this peace we can find our true self and all the answers which are present for us, we just have to see them. Through this practice we can reach the Divine. I think yoga is an amazing gift that if you can embrace will help you to blossom. Some people tell me they are too busy and have no time for yoga. No time for yoga? No time to connect to yourself and to the Divine? Really? Think about that, what is important in life? To me connecting to self so I can truly see and be, so I can find and see the Divine is vital. Besides I believe that yoga warps time. When you do a yoga practice all the "stuff" that you must do seems to get done easily and in less time. The more we can take time for connecting the more we can connect to what we think is true, what we think is real and see through all that has been told to us. If we just follow along a path that is laid out for us, we are not living life through knowledge, we are living life though someone else's eyes. Open your third eye and see with YOUR yoga sight, YOUR heart, YOUR soul. Close your eyes and see with your third eye. What is real to you? Do yoga, it will change your life.

CHAPTER 14

DANDELION

There are magical healing tools that pour out of Mother Earth to help heal us. They are called herbs. Those beautiful plants that appear everywhere on the planet. Some people call them weeds and get weed killer to destroy these powerful healers because they prefer grass. Now here is my theory about why you would want grass and no other plants. As one who has alpacas or anyone who has animals who eat grass, you want your animals to be healthy and graze on grass, clovers and other plants that are the best thing for them. You work hard to get the proper PH in the soil and even mow the grass or other plants to let the grasses take over. If you do not have animals there is no need for this procedure. We don't eat grass. On the other hand, we can and should eat the other plants growing in the yard. I cringe every time I hear the commercials for weed killers. "Kill the dandelions," they state. What!? I ask. Besides killing the medicinal plant, you are also filling Mother Earth with toxic chemicals which are detrimental to the bees, the birds and all insects and guess what, if they are gone, so are we. Dandelions, Taraxacum Officinale in Latin, are amazing. The root is great for your liver, and they are filled with iron that is easily assimilated into the body. I make a decoction and a tincture and take it all through the spring. A decoction is when you take the roots of a plant and boil them for a period of time. Never boil leaves, you will destroy a lot of their energy. The roots are great for your blood, your liver, your kidneys, your heart. The leaves of the dandelion are great in salads, a little bitter, but when mixed with other greens they give a nice added flavor. They contain calcium, potassium, zinc, and vitamins A, B, C, and D. Dandelion root helps remove the fat in your liver, cleaning it out so you can digest food better. When you digest food better, you absorb more nutrients and thus are healthier. Dandelion also helps to clean your blood. Every spring I wait until the beautiful flowers appear, filling my lawn with medicine and healing. On a sunny day I harvest them for they are flowers of the sun, opening their bright yellow petals to the glorious rays of light. Before harvesting I ask the plant if I may use it for medicine. If they are waving toward me, I will pick those, if they seem to turn away then I do not. I also thank them for their healing. I harvest a big bowl of dandelion flowers and some violets which are filled with vitamins, to make Dandelion Wine, the brew will take 6 months before it is ready. I also make a yummy and healthy Dandelion Summer Cooler. (RECIPE at end of book)

I knew Dandelion was powerful, but I did not know how amazing it was until one day when I was faced with one of the most difficult parts of healing, which is to heal yourself, your family and your animals in a crisis. It can be trying to keep your energy and spirits aiming in the right direction. It is so easy to let fear and pain seep in and often hard to focus on being positive, but we must. If we fog our brain with fear and worry it creates that energy. This became a challenge for me. Sofia, my pug had a severe case of Lyme Disease about four years ago. One day she woke up and she was paralyzed from the neck down. I carried her into the vet, and she did a blood test. She said the levels for Lyme were the highest they could possibly be, and that Sofia would have to go on heavy duty antibiotics for at least three months and they would probably make her extremely ill. I told her that I would treat Sofia at home with my remedies. The Vet said she trusted what I did with herbs, but this was very serious. She said she would give it two days with my treatment, and I should go back at that time, and we would discuss it. I began my Lyme Remedy which includes Frankincense and Turmeric and returned to the Vet two days later. Sofia walked right into the office, not perfectly at first, that would come a week or so later, but she did indeed walk. The Vet was shocked.

Sofia was back to her normal, healthy self within two weeks, aside from a couple small flare ups over the years, at which time I redid the remedy protocol. I also had to create a daily herbal regimen for her. I caught the flair ups earlier each time and started at a better point, but it still always seemed to take about eight days of remedies. When she had flare ups it was hard to be positive, I got sad and discouraged. I keep trying to get to my higher self but when I see MY little pug not feeling good, doubts can creep in. I had to keep telling myself that she was improving daily, taking steps to her recovery. Daily I checked how she walked, her eyes, were they brighter? How did she eat, poop, pee? I wrote everything down because believe it or not we don't always remember perfectly and clearly.

This past year, about 4 years after Sofia's first bout with Lyme, was a trying year, to say the least. Salvatore's appendix burst and I was dealing with his illness, the farm and stress. I could not give to Sofia and each individual animal what they needed in the way I normally would have. I know I missed signs. Sofia is also very connected to Salvatore, and I am sure she experienced much of his pain in her energy field because as soon as he got better, I saw that Sofia was showing symptoms, but this time they were different. She was then 13 and a half years old. She got up and could not walk well, it was almost like she was drunk, she was wobbling, and I had to hold her steady. She would not really eat, pee, or poop but was drinking ridiculous amounts of water. Her eyes looked foggy, and she was totally out of it. I took her to the Vet who did some bloodwork, and I immediately got the bad news. Sofia had kidney failure, her levels were over 260 and should be in the 14 range. The Vet also had done an x-ray and said that her upper stomach looked very strange, very thick. What it was she did not know.

Tumor? Thickening of the stomach lining from irritation? She seemed to be very unfamiliar with this sight. Sofia, long ago had a fatty tumor in her chest and that was a big scare which sent us to Tufts University for testing. They said it was huge and wanted to operate. We chose not to and had a Vet that did Chinese Herbs and he said he could treat it. This was many years ago, before I felt as secure as I do now with my own remedies. Slowly but surely the fatty tumor dissolved. Could this be a remnant? She thought not. There was nothing she could do; no medicine would heal all this. Not the kidney failure or the possible tumor in her stomach. Nothing. She said that Sofia was already in a very bad state and would get worse. She suggested we put Sofia down. I told her that I had to try my remedies and not give up. She said to call her if I wanted her to help Sofia pass along. I felt my heart break as I walked out the door with Sofia in my arms. Sofia is my little baby; I knew that Salvatore and Nico would feel the same and the sorrow began to feel overwhelming. I took her home and she ate just a tiny drop after I added some dried Salmon to some cooked Salmon. I felt scared, I feared losing her. I feared watching her be ill. I thought back on all sorrow at once, my mom's death, my dad's, my animals, Salvatore's illness, Jimmie, but then I remembered Jimmie and how she passed, and I saw a bit of light.

Jimmie was our pug who lived to be sixteen and a half. She was healthy and happy until the last 4 months. She got skinny and had trouble using her back legs and she lost a lot of her vision. I had to carry her around. It was so hard to see her not being the happy Jimmie who used to jump up off of her front legs and bark every time you fed her. As time went on, we sadly realized that it was time for Jimmie to go but she was being so strong spiritually she was hanging on even though her body was done. One day I sat outside with her and did a healing. I said "Jimmie, what do you need to move on, your body is not healthy any longer." I held her close and felt her energy not wanting to let go. I heard her speak in my mind. She said she had to say good-bye to the alpacas. I looked at her and told Nico and Salvatore to say goodbye. I then walked her up to the boy alpacas who came to her one by one and sniffed her head. Jimmie seemed content and stayed calmly in my arms. Then I went back to the girl alpacas, and they did the same. I told you, they know better than us when it is time. When the last alpaca had said her good-bye, I told Jimmie it was time for her, and I walked to the field behind the girl's barn, and I stared at her beautiful little face. I told her I loved her, and she passed right there. She had indeed wanted to say good-bye to the alpacas before she moved on in her journey. That memory gave me peace. I knew that I had to open to where I was being guided and try to help Sofia as best as I could with herbs and healings but also help her passage spiritually, if that was what she chose.

I stayed up most nights with her and fell asleep when I could no longer keep myself awake. One night I awoke and felt a lot of animals sleeping on me. I did not open my eyes right away, but I felt Jimmie, Lucy, the first Max, and all of my cats and dogs that were in another realm now. They were there, it was wonderful but made me ask if they came back for Sofia. Then my dad came, I feel him often, but it had been a long time since I really felt him like this. This time it was an actual conversation in which he was doing most of the talking and I was listening. It was as if he were right in front of me. He said to remember when Lucy died. I asked what about specifically. He said that after Lucy died, I had told him that Salvatore had been so hurt and angry that he punched the wall and hurt his hand. Lucy was his little baby and that was the way he wound up expressing his deep pain. My father said that he had wanted to talk to Salvatore about that at the time, but it was a conversation that did not happen, so it had to happen now. Ok, I said and listened. He said that Salvatore, or anyone, should not get angry about death, that we had to connect to the soul which is eternal. He told me that I could not even begin to imagine the beauty of where he was and if I pictured the most beautiful nebula filled with colors and stars it would not even begin to compare to what it was like. He said he was with my mom and that was beautiful. I then told him that I missed actually seeing him and asked if he missed me. He laughed and said he was able to see me anytime he wanted to, I just had to see him better, although now was good. He said that the spirit, the soul, becomes one with the Divine Light and the beauty is beyond belief. He wanted me to help Salvatore connect to the soul, the spirit and Nico too. He also said it was something that, I too, needed to keep in my heart and mind or I could get myself sick with worry. We talked a long time and I understood and conveyed the message to Salvatore in the morning. Some would say "this is your mind, let's analyze what the brain was doing," or this was "your imagination," but I had completely forgotten about Salvatore punching the wall and it was a clear conversation where I was mostly listening. That is not MY MIND.

Synchronicity again stepped in and somehow, I wound up looking for something on the internet and arrived at a Ted Talk by Doctor Siyaram Pandey. He was taking about using Dandelion Root to cure cancer. He found that in test tube studies the root ground up in water killed cancer cells (apoptosis) and did not destroy the healthy cells. He then tested it on a dog that had a cancerous tumor, he ground the dandelion root and put one teaspoon per day into the dog's food and the tumor disappeared. Canada approved to do a clinical study on Dandelion Root due to the fact that a 70-year-old man with leukemia was in remission for 18 months from dandelion root alone. Another patient with cancerous nodules went into remission within 24 hours. I ran outside and dug up a very young little dandelion plant (it was March so there was not much growing yet, but I found a small one) and crushed it. I mixed it with some probiotics and made a little ball. At first, I had to mix it with a little food and slide it into her mouth because she would no longer eat and was scary skinny. I continued doing this three times a day. We also did regular healings for Sofia and would try to get her to eat by sitting around her and then we would envision a bright light between our heart chakra and our solar plexus chakra. We sat and focused on the light. We then connected our lights to each other in a circle and also like spokes of a wheel, then like a star, connecting all to all and finally to Sofia. Then we imagined the light in each of us and in Sofia, Penny and Butterball and made a circle connecting our lights. This was our soul connection. Sofia felt it, she started to take little nibbles of food and finally I could put her remedies in there and she ate it. It was tiny little amounts but at least it was something. I tried to fill it with as many nutrients as possible. Three times a day I gave her a NUTRITIONAL BOOST with SLIPPERY ELM BARK BREW (RECIPE at end of book) This I had to syringe in her mouth also. 1.5 cc every 5 hours.

She was looking frail and thin but was now starting to walk a little better. She finally peed but had no bowel movement because she had no food. On the 6th day she started to look a lot better. No miracle here but her focus seemed clearer. Salvatore made his wonderful homemade pizza for dinner, and she became very interested in the smell in the kitchen and walked herself in. We kept giving her little bites. She wound up eating 1/2 a piece. After that she started eating again, only pizza, dry food and healthy O's cereal, at first but at least it was something. The fog lifted and she was perky again. Nico asked me if she was passing. I said she was still very sick, but it was up to her. I did not feel she had much time left at all. He said that he had seen, so many times, on our farm, that the animals get better before they pass. This is true. I talked to him about keeping the connection to Sofia.

So how do you find the soul through this physical body. The body that wants that other physical body there, to stay with them. The body that finds it difficult at times to see the soul. I think the answer was put beautifully in the film Dr. Strange. Dr. Strange was an incredible surgeon and very full of himself. He got into a car accident, and it destroyed his hands, his surgical hands. He then heard of a healer in Nepal and journeyed to find the answer. When he met the healer, he did not believe until she showed him his astral body. He was in awe and asked how he could learn this. She calmly looked at him and asked how he had learned about medicine, how he learned to perform surgery. He responded that it took a great deal of intense study and practice. She told him it was the same. I think we need to constantly remind ourselves of the soul, of the Divine. We can get so easily distracted. We must live and breathe it and practice and study. So, with Sofia every time I felt sad, I reminded myself of divine healing. I pictured myself as one with the Eternal Light and I sent it to her. We gave her healings daily.

I had not set up a Transmutation in a long time. I had done this with Nico when he was little, but I knew he did not remember. This time I knew we, (Salvatore, Nico and I) had to set one up for Sofia together. The place for this was my altar. I put out my healing stones and sacred objects. We surround ourselves in the white, violet, and silver light and proceeded to set up the transmutation. I told Salvatore and Nico to pick out which healing stones and crystals they felt would be important for her on her healing journey or her passing to the next realm journey, we did not know yet. We slowly, quietly and carefully picked the stones we felt were important. I then told them to create statements, as many as they wanted, to present to the Divine Energy to aid Sofia. I told them not to wish she got better but to create statements that were of the highest and the best. In other words, don't say "I want you to heal Sofia," You activate the energy in the stones, which are connected to the One Divine Light and make a statement. "If it is best for Sofia create an easy healing path for her in which she will not suffer but if it is her time to move on than create a painless path through the light." We did many such statements for our clear wishes for Sofia.

Then we created statements to help Us, including Penny and Ball, (we had not gotten Max back yet), to stay mentally and spiritually strong. We wrote them all down. The next step was to place the stones in a pattern as I explained previously that would vibrate for Sofia. We then lit a candle and incense and said each statement three times. The day after the Transmutation Sofia started eating more and each day after that more and more. She was peeing and pooping, walking and even running a little, she started wagging her tail.

Just as Sofia was feeling better, Penny started limping, a lot. Penny had a tough life before she came to us. For the first two years of her life, she lived in a barn, down south, with about 30 other dogs and they were all chained up. They had given them food and water daily. The cats lived in a big cage and were also given food and water. When a real rescue center found these animals, they concluded that the woman who took care of them was crazy, and they removed them all from the premises stating inhumane conditions. Penny was then adopted by our friends who loved her dearly. She had a fenced in area to run and one day jumped the fence and got hit by a car that broke her leg. The family was dealing with some personal trauma, and we took Penny. By the time we adopted her and got her to surgery the doctor said she could have trouble with it throughout her life since it was broken and not repaired for so long. I give her remedies and do pain salve packs from time to time when necessary but overall, she walks well and is very happy. This particular night, she would not even put her leg down. I could tell she was in a lot of pain. She jumped off the bed, slipped and fell. That is when I broke. Salvatore took her outside for her evening bathroom break. As she limped out the door I ran into the bathroom and fell on my knees. I screamed and I called to Jesus to fill me and my family and keep evil away. I felt a light come over me, through me and I felt better. I pulled it together and went out. Salvatore told me she was ok; she had slipped but was the same as during the day. I did not sleep all night. I had given her homeopathic belladonna for pain, but it did not help. I wrapped her leg in my pain salve and that helped a little but not enough this time, usually it did the trick. Later in the day I made a tea of willow bark, but she was not feeling better. As I sat there in the dark, I took a deep breath, and it came to me. I did not give her the Lyme Remedy. I got up at midnight and gave it to her as she lay under the covers with Nico. She looked so sad. About an hour and a half later she came running into my room and jumped on the bed putting a little pressure on her leg. I breathed a sigh of relief. I continued the remedy every 4 hours and she got better and better. I prayed that with all the trauma that had been happening that I could see signs before all fell apart.

The main ingredient here is Castor Oil. I used to tell people to do a castor oil pack if they were in pain, they would nod yes then never do it. When I asked them why, they said it was too messy, which, it is very messy indeed. Castor oil is a very thick oil and stays on your body for a long time, it will also stain your clothing which is why I decided to make a salve. Castor Oil is an old Edgar Cayce remedy. Edgar Cayce, better known as "THE SLEEPING PROPHET," was born in Kentucky in 1877. He was not doing well in school, so his father told him to stay up and study. He did but fell asleep on his schoolbook. The next day at school he remembered everything from the book, word for word, including what page it was on. No one believed this until the occurrences kept happening. He had absorbed the book into his brain. Later he would go into a sleep state and diagnose people and then give them the cure. He did not remember anything when he awoke. Later in life he became a photographer, the old-fashioned kind with gunpowder in the camera. His young son was with him at work one day, playing around and got a flash of gunpowder in his eyes and was blind. The doctor said there was nothing to be done. Edgar went into his trance state and prescribed a remedy. When they asked the doctor if the remedy would do anything he said the remedy would cause blindness, not cure it, for sure. Since he was already blind and could not be more blind, Edgar and his wife did what was in the "reading" and his son's vision came back. Edgar also saved his wife and healed many local people. Before he knew it he was getting visits and letters from around the country. He did over 30,000 diagnosis and cures during his life and had hundreds of affidavits about the accuracy of his work and the cures. Many people just did not write an affidavit but would swear that he had cured or helped them. He often recommended castor oil packs for cancer, pain, and many other things. Castor oil goes deep into the body healing bones, muscles tendons and more. I added the cayenne in the pain salve because it is warming, and the ginger and burdock leaves are great for inflammation.

Sofia was getting a little better each day, but it was still difficult for me. I awoke in the middle of the night, one evening, and was reading SHADOWS OF THE SUN DYNASTY a beautiful adaptation of the first part of the Ramayana by Vrinda Sheth and illustrated by her mother Anna Johansson (friends of Sharon and David). The story of the Ramayana is not considered a myth to those of the Hindu faith, but rather a historical account, of Rama. It was originally in Sanskrit and believed to be composed around the 4th or 5th centuries B.C. One part in particular, caught my attention that evening. Sita was to be wed to Rama who would be king of Ayodhya. Her father was talking to her about how she was different. As a child he reminded her "When you cried, it rained. When you were angry, the fires crackled. When you screamed, the Earth trembled." (Sheth) Sita had fond memories of her youth. A time when she was one with the elements. When Sita mastered language it seemed to stop, and her father asked her why. She said the humans had come around her "emanating big tangles in their energy." (Sheth) Her father would hug and protect her, but he was anxious and she felt his energy. She changed her connection with the elements. She began to realize that she was NOT her emotions, she was NOT fear, sadness, anger. "She was the WITNESS, very much like someone standing inside while a storm raged without. She could control and subdue her feelings. She could walk away from those storms." (Sheth)

I thought about this and put the book down so I could heed her words. I stepped away from my pain. I was not sadness, I was not fear, I was a witness to those things. I, Judy, am a being of light, in this incarnation I may experience things, but they ARE NOT ME! This revelation made me feel better. I looked at Sofia and Penny sleeping and realized I was not being of any help to them, myself, or anyone if I was sorrow and fear. I was just tearing myself apart and sending out negative energy. Instead of letting fear creep in I had to look at the way Sofia was getting better and better since the transmutation, since the healing work and dandelion root. Once I thought, like Sita, and saw myself as a strong whole being of light, connected to the Divine, having earthly, material experiences. I could control my pain and fear. I stepped away from it. I recommend trying this. It helped me greatly and I still practice it. You are not fear and pain, you are not anger, you are experiencing them and if you step back and watch it, remove yourself from it, you can actually see yourself from outside of yourself. It becomes clearer, easier. I also thought, if Sofia did not last long then I did not want to spend her last days with bad energy. We started incorporating the words "Already healed!" into her healings and seeing her as such. Sofia steadily got stronger, healthier, and happier.

About a month and a half after Sofia's visit to the Vet we had to have the Vet come to the house to check on one of our alpacas, all turned out to be fine, but we wanted to make sure. She turned to me with a sad look and quietly asked if Sofia was still with us and if so, how she was doing. "Great!" was my reply. She did not really believe me and asked to see her. I brought Sofia out and she ran up to the Vet with her little wiggle, jiggle. The Vet said she had never seen anything like this. Sofia was indeed doing great! Over the next couple of months, I continued the remedies, I think the dandelion root is a key here and I still do it.

She was doing so well that we took down the Transmutation and set up a new one. This one was to bring her back to the health of an 8-year-old dog, or younger, with all of her organs and cells perfect. Nico said she was still too thin, and his statement was that she get Fat. I told him to say fatter than she was as opposed to FAT, which is not healthy. He changed it and within 2 weeks Sofia started to put on weight and quickly too. She got to a great weight, for her. I then started looking in her eyes, for over the past few years they had filmed over with cataracts. They were now clearing up. She was waking in the morning, doing the "Sofia Roll," which is when she dives, happily, toward you, sticks her head in the covers and flips so you can rub her belly as she wiggles. She only does this when she feels good, and she was doing it every morning.

The last time I saw the Vet, I showed her a video of Sofia and she said it was a "MIRACLE." It has been over a year and a half now and Sofia just keeps getting better. The Vet asked if I wanted to do some testing because she was so curious about this. I said no, for two reasons, one, I don't want to put Sofia through anything that she does not have to go through and the second is because it really does not matter what shows up or does not show up. What matters is that she is now healthy and strong. I think she is a miracle too and I cherish every moment that I have had with her and will have.

CHAPTER 15

FLOWER POWER

Herbs heal the physical body, our organs, muscles, bones and more. Flower remedies heal the emotional body. Flower essences were discovered by Dr. Edward Bach 1886-1936. He grew up in England and studied medicine, receiving his diploma from Cambridge University. He was a surgeon and then researcher of immunology and bacteria for over 20 years. He then went on to study Homeopathy and joined the laboratory of the Royal London Homeopathic Hospital. He created seven bacterial nosodes there. Nosodes are remedies used for prevention of a disease or illness. He had a problem with the world of allopathic medicine's concentration on the disease and not on the person. He felt that illness went much deeper than the physical and was created when the body and mind were out of balance and were no longer in harmony with each other. He felt illness came from negative emotions. So, he turned to flowers which he tested to see how they could heal emotions rather than physical symptoms. He followed a seasonal pattern of living, which most herbalist do. Spring and summer were for harvesting and preparing remedies and winter was for healing yourself and those who need assistance with the remedies you preserved and created.

As he began his early experimentation, he found that his

remedies were working. Those who he gave the essences to were feeling relief from their anxieties and negative emotions which, in turn, began to heal them physically. Dr. Bach created 38 emotionally healing remedies including Rescue Remedy which contains Star of Bethlehem. Others have followed his path and created new flower essences since.

A wonderful spring flower that you will never see if you mow your lawn is Star of Bethlehem (Ornithogalum). It happily burst forth from the ground in late May. These flowers possess a lot of emotional healing power. If you do let them grow, they will rise to about six inches and have 6 white petals, like a star. Inside is the yellow stamen. (See white flower in picture next page) Dr Bach called Star of Bethlehem the "Comforter and soother of pains and sorrows." It is a remedy for shock and trauma, past or present. It brings comfort to those who need to be consoled and helps heal animals and people. I give it to my family, my dogs, alpacas, pigs. My cats don't seem to need it, they are always happy. You can make your own flower essence: (RECIPE end of book) Here are some of the other flowers that I use to make essences.

Dogwood (Cornus nuttallii) - the beautiful cross shaped flower from the Dogwood Tree helps to fill us with balance and harmony and works to unite our etheric, higher self, with our physical self. It is also useful for those who are accident prone and feel awkward in their movements.

Self-Heal (Prunella Vulgaris) This flower enhances the energy and healing power of all flower essences. It helps us to believe in the ability to heal ourselves, physically and spiritually and unite those forces so we live as ONE HOLY BEING, who takes responsibility for self.

Violet (Viola Odorata) Is wonderful for those who are shy, fragile and also perceptive. It opens them to raise their spiritual insight.

Buttercup (Ranunculus Occidentalis) - Just as this lovely yellow flower reflects the sunlight and radiates it outward it helps us to radiate our light with confidence. It is for those who put themselves down, so they stop doing so and shine their light.

Dandelion (Taraxacum official) dynamic physical energy, inner ease at work and play.

Crab Apple (Malus Sylvestris) I use this for urinary and bladder infections. It is cleansing and creates
inner purity.

Celendine (Cheliodonium Majus) Helps transfer information from person to person and cell to cell. Helps us to be clearer in our thoughts and articulate them better.

Queen Anne's Lace (Daucus Carota)-This Flower Queen offers sacred geometry. The color in the center is the spiritual eye. It helps us interconnect our physical senses with our higher consciousness and see our "true self" rather than the one we think and create in our minds. This delicate queen is a radiant white mysterious flower.

Lilac (Syringa Vulgaris) Helps with depression, to find peace within and joy to accept help from others. It helps with low energy and aids us in connecting to ourselves by relaxing and finding peace, easing painful memories.

Yarrow -Achillea millefolium- White Yarrow is similar to white light, which contains all the colors of the spectrum. It relates to all the chakras and helps you connect with the white light, your own and the Divine. It assists those who are overly sensitive. It detoxifies, clears, and aids with energetic protection.

Jewelweed (Impatiens capensis): Helps with those who are impatient and creates stillness.

Stinging Nettle (Urtica Dioica)- This flower essence is good for those who cannot remove themselves from a toxic relationship, it aids in helping you change a pattern in your life that is hindering you.

Nettle flowers come out if the plants get too tall. Stinging Nettle is one of my favorite plants. It's uses date back before 3000 BC as a medicine and as a fiber. In the stem are long strands which can be woven. When I began my herbal journey with Barrie, I decided that to truly know an herb I would study one herb for at least 6 months, intensively. My first adventure with this idea was with Nettle. I lived and breathed Nettle for over a year and still spend much of the spring and summer with it. Nettle Infusions are a great remedy to fill your body with nutrients. (Recipe in back) Nettle is one of the most nutritious foods (not herbs, but foods) on the planet. It is high in iron and therefore great for anemia and strengthens your blood chi (vital force). It is rich in Chlorophyll, Magnesium, Potassium, Phosphorus, Calcium, Sodium, Zinc, Manganese, Copper, Selenium and is filled with vitamin C, E, A, B3, B6, B2, B1. Now many of you may ask why you need copper. Copper is essential to help iron absorption and transport. A copper deficiency can cause iron anemia.

The Nettle plant is covered in tiny hairlike structures that actually "sting" when you touch them, thus Stinging Nettle. Now here is the magical part. If you grab the plant with intention, it will not sting you but brush against it and it will. Once you cook, add boiling water, dry or macerate nettle, it loses its sting. When harvesting fresh nettle, I recommend wearing gloves. Nettle is great for allergies, especially Hay Fever, enlarged prostate, eczema, arthritis and gout, urinary tract infections and pain. It helps to purify the blood, so should be added to your diet during times of any infection from a tick bite as well as other infections. It is also great for kidney and bladder stones (so is lemon so add some of that). It also helps if you have a heavy menstruation.

When Salvatore was very young, he had problems with bed wetting, thus his bladder. His Aunt gave him daily nettle infusions and he was cured. Nettle helps to strengthen the bladder. I also make Nettle Pesto which is yummy. (RECIPE at end) Another great use for Nettle is Urtication. This is basically smacking yourself with fresh Stinging Nettle to bring the circulation to the area of your body which is in pain. It really helps. Urtication was used in tribes in America and Canada for rheumatism. I use it for pain, sciatica as well as circulation. It does not really burn when you hit yourself with it but rather gives a little sting so you can feel the blood going to that area. Nettle is all around amazing and once it grows near you it will come back in abundance. I harvest it when it is about 6 to 8 inches tall. Never cut lower than 3 inches above the ground or the plant will die off. In my opinion the healthier, more nutrient filled, pure foods you put into your body, the healthier you will be. There is a reason that cancer is rampant in our society. Sugar, refined flour, GMO, pesticide foods can all lead to poor health. Eat organic, no GMO, eat of the earth and connect more with her.

We were ALL, long ago, more connected to the Earth but that was another place and time. We need to return to that for the sake of the earth, our future, and our true selves. We need to return to the spirit of the plants, water, crystals, and animals. If we can connect to all of this energy of the earth with love and without judgement, then we will be one. I love animals and as I said on our farm sanctuary we have a lot, 29 alpacas, 1 pig, 1 sheep, 11 cats, 2 dogs. They are all my family and I care for them with my heart and soul, and they care for me. There are also a lot of wild turkey and deer that are on our property. I love them too. I feel them and hear them. I know them. They tell you things if you listen. They come to you as a sign, a totem, a spirit guide, but you have to see them, you have to take the time to look and be in tune. I mean truly look, truly see. We often run, run, run and miss all of the signs that are presented before us. We must connect and be more aware.

CHAPTER 16

ANIMAL TOTEMS

In October, Salvatore's appendix burst. We did not know this at the time. I thought it was a bad stomach flu. I gave him remedies, slippery elm bark, nettle and my Lyme be gone which is a natural antibiotic and placed him in yoga postures to cleanse his colon. He began to detox and feel a little better but after about a week, I realized he was not healing as he should for a stomach flu and that it was something much worse. I took him to our naturopathic doctor who sent him to the hospital. It was a very hard road for him and hard for Nico and I, in a different way. The doctors, of course, kept saying "why didn't you come to the hospital earlier, you could have died." We of course were thinking, how could we have known it was the appendix for one and for two the remedies seemed to at least stabilize him. The doctors, of course, went full force with medication and I had to step out of the picture. I have to say they did get him better, but I worry about all the meds that were pumped into him and their long-term affect. I also felt guilty for not taking him to the hospital earlier, but I really did not know and apparently, he did not either. The whole time he was in the hospital Nico, and I kept seeing Red Tail Hawks everywhere we went. I mean everywhere. By now it was winter, and snow was all about but we saw them flying over our farm, we saw them flying in front of the car when we left the driveway, we saw them sitting on a post near the hospital, sitting on a wire on the way to teach my yoga class. We are very aware of nature and saw the signs right away. The significance of a red tail hawk is very powerful. These beautiful raptors are signs of help from the divine realm, they are messengers who bring guidance from the heavens to the earth, and they have many layers of guidance and understanding. They are bearers of gifts, gifts showing their support and unconditional love. Just as a hawk sees its prey, you must look with clear focus and see what the divine message is. I felt that this whole illness had more to do with the spirit, the divine, than the physical. Salvatore had to make a breakthrough, become more in tune with his divine self and Nico too. When Nico was young, he was earthy, magical and divine, as he was getting older he was becoming more…. well, human. It surprised me because I am not so, well, human. C. S. Lewis said, "One day you will be old enough to read fairy tales again." Nico had to get that back, (which he began to do when Max' returned), Salvatore needed to find his Divine connection. Nico was helping me on the farm and becoming a man quickly for there was so much to do and we had to just keep doing it. Nico stood firmly by my side with strength and support. I am very proud of him for that, he never complained once about it. I felt protected when I saw the hawks, I felt they were comforting us, supporting us, and guiding us to help Salvatore physically, mentally, and emotionally and help us too.

One day when Nico and I were visiting Salvatore at the hospital we put on Krishna Das' - *My God is Real*, a song that fast tracks us to the Divine, and we gave him a healing. He seemed very peaceful after that and came home a couple of days later. When Salvatore got home, I told him to find the divine meaning of his illness. He said he tried but it was difficult for him. I am sure it was, physically he was very ill, and my heart went out to him, and I so wished I could take away his pain. I suggested he meditate, and the answer would come but it did not come to him. I tried to talk and read him various spiritual texts but came to realize the chanting was what was bringing him somewhere else. So, I put on the chants often. One night the three of us sat in a candlelit room and listened and went on our respective journeys. When we "came back" Salvatore said that he had seen his wolf again and the wolf had brought him to the edge of a cliff where he looked out, peacefully, at land below. I would interpret that as he has come to the end of one road and was at a place where he has a whole world in front of him but could go no further unless he took that leap of faith. It is like the Fool in the Tarot. It is the beginning of a journey. All this was very challenging, seeing him so ill and in so much pain. I knew this step on his journey was a difficult one and it was not something I could do for him, but I could try in small ways. I wanted so much for him to see the light but sometimes the more I talked about my spiritual thoughts the more he resisted so I stopped, again physical pain was also greatly at play here. I was also physically overtired from all the work on the farm. I began to see Red Cardinals everywhere. Red Cardinals have a strong whistle or voice that commands attention. They are strong in spirit and nature. They teach us to balance out our masculine and our feminine sides. They help us vibrate what we have to say with confidence and strength. They are strong, bold, helpful, cheerful, and grand. This was the energy I needed to be holding at this moment in time. Strong, bold, cheerful, with hope and renewal. I had to continue to give a strong whistle at times and then be silent.

One night after doing all the farm work and filling the outdoor wood burning furnace with giant logs that weigh about 20 - 45 lbs. each, for which it takes at least 15 of to fill, I felt like I was going to break. One important note, we use trees that have fallen down or are dying on the property, not healthy trees that are living. I sat on the little hill in front of the furnace and looked up and saw a beautiful full moon smiling down at me. I stared at it and began to cry. I felt the moon's presence, a comforting one that allowed me to pour out my emotions as she quietly looked on. I felt her sending me light and peace. I looked at the planets and the stars for they seemed brighter, more vibrant. They were comforting me too. I walked up the big hill to where Salvatore had put a Christmas laser light, before he got sick. It shone out onto the land filling the trees with tiny orbs of green and red light. It extended back to the tee pees and up to the highest branches of the great pines. I knew that I had entered the Fairy's Realm, so I laid on my back in the snow and stared at the sky and the little green orbs. It was a magical ritual which I continued each night for it gave me great peace and made me look forward to going out to do the furnace at night. When I went back into the house I fell straight into bed and was asleep in moments. I awoke, as I usually do, in the middle of the night and I felt a tingling up and down my arms from my neck. My hands were numb. I had been overdoing it with the farm work and heavy lifting and my spine was rebelling. Night is always a time of peace for me, so I thought about the moon and the energy that filled me, I thought of how Jesus said that if you ask, he will be there to help you, so I asked. I was actively involved in the healing, holding my hands on my yellow chakra and I felt a fireball of light, shoot into me, and fill me. I could see it as well as feel it. It began to fill my heart, my head, my whole being. I felt a vibration of warmth fill every cell in my body. All the tingling and pain was gone, and I went to sleep. When I awoke the next day, I was a burst of energy. I don't drink coffee or have any caffeine in my life, but it was like I had some. I was ready to go, no tingling, no numbness. Nico kept laughing at me because as we were doing the animal chores in the morning, I kept doing more and more added things, I was charged.

We have the power to change our lives, to create the energy around us, in us, through us. We can play the victim, or we can hold life and mold it, shape it with faith, love, and light, finding happiness in all we do. Nico and I started seeing black crows and Ravens, big ones. I did not tell Nico about the moon and the fairy lights, but he must have felt it because every night after that when I would go out to do the furnace he came. I kept telling him he had done enough all day and he could rest but he happily accompanied me and after we would visit Fairy Land and stare at the moon, the stars, and the planets.

What words of wisdom did the Crows and Ravens wish to share with us? Look for your spirit guides, your totem animal guides and see what they are telling you. One website I love is the Manataka American Indian Council. They tell us that man was meant to be the caretakers of the Earth. We should never use more than we need of the earth's natural resources for that is greed. The earth provides what WE NEED. The Crow (according to Manataka) "knows the unknowable mysteries of creation and is the keeper of all sacred law." "Crow is also the guardian of ceremonial magic and healing. In any healing circle, Crow is present. Crow guides the magic of healing and the change in consciousness that will bring about a new reality and dispel "dis-ease" or illness. You can rest assure whenever crows are around, magic is nearby, and you are about to experience a change in consciousness."

Ravens, according to Manataka "are often referred to by some indigenous tribes as the 'secret keepers' and are the subject of many stories. The raven spirit guide is not chosen by those who seek its wisdom. The raven only comes to those to whom it may speak in private, sharing secrets and knowledge, it is for those who already possesses wisdom. The raven can transform, move into other dimensions, or shape shift. "AH, exactly!

It is also important to cleanse your energy in your home after and during an illness, after trauma or an encounter with negative energy and after people who are not positive enter your home, although you may want to consider not inviting those people anymore. A general cleansing, at least once or twice per year, is what I consider a necessity. You can do this with sage, by burning the dried leaves in a seashell or use Frankincense, Myrrh or Dragon's Blood incense which are my preference. Light the incense and start at the entrance of your house. First cleanse yourself by moving the incense in circles around your body, starting at your feet and then moving up. All the while say a prayer or a chant. Something like "Begone all that is not of the highest and the best. Begone all that is not of love and light, you are not welcome here. Enter love, enter light, enter healing. OHHHHMMMMM! Then open the front door and start there. Walk around the room, starting to the left, hugging the walls, moving from room to room until you come back to the starting point, continuing to say prayers and chants as you go. Cleanse your family members and those in your household by swirling smoke around them. This purifying Ritual was and is used in various ancient and present-day cultures from Native American to Ancient Egyptian. Cleansing with incense is incorporated in most religions. Sacred scents help clear negative vibrations.

CHAPTER 17

SIGNS

As I said before, whenever a dove came around and stayed near me and did not leave it was a big sign. This past summer, Nico was 13 and he and Salvatore went on a week-long Marine Biology Trip to Florida through Kent Prep school. I felt after all they had been through it would be good for them to get away, so I set it up for them. I stayed at the farm taking care of the alpacas, dogs, cats, pig etc. I started to get very agitated near the middle of the week. I began to feel fear, intense fear. I am not a fearful person, I never felt like this. What was happening? I looked outside and a dove was there. I got scared and asked if someone was going to die. The dove flew away so I felt that the answer was a clear no. The next day I began to feel very protective of my home, my animals, my family. My morning protection ritual got stronger. I felt I could not leave the farm. I even canceled my yoga class that I teach. I thought, this is crazy. The next day I saw another dove when I walked out the front door, it was a light brown color as was the one from the previous day. I asked again, if someone was going to die, it flew away. I felt more fear build up through the day. My lower back started to hurt so badly that at times I had to stop and just lean over. I did some yoga stretches which usually heal my body quickly, but the pain was not going away it was getting worse. All the while the fear was getting more intense. Was it their plane, the flight home? I meditated if I should tell them to switch their flight, I got that the flight would be fine. When they called and said they had landed I thought I would feel relief, but I did not. When they arrived home, again, I thought I would find relief but there was none.

Every time I went to the girl alpaca's barn something was buzzing in my ear. I did not feel like it was an insect I kept thinking it was a fairy trying to convey a message to me. I thought it was trying to tell me something about Sofia, in that this was after her illness, but she was doing really well. I said, "fairy this buzzing is annoying, if Sofia is going to die buzz in my left ear, if not, in my right." The buzzing had been in my left and quickly went to right. I then, stupidly, got annoyed and said, "then leave me alone." Then I felt bad and said I was sorry but if the information could be given without it being so annoying, I would appreciate it. The buzzing stopped after that.

I also saw crows and Ravens again, everywhere. Really big ones. They were sitting on top of the alpaca's fence, sitting in my back yard, sitting in the trees. They were huge and very present. Crows, as spirit totems are giving you a message to help guide you. To help show you the next steps on your path. They tell you to pay attention to your thoughts and the omens that present themselves to you.

Diana came to visit for the weekend and asked if we could set up a transmutation for angels to come and help us. She remembered doing it but forgot how. It was funny because I had just cleansed all of my stones out in the sun for days, which is the preparation for what she asked. You write down your prayers/needs. I wrote that I had to remove this fear from my life, it was overwhelming. That night I had a dream, in which Salvatore was floating in a big glass tank (at one point I thought it may have been Nico, but it kept going back to Salvatore). I looked at him and he was totally unconscious and out of it, just floating. Was he alive? I wondered. I was so frightened. Then someone took a giant syringe and put it in a hole in the tank and pushed it hard and quick into the tank and into Salvatore. I screamed NOOOOOOOOOOO! Then I woke up. I was going to tell Salvatore the next day, but something distracted me. I thought I was screaming no because I did not want that medicine injected into him.

I had signed up for my yearly retreat at my yoga teachers wonderful Wild Woodstock home for a week of yoga and I told Salvatore I was not going to go for all of it. Shocked, he asked why. I told him something was happening. The animals and wildlife were acting strange. I had to be at home to protect everyone. I was adamant about it.

Salvatore went out to mow the field on the riding Kubota tractor and the next thing I knew he came in the house and said he had gotten stung. Salvatore is allergic to bees, wasps and hornets and has gotten stung every year since we have been here. Nico and I are rarely stung. His worst reaction was 5 years ago. I had given him homeopathic apis but within minutes he laid down on the ground and was weak and in pain. He was awake but could not get up and was in really bad shape. I called an ambulance. They came and took him to the hospital for a few hours. They asked if he had ever stopped breathing or lost consciousness and we said no. They said, even though I did not like medicine, to take a Benadryl if he ever got stung again. I had him carry Benadryl everywhere he went, and apis. I said he should keep it on the tractor, in every barn, in his truck, in his pocket. This time when he walked in the house, I realized he had not taken anything, nor did he have it with him. I ran and got the apis first because that was for breathing and was trying to open the Benadryl which seemed like it took me forever to open the thing and get the pills out. Salvatore sat in the chair and moaned, "please, the Benadryl." I was trying to go as fast as I could. I got it to him, and he swallowed them and then said he was nauseous. Then the worst happened. His eyes rolled to the back of his head, and he was out. I felt that it was not just passing out, this was something far worse. I yelled to Nico to call 911 and he calmly did. I don't know how this brave boy kept his cool, but he moved quickly. In the meantime, I was compelled to open Salvatore's mouth. His teeth were clenched together, and I pulled them apart and stuck my finger in. I felt his tongue towards the back of his throat, and it seemed swollen. I did not feel like he was breathing. I shoved my fingers into the back of his throat to pull his tongue down and he gaged for one brief moment and got a sip of air, then right back out. I got some water and threw it on his head, nothing. I poured a little down his throat then leaned his head forward and he gagged again, another quick breath, then out again. I kept repeating sticking my fingers in his throat to make him gage/breath and pouring the water to do the same. He bit down on my fingers, and I had to pry his mouth open. I was screaming the whole time NOOOOOOOOOOO, like in my dream. I screamed, "you come back to me! Don't you leave me!" Then I slapped him and nothing. I finally heard Nico pause in his phone call and ask me if we had an Epi-Pen. An Epi-Pen! Oh yes! It had fallen from my consciousness for I had never had to use it. We did have an Epi-Pen. In her brilliance my dear Jen Jen had told Salvatore to have one on hand just in case and her mother who is a doctor, amazingly provided us with one as a gift. Oh, what a gift. I got it and stabbed it into his leg. This was so similar to the syringe and my dream. I was screaming NOOOOOO. One second later he regained consciousness. A couple of minutes later a man arrived who was with the medical emergency team and lives right on our street, so he got there quickly, to me it seemed like forever. The rest of the team arrived and said their thanks for the Epi-Pen, which is adrenaline. They took him to the hospital and said he would be fine.

Our neighbors had run out and Nico was talking to them. I did not know how he could be so very strong. They told me, as we left, that he was amazing. I agreed. Nico and I hugged for a very long time and talked. When we got to the hospital Salvatore looked much better and was talking and moving around. I asked him if he remembered anything. He did not. He felt like it was one second that he was out then came back. I felt like it was 20 minutes, Nico felt like it was 5. Oh Einstein, time is indeed relative.

I do not know what happened. Did he pass out? Did he stop breathing? Was he still with us? I don't know. The fear I felt the previous week was nothing compared with the fear that I felt watching my husband in that state, not knowing if he would live or die or if he was already dead. I blessed Nico, I blessed Jen Jen, I blessed her mom, I blessed the Fairies, the Ravens, the Crows and Jesus. I pondered why I was given so much information about what was going to happen. Why I was guided to stay at home and protect. How I knew something traumatic was approaching but still could not prevent it. I felt maybe it had kept me at home that day to do what I did but I was not sure. I again asked why I had this gift if it did not truly help. Nico and I sat down and read our Tarot cards. It was all about how Nico and Salvatore had to find a more spiritual path. I know illness and things like this are a sign. I began to think that I needed a mentor, someone to guide me through my visions but I have come to discover, during the past few years, that I am always led back to me. They are all things I need to find out for myself through meditation, reading and connecting to the Divine. The more I thought about the signs I had seen the more I realized I had not really taken the time to stop, to ask, to meditate, to read my cards. I just let myself be filled with fear. I must be more mindful. I knew I must heighten my practice. I knew I had to go deeper. I thought of Dr. Strange and how tragedy can sometimes propel you into the deeper spiritual consciousness but now I felt I was living in fear, fear of the entire summer and fall, fear of Salvatore being stung. It is a monumental thought and one that is extremely difficult to release, but I must try. I also must try to be more in tune with my foresight, I must tune that skill. Salvatore must carry an Epi-pen everywhere and bought a bee suit for when he mows the lawn, but the fears and threat remain. Life is filled with challenges. Life is a challenge.

CHAPTER 18

CHARIOTS OF THE GODS?

Prior to Einstein a physicist named Schwarzschild described the universe as being finite, possibly in a circle or black hole. He thought two black holes could be connected by a tunnel or Wormhole. Einstein later used this idea in his work with Nathan Rosen and their theory was that this wormhole could connect two flat regions of space-time which could even be at opposite ends of the universe. They called this the Einstein-Rosen Bridge and thought if the entrance to the tunnel were big enough someone could jump through it and wind up at the other point, maybe across the universe. This idea is used in many films and shows from Star Trek to Thor to The Flash. Now some scientists believe this bridge could also bring you to other places and other times. They do not think that time travel is impossible, merely difficult. So, what is time? Do we create it in our material realm? I don't think the soul knows time. Does it only exist because we create it in this physical existence? Why do we think in such a linear pattern and not see the Wormholes, not see a timeless realm? Perhaps it is because we don't try.

The more we can create ritual in our lives, the more it will help us to find something higher. Through yoga and meditation, we can become leaders and not followers. I think many people in this country find someone or something to follow and do so without questioning or without studying the facts for themselves. Often, we do not really look. Question everything! Seek your path. One such person who is an amazing example of questioning everything and who has influenced my life is Erich von Däniken. In 1968 he wrote the wonderful and controversial book *Chariots of the Gods?* In this book he introduced the thought of ancient cultures having some kind of interaction with off planet intelligence. Throughout the book he asked many rhetorical questions, note the name even has a question mark. He gave evidence for his thoughts by citing various monolithic sites and religious texts around the world. He asked that people take a fresh look at history, with an open mind, a new mind, as did all of the great thinkers who changed the world by challenging the norm. Of course, Daniken was attacked for this by some but others felt there was something to what he was posing and his book sold over 500,000 copies in the first year.

Von Däniken attended a Jesuit (Catholic) school in Switzerland in his youth. When he read Exodus in the Bible- *(16) On the morning of the third day there was thunder and lightning. A cloud covered the mountain, and a very loud horn sounded. All the people among the tents shook with fear. (17) Then Moses brought the people from among the tents to meet God. They stood at the base of the mountain. (18) Mount Sinai was all in smoke because the Lord came down upon it in fire. Its smoke went up like the smoke of a stove. And the whole mountain shook.*

This made the young Von Däniken think, why would God need to come down with smoke and loud noises? He thought it sounded more like a vehicle than God manifesting. He asked one of his teachers, who told him to read the book of Enoch. Enoch is Noah's great-grandfather; this amazing text is part of the Ethiopian Bible but not the Catholic Bible. Enoch was taken from the Earth in a fiery chariot and shown many wondrous things. He asked many questions and the beings he was with asked him why he wanted to know "all these things." Von Däniken, who believes in GOD and still prays every night, thought this sounded more like a sci-fi space adventure and went on to investigate further. As he read Ezekiel and the wheel within the wheel, he felt like he was reading a description of a technological vehicle and once again asked his teacher who told him it was a vision that Ezekiel had. "But" Von Däniken stated, "visions don't have sound."

He decided to go to Egypt and see another mystery for himself, the pyramids. The pyramids are the only remaining Wonder of the 7 Wonders of the Ancient World. To this day, no one can explain how they were built. They can guess, they can theorize but never believe anyone who tells you they KNOW. Egyptian history tells they were built with help "FROM THE GUARDIANS OF THE SKY." A thought you will hear repeatedly. Von Däniken then began to travel the world with open eyes and a totally open mind, studying cultures, religions, mysterious sites. He learned from a Sanskrit Scholar at the Sanskrit College in Kolkata India that the ancient texts refer to Vimanas or flying machines through which the gods descended to earth. They had very technical and specific detail. He noticed the many stupas around India seemed to be replicas of these Vimanas. There were also references to battles in the sky, in which the gods carried and used celestial weapons. The description sounded like nuclear weapons to him.

The more he learned, the more he wanted to see. He visited Puma Punku in Bolivia which was said to be built about 2000 years ago, but many believe it was more like 17,000 years ago. The stones were cut with laser precision. There are H shaped, giant blocks of granite which fit together to create walls. Stone cutters say it would be impossible to do this without high tech construction tools. When he asked the Indigenous people the history, they told him this was built by the gods. Von Däniken has been exploring these mysteries for years and continues to do so. His show Ancient Aliens is a favorite of mine. He states that if we never question things and research them, we will never grow. He says that we need to continually ask the questions so we can change the thinking and consciousness of our society. I wanted to know. I wanted to see, so I read, I read the Old Testament, the New Testament, Parts of the Mahabharata (the long one that is about 12,000 pages), some Vedic texts, Buddhist Texts, part of the Koran. I explored, through Ancient Aliens, the mysterious sites around the world. I had visited Stonehenge and wanted to visit another megalithic site. I knew it would happen one day but did not feel it was in my near future, so I kept exploring in the ways I could.

I had two visits to Stonehenge, both quite mystical. The first time I was with my Aunt Dee Dee and we took a bus trip from London. The day was warm and sunny. The minute we arrived at Stonehenge it began to snow. Big, giant flakes. The whole area seemed to be apart from the rest of the world and was swirling with magical white stars. I felt I had gone somewhere else which was not of this realm. The minute we left the snow stopped. The second time I went I was with Salvatore, Nico, who was very little and Joyce. We took a bus trip from London this time also, but this was a bright, sunny day. We departed before sunrise so we could step inside the circle. When we got there the feeling was once again, other worldly. We decided to sit and do a healing for Sofia (this was when she first got her fatty tumor). I felt the energy of the stones, of the circle. I felt their power and I was transported.

As Enoch, I wanted to know more. I was a seeker and found many amazing things that I was never taught in school. Through my explorations I encountered two old and mysterious books which are now among my favorites. They were both handwritten in pen and ink long ago. The first is the Voynich Manuscript. A small book that resides at the Beinecke Library of Rare Books at Yale University. Although you will probably never see it for it is rarely out on display. The only way to really view it is on their website. As you flip through the pages of beautiful images of plants painted with lapis lazuli and other plant-based materials you will find it very difficult to read the text, which there is much of. You may understand a word here and there in another language but for the most part you will not. That is because no one, not even some of the world's greatest code breakers have been able to crack this mystery. To date, no one knows what it says. It dates back to around 1400 AD, most likely from Europe. I believe it is older, perhaps from the 12th century. The first part of the book is obviously about herbs and plants. I think it may be herbal recipes and healing scripts.

Even trying to identify all the plants in the book is a challenge, some of which we don't have on our planet now, at least not that we know of. The next part of the book is more astrological. There are circles with planets and stars. Some of the circles have women surrounding them and astrological figures in the center. There are a few pages where these women seem to be bathing in a green fluid which flows up. When I stared at the pages, I felt very connected to this book. I again, got flashes of a time when you would be put to death for the use of herbs and astrology and were deemed a WITCH.

The other mysterious book is called the Codex Gigas, Giant Book or most often called The Devil's Bible due to the large illustration of the Devil near the middle. It is thought to date to the first century AD. and they believe it came from a Benedictine Monastery in the Czech Republic. It is the largest Medieval manuscript in the world. It is 6 feet long, almost 2 feet wide and about 8 inches thick. It takes 2 people to carry it. The book is bound in wood with leather and ornate metal decorating it. Legend says it was written by only one scribe. The codex has many sections including the Latin Vulgate Bible, a historical section by Flavius Josephus who wrote the history of the Jewish War, Isidore of Seville's encyclopedia *Etymologiae*, which is amazing, in and of itself, just think Pliny the Elder, geometry, music, metals and stones, cosmology and astrology as well as medical journals, including those of Hippocrates, the New Testament, magic formulae, conjurations, and more. But the real kicker here is the giant painting of the devil on one page with a drawing of the kingdom or Jerusalem on the opposite side.

The legend states that a monk wanted to glorify the monastery to repay his falling out of grace and said he would write the document in one night, (as you will read later, many things are said to have been created in one night), which most say would have been humanly impossible. During the evening he realized this task could not be done and called upon Lucifer Morning Star, the fallen angel and asked for help. They say this was his tribute to Lucifer. I think otherwise. I think that the devil points back to the Old Testament. You will see further along in the book what I mean.

CHAPTER 19

JESUS

Ok, so here is the part of the book where Witch Judy/Which Judy will probably be dragged into the town square again and burned at the stake, angering a lot of people in the process, but here me out, ALL THE WAY THOUGH PLEASE. I believe there is a Divine-ONE being that is pure energy and light, that we are all a part of. I believe that Jesus is a physical manifestation of this light and this energy, the son. I believe this Divine light is in all of us, not a physical manifestation, like Jesus but a soul one, a part of us, the base of us, or I should say we are a part of the Divine. I believe Jesus was and always will be, as he WAS before he came into the human manifestation. You can call this Divine Energy, God, Divine Light, All One, whatever name you like. Now let's say God with a capital G and god with a small g for writing clarity here. God, that I believe in, is all loving, all healing, and is in ALL. There is no hate, no anger, no vengeance. The anger, vengeance part was always baffling to me. I would be in church and hear the story of Abraham from the Old Testament. God told Abraham to bring his son to be sacrificed, to test him. Abraham was just about to kill his son and god said, no stop, I was just seeing how much you loved me. I am so sorry, but I hate that story and, "MY" God, the one filled with love, the one with the capital "G", would never do that. Why would this be done, this is not love? So, I read, and I read, and I read. I read the lost gospels, I read about Krishna, Shiva, Ram, Buddha, and all that I could. As I read the Old Testament, I could not believe it, story after story was "god" telling "his people" that it was ok if they killed other people who didn't follow him. Now wait, weren't all people god's people? Didn't he also say, "Thou Shall not Kill?" Wasn't God supposed to be love? Why did god need an animal sacrifice brought to him? Why did he need human sacrifice brought to him? Why could only a couple of people see him? Now don't get me wrong, I believe the stories of the Old Testament and I believe this being really existed, but here is where some of you will get mad but just read on a bit, I don't believe this being was GOD. When I read John in the New Testament everything became clear to me. Jesus says in John 8 31-32

If ye continue in my word then are ye my disciples indeed:
And ye shall know the truth and the truth shall set you free.

I had heard this many times in my life, a great thought as a child, don't lie, tell the truth, the truth shall set you free but now I started to see something else, something different. In the Old Testament there is much talk of gods. Exodus 20:3-4 *I am the lord your God.... you shall put no other gods before me.* Doesn't that make it very clear that there were indeed other gods on the earth at this time? Who were they? Why would God be worried about any other gods? Why was he a "he" and not just energy and why was "he" so angry? Wasn't GOD beyond this? Isn't GOD energy like we can't image? So I went back to John, what is the truth? What was Jesus saying? John continues, as many got very upset and said, hey we are from Abraham *we were never in bondage to any man (John 8:33)* how can you set us free? Breaking this down got me thinking. How can they say they were never in bondage? I had visions of Charlton Heston in THE TEN COMMANDMENTS saying, "free us from bondage." Jesus went on to say that if you sin, you are a servant of sin. He said,

I know you are Abraham's seed; but ye seek to kill me, because my word hath no place in you.
I speak that which I have seen with my Father: and ye do that which ye have seen with your
father. (John 8:37-38).

I thought about the image of Abraham going to sacrifice his own child, about the call to kill others throughout the Old Testament and how Jesus was all about healing and peace and they did not go together. Were we talking about two different fathers here? "I have seen with

MY Father….ye have seen with *YOUR* father"? He then goes on to say, *But now ye seek to kill me, a man that hath told you the truth, which I have heard of God: this did not Abraham. (John 8:40)* So, in my opinion, Jesus is

saying, I have heard things from God and I am telling you the truth, but Abraham did not hear the truth from GOD because he was talking to a god. Then Jesus tells them that their god is not his father, or they would understand and love him because he came of God and for God. Then he gets upset *Why do ye not understand my speech? even because ye cannot hear my word. Ye are of your father the DEVIL, ….he was a murderer from the beginning, and abode not in truth, because there is no truth in him. ….. he is a liar, and the father of it. And because I tell you the truth, ye believe me not. (John 8 43-45)*.

Now this seemed pretty clear to me. I always felt Jesus was of God and the contrast between him and the god of the Old Testament was so vast I could not comprehend it. There is a big difference between "love one another" and you did not obey me again so I will wipe you out in a flood. Was Jesus telling us clearly here that the Old Testament was not God? That God did not come down and take that form (although I think Jesus did), did not tell others to kill, did not just support "his people" and not care about anyone else. This started to make sense to me. Jesus was saying clearly, this guy, this killer was the devil that presented himself as God and tricked you. I am now telling you the truth, God is really awesome, he is love, he doesn't need sacrifices and does not want you to kill. He loves all people. WOW! This blew my mind and brought me into a whole new area to explore.

So, who was this being of the Old Testament? I sat up many nights contemplating this. I thought of the stories of Lucifer Morning Star and the fall from grace. What was the fall? Was the fall "spirit", attaching to matter? Creating matter? The more we get attached to matter the more that is the matter. We create greed, need, anger. Did the fallen angel or some other being or beings, that had great powers, magical powers, if you will, make people think, due to this power, that he was God and made many promises that were not kept. Yes, not kept, that is another thing that really bothers me about the Old Testament. He would promise them the land of milk and honey, give them hope and then blame them because he did not give it to them. Wouldn't God keep a promise? Why would God need an army and why did he not clearly state, I will only give you this if you do x, y and z?

Jesus went on to say *Before Abraham was, I am (John 8:58).* Doesn't that make sense, that he always was, because he is part of God, the God that is energy and light, something that always was and will be, something that is difficult for us, in this human form of matter, to understand. Doesn't this also make a lot more sense of why they wanted to kill Jesus? They thought this blasphemy. Why they wanted to kill the followers of Jesus? They believed they were going against their god, calling him the devil or a "god".

I see many people who say they don't believe in God. Often when I ask them why and talk to them about it they say they cannot get on board with a God who is vengeful and destructive like the Old Testament. Many went on to explore religions in India and Tibet, as I did, and they found more loving beings that manifested. I think, perhaps, we need to separate the Old and New Testament and see what Jesus is saying. It is beautiful, it is love and it is amazing. It is compassion. It is not of this world. Many people seem to get angry with him or about him, but I think if you take a "separate" look at what he said there is no way to be angry, he just taught us to heal and love one another. There are some that say the gospels are not true because they were written 30-200 years after he died, but that does not make them wrong. The gospels were the stories handed down, as were most other stories of the past. We do not know who wrote most of the ancient text or if there were earlier copies or notes, but why would we disregard them, why would we disregard any religious text? Why would we call them myths? Look at them, read them, not as a mythical story but as real and see what you think. There are even some who say that Jesus did not die on the cross, I don't think Jesus wanted us to do this. To me what matters is how Jesus lived, not how he died. For, to me, that is something we can't even comprehend, for we are too much of the body, and he was NOT. We need to be more like him and stop getting angry with him. We need to remember how he lived on this planet and how he is still ever present in another realm and this one, if we open to him.

I do have to say that although I say read and believe and decide you must also understand that "adjustments" were made to the gospels in the Bible by the Council of Nicaea in 325AD, led by Emperor Constantine. We don't know what they edited but we do know that they disallowed a lot of stuff which was later found in Nag Hammadi and elsewhere in the "LOST GOSPELS," which I will get to in a moment. I find that the deeper I go into this journey the clearer everything becomes.

I think it is also important to understand all religions and all faiths, looking with an open eye, an open mind. I attended a yoga retreat with Nico when he was 12 because my wonderful teacher Sharon Gannon was a part of it and I love her. There I met Radanath Swami. He arrived later than the rest of the presenters. Nico and I were walking through the halls and stopped because a glowing figure was before us with the brightest smile you could imagine. It was him, Radanath Swami, dressed in his simple saffron robes. He was so warm and wonderful and through the weekend Nico felt such love for him and he fell in love with Nico. They became friends. I got his book THE JOURNEY HOME and adored this being even more. He was born into a Jewish family. When he was a child, he was at a friend's house, and his friend showed him a gun, owned by his family, he then turned to Radanath Swami and said, "my parents hate Jews, they hate you." Fear fell over him and he went home to contemplate this hatred. It sent him on a quest to discover unity and love.

When he was in his teens, he took off on an amazing journey that brought him to India, where he met many "Holy Men" and "Swamis". He meditated on a rock in the middle of the Ganges River, every day, watching the water flow around him with all its strength. He contemplated the many magical beings he met and knew that when his guru appeared he would know him. He felt that some of the beings he encountered were not pure of heart, some even did their magical tricks for a purpose that he did not feel attached to. When he met his guru, he knew it was his destiny that he help the world. He became a Swami, and he travels the world teaching of love, which he radiates. He helps people in India and everywhere.

I feel that if you are not trying to love, trying to give, trying to help and to heal than you are not on the path to the Divine One. I also think that these beings had powers, they are not myths in one religion and reality in another, I think the gods of many religions could have been something else. Something other worldly, or other realmly. When I read the texts, I was amazed at all the EXTRAordinary things that were present and there were many. In the story of Sita and Ram, Ram's father would go to war and the battle would last for a few days but back home his wife had been waiting for years, a clear time difference in the realms. The beings that they encountered were monsters, not of this Earth. There were weapons in these stories that we cannot even conceive of at this time. They seemed like lasers and nuclear bombs. There is evidence around the world that supports the presence of nuclear weapons in the past. In Egypt vitrified stones were found, which are difficult to explain. Vitrification (turning something into glass) needs intense heat which would either have been a meteor, for which there is no evidence, or a nuclear detonation. They are very similar to stones found in Japan, after Hiroshima. In Mohenjo-daro (Pakistan) the radioactivity is off the charts, but why and how? The old texts describe weapons whose intense heat could destroy. What if we looked at the stories of Zeus and lightning bolts, not as myth, but as "Ancient Aliens" who had technological power and so impressed man, at the time, that they thought these beings were gods. I thought of the opening scene from Star Trek's INTO DARKNESS, where they land on a primitive planet and are seen by the beings who think they are gods. I suggest you explore Von Daniken and Ancient Aliens with an open mind.

I also think in this same respect that we must look at all religions as fact. I think that The Divine One manifested as Jesus. I also think that the Divine One came to other places in the world and manifested with different names. The Divine One is ALL, so can manifest and shine at any moment, coming to teach us and bring light. Read about Krishna and Rama and Jesus. See for yourself what beings you think are manifestations of the ONE and which may be Other Beings but see with an open mind, with love, for perhaps many of these being are ALL ONE!

CHAPTER 20

HATSHEPSUT

As I contemplated "which reality or witch reality," is this? I thought how we, too often, take what we are told as TRUTH, but should we not see for ourselves? Why are so many things assumed? Why is much hidden? One "fact" that I had learned in school was that the pyramids were tombs, but were they? Aside from the Step Pyramid no bodies were found in any of them. The mummies were, most often, in THE VALLEY OF THE KINGS. The paintings on the walls are beautiful and were thought to help bring the Pharaoh to the afterlife. They were buried with many of their treasures and their vital organs were preserved in Coptic jars, but these were not found in the pyramids. Many historians said that thieves had robbed the pyramids, but that does not make sense. Think about it, why would they want the Coptic jars?

The Great Pyramid also holds many other mysteries. Many who have lain in the sarcophagus say that it fits perfectly to their body, and they feel that as they lay there, they are opening to another reality another state of being. These people range in size from under 5 feet to over 6 feet. How could it fit perfectly to all? Many say they see beings inside, ethereal beings. Napoleon spent a night in the Great Pyramid and came out white and shaken the following morning, when asked what he saw, he said no one would believe him. Even on his death bed he felt it was too crazy to share. Many Archeologists are now questioning the use of the pyramids and the dating of the Pyramids, as well as, the Sphinx, believing they could go back to 10,500 B.C or more. The Sphinx shows signs of water damage and weathering that supports this. Why did no one see it before. There are 3 shafts in the pyramid that align with the stars in Orion's belt, or I should say, did perfectly align with where they were in 10,500 B.C. Which is also the time many have dated "THE FLOOD," to.

One fascinating story is about Sir Siemens, a British Inventor, who was visiting the pyramids and had Egyptian translators and guides who took him to the top. As he began talking, he noticed a vibration between his fingers as he moved them. Being a scientist, he knew this meant energy. To test his thoughts, he took an empty wine bottle he had with him and a newspaper which he wet with water. He then wrapped the wet paper around the bottle, making a capacitor. He held it above his head and sparks began to fly out of the top of the bottle. Thinking him a wizard of some sorts the guides threw their arms forward in fear and as he tilted the bottle toward them, they received an electric shock. That was the end of the tour for him, but it pressed him to conclude that the pyramids could have been used as an energy source of some kind. This led others to investigating whether the pyramids were indeed a power source, an ancient Tesla Coil, to supply energy to all?

That brought me to another thought, an ancient one for me. Every time I thought or heard about Ancient Egypt, I always felt like I was actually there. I could see it, feel it, smell it. One time when Nico was about 3 years old, I took him to NYC. While we were there, we decided to go to The King Tut Exhibit at the Discovery Center. I had a feeling he would like it, but he was young, and we had been walking around NYC all day. I did not know how long he would last but thought it worth the try. For some reason there were not a lot of people there that day. Every other time I had been there prior it had always been full. As we entered the first room we were greeted by a large, golden sarcophagi. We approached without saying a word and just stared and stared for the longest time. We went through the whole museum that way, seeming unable to move at times. I started to feel like I was somewhere else. I was no longer aware of NYC around me. I felt like I was in Egypt, actually Ancient Egypt, transported through time. Maybe we were for what is time, what is space? Nico felt the same way. Everything was very real and very familiar. We stayed for hours but it felt like minutes. I know time is relative, but this was different. We were in another place and time. When we left there was a gift shop and Nico chose a small replica of the sarcophagi to remember the day. It felt a little strange as we stepped out onto the streets of the city afterwards. It took time to get back into that reality.

My family loved to watch documentaries on Egypt and there was a great series with Dr. Zahi Hawass, which would follow him on archeological digs. It was wonderful to see his journey of discovering the tombs, mummies, and various sights. One time, when Nico was a bit older, around 8 years of age, we were watching Hawass as he was looking for the tomb of Queen Hatshepsut, who was one of the few female Pharaohs of Ancient Egypt. She came to the throne around 1478 BC. He showed three possible mummies, which he thought could be her and was going to investigate them through the show. I did not know there were female Pharaohs and had never heard of her before this. When Hawass got to one particular mummy I said to Nico "oh, that one is me." Nico stared at me for a moment than asked if I realized what I had just said. I paused, for I actually had not. He said, "you said, 'THAT one is ME!'" I did!? I thought. I had not even realized what I said and just brushed it off. The narrator told the story of Hatshepsut's divine birth as it was depicted at Deir el Bahari, which was her temple. The god Amun called together the other gods to announce the birth of a great Queen for whom he would unite the two lands of Egypt in peace. He breathed the breath of life into her Mother, Ahmose, and presented her with the ankh of life and the new queen was blessed with divine power. She was given the royal title, friend, and consort of Horus (the falcon god). As they showed the temple of Deir el Bahari, I saw the entire temple and landscape before the camera panned to that area. I knew this place, although I had never seen it before.

I felt like it had been my home. It was the same feeling I had gotten in the Discovery Center. Again, I was transported through place and time. Hatshepsut was the longest reigning female Pharaoh in Egypt and was one of the most successful Pharaohs, reigning for about 22 years. She was not a conqueror, she believed in peace and prosperity for Egyptians. She built and restored monuments in Egypt and Nubia. She only had one child, a daughter, Neferure. As they showed her image on the walls of the temple, I grabbed Nico. I looked at him and asked if he felt anything, which I knew he did. A simple yes was all I got. I learned that Hatshepsut had a lover, Senenmut, who was her architect. He designed and built Deir el Bahari for her, another strange and familiar feeling. I started to feel like I was partially in a dream state and in this state, Nico was Hatshepsut's daughter and Salvatore was Senenmut. I felt our family together in a different way, in a different life. This is crazy, I thought, then Hawass discussed how he had found a Coptic jar that was labeled Hatshepsut with her tooth inside, he then matched the mummy that had the tooth missing with the tooth in the jar and discovered which of the three was Hatshepsut. It was MY mummy, the one I said was me. This was crazy, even for me. That night I dreamt about Hatshepsut and Deir el Bahari. I could not stop thinking about her. I got flashes of my death, as her, which was different from what Hawass felt for I saw that I was murdered. I told Nico that he was Neferure and his only comment, calmly stated was, I was your child there, I felt that "But I WAS NOT A GIRL!" I told him he was, and he made a face. I thought about my drawing and went to my old college portfolio and pulled it out. It was Hatshepsut. The ankh I had since high school, Hatshepsut again. In this life Salvatore loves to build and is always building me things. I told him my thoughts of my Pharaonic past and thought he would surely think I was crazy now. He said he wanted to watch the documentary with us. As we got to the temple, he said he felt connected to it. I asked if he felt too, that he could have been Senenmut and was surprised to hear him reply yes. Again, he is not as out there as I am, so he did not talk a lot about it but the simple yes said it all.

I remembered a time, years before, when Lilith had done a billet reading for me, and told me that, in a past life, I was in the history books. Now it became clear. I was Hatshepsut. This was something that blew me away. I did not talk to anyone but Salvatore and Nico about it for many years and even after that only one or two people. One of those people told me to write this book. Again, I am not big on the thought that in a past life you were famous but here I was or there I was, I should say.

I have a great love and affinity for Frankincense and Myrrh, on the walls of Hatshepsut's temple there are scenes of a journey she made to the Land of Punt during her ninth year as Pharaoh. She went with five sailing ships, 70 feet long with over 200 men. Hatshepsut returned from Punt with over 30 Myrrh trees, and Boswellia (Frankincense) trees. This was the first attempt at transplanting trees from a foreign land which she placed at Deir el Bahari and was the first recorded use of Frankincense resin. I am glad to have that memory of this sacred resin from my past life which has brought so much healing into this one. Frankincense is great for inflammation, cancer (lots of research being done here), wrinkles and more. It comes from the resin of the Boswellia tree and can be used in many forms, essential oil, incense, tinctures.

Myrrh is a resin from the Commiphora Myrrha tree and is great for mouth and gums, infections internally, externally, and much more. Frankincense and Myrrh are two of my favorite incenses, essential oils, and resins which I use on myself, my family and my animals with great success for various ailments. Frankincense was used in the Middle East and Northern Africa for over 5000 years. The Babylonians used it for ceremonies and the Egyptians brought it in boats from the Phoenicians using it for everything from embalming to skin and wound healing. It was also used as the dark eyeliner you see marking the dramatic shape of the eyes of the ancient Egyptians. It was brought to the baby Jesus because its value was greater than that of gold. It's healing properties were and are invaluable. I make a toothpaste with myrrh which is great for your teeth and gums (although it does not taste good). (Recipe at end)

Hatshepsut was also a prolific builder and restored the Precinct of Mut, the goddess Mut was the wife of Amun Ra. Mut was known as The Lady of Heaven, The Mother Goddess, Mother of the Moon god Khonsu. She represented motherhood and the cosmic waters.

Hatshepsut had twin obelisks built that were the tallest in the world for their time. One still stands at Deir el Bahari where there is a temple with many columns called Djeser-Djeser. It once housed beautiful gardens which had many plants and herbs. Between these plants were crystals and stones. As I read this, I looked out at my garden which seemed the same as Hatshepsuts', plants, crystals and stones. When I first watched the documentary and saw Djeser-Djeser, I felt drawn toward the cliffs above, slightly to the left, if you are facing the temple. There was an area which I felt was part of the complex, although it just looked like a cliff. I cannot prove this, but I feel that this maybe where Senenmut is buried (for they have not found his body) but I am not sure.

Salvatore also had a strong connection to Egypt. His came to expression when we first started dating and we went to see Aida on Broadway, with the wonderful music of Elton John. He felt so connected to the show that we saw it 3 times and for our wedding, our friend Arthur Matera, who made the costumes for the show, make him the priest's coat for our ceremony. If you do not know the story of Aida it is sad and beautiful. The prince is to marry the Pharaoh's daughter in ancient Egypt. One day the prince meets a slave girl from Nubia, Aida, and falls in love with her. He later learns she is the princess of Nubia. He will not forsake her and would rather die, buried alive in a tomb with her, than live without her. When I think about it now, it made sense that Salvatore would connect to this show for the story is so similar to that of Hatshepsut and Senenmut who had a great love but because of her status as Pharaoh they could not be married. I also know that he was Neferure's father although this has not been proven. I felt he was connecting to Aida because of our past, a memory of that time and space.

CHAPTER 21

DRAGON CIDER

Another thing I learned was vinegar residues were found in urns in Ancient Egypt dating from before 3000 BC. Vinegar also plays a very big part in my life. Vinegar in the form of something called Fire Cider or now Dragon Cider. I began making Fire Cider many years ago. Fire Cider itself is an old recipe that was re-created by a wonderful herbalist named Rosemary Gladstar. I never had the pleasure of meeting her but her legacy is strong and she has written many wonderful books. Back in the 80's she made "Fire Cider" using Apple Cider Vinegar, Onions, Garlic, Horseradish, Ginger, Cayenne, honey, and lemons. She freely shared this wonderful remedy with the world and was happy when other herbalists made it and added their own ingredients and even sold it. One day a company decided that it was their remedy and trademarked it. Herbalists were in shock. How could they trademark something as their own that Rosemary had re-created and shared long before?

There were various incarnations of this recipe through history, Hippocrates had one and the 4 Thieves Vinegar, which was said to have prevented thieves from getting the plague in the Middle Ages, is another. It is great for detoxing the body, and wonderful for flu prevention and recovery. I bless my herbal ancestors and thank them for their lessons. I began experimenting with my own recipe for Fire Cider and let the energy move through me to create its own name. Dragon Cider was what presented itself for I love and believe in Dragons. I began to sell it at local farmers markets where I sold my other remedies and our alpaca socks. One day a young man named Justin came by, tried some and loved it. As we talked, I discovered he worked in our local health food store so I gave him a bottle and he said he might be able to interest his department in carrying it there. Within a week he wrote and told me that they wanted, very much, to have it at their store. I was happy but not overly optimistic. I find many people think when an opportunity arises "OH! This is it" and it is their ticket to financial wealth. I was thinking more realistically, it may be a nice addition to what I already do. We moved along in the process over the months that followed, discussing pricing, tax ID info, the works. Then we got down to sealing the bottles, so they were tamper proof. I started feeling like this was too much work for an unknown outcome and thought I might just take a step back. Just as I was thinking this Justin called and said I needed a license to sell in a store. I told him forget it, it was too much. He said he thought I would do well and had faith in me and I should keep going. He called a friend of his, unbeknownst to me, and had her call the Department of Consumer Protection, so they could contact me and discuss it. I got very nervous and felt like pulling back. What would they say about my old-world process of making it in my kitchen, harvesting my herbs from my garden?

I sat down feeling quite overwhelmed and decided to read my Tarot Cards. Now let me just say here, that many people fear Tarot Cards, but I think that Tarot Cards are a tool to help us get in touch with other energies. Energies that we could tap into without the cards but need a little help to get there and higher energies that are guiding us. I laid out the cards on the floor and although the message was somewhat clear it was not really in order. My cat, Ball, my familiar, it you will, walked over to the cards and laid on top of them. Then he started skooching his butt around and the cards were moving with him. I stared at him thinking, "what the heck are you doing? Why are you messing up the cards, I need an answer?" He then looked at me like "THERE," and walked away, like a magical Garfield. I looked at the cards which now were in an order that was perfectly clear and made total sense. I looked at him and he nodded. I thanked him and then went back to the cards. They clearly said that I had to get over my fears and take this step. They said that I was afraid of spending more money on another business, afraid I would not flourish but that I must overcome that fear and proceed. It said that I would be successful should I move forward. I took a deep breath and then called the Department of Consumer Protection.

I first talked to an inspector who was wonderful. She answered some questions and then told me to talk to her supervisor, Virginia.

Virginia was also extremely helpful and told me that to obtain a license I would need a commercial kitchen. I told her I did not have one and thought that was the end of the line. She said I could rent one and that many churches rented them out for a reasonable price. She then gave me all the info I needed and said I should think about if it would be worth the money for the license. I thanked her and got off the phone thinking about the expense of the license, it was not cheap. As I then moved along with each step, I felt I was guided, pushed, helped. The next step was a lab that would test it. I was wanting to give up again on this big, expensive adventure but every time I did the woman, Abby, from the lab would call me with a gentle guiding nudge. The results from the lab test showed that my Dragon Cider was so powerful that it killed E. coli. It is great stuff! I also had to take an intensive course, on-line, which involved microbiology and various bottling procedures. Then finally I had to get inspected by the Department of Consumer Protection. All went well. I list the ingredients below and their healing power here.

Organic apple cider vinegar- Fire Cider/Dragon Cider will help to rid your body of toxins, it assists in healing flu, allergies, gout, and colds.

Red onion (Allium Cepa)-Red onions are a great source of quercetin which is great for helping to reduce free radicals in your body -bad things that cause disease and damage in your body. Onions also contain allicin which is great for high blood pressure, cardiovascular health. They also help fight bacteria and fungi.

Garlic- allium sativum - Garlic has been used for over 5000 years in Egypt and Mesopotamia for battling infections and was thought to fight the plague. It is a natural antibiotic and antibacterial agent. Louis Pasteur studied garlic and found that it killed bacteria. Research has shown that garlic is affective as an overall antibiotic. When you take antibiotics too often you build up a resistance to them, you produce a resistant strain. Garlic does not appear to do this. (Please note that there are times you may need an actual antibiotic.)

Horseradish -Armoacia rusticana - Great for sinus infections and also a natural antibiotic, great for bladder infections, kidneys, lungs, cough, cold and digestion.

Ginger - zingiber officinale -In Sanskrit singabera means horn shaped. It has been used in Chinese and Ayurvedic medicine for centuries. It was so valued during the Middle Ages that they said it was from the Garden of Eden. It is great for digestion, nausea, arthritis, colic, and heart conditions. It guards against intestinal parasites, colds, flu, bronchitis, stimulates digestion, helps clear arterial plaque (remember the dream about my dad) and helps promotes circulation.

Goji berries (Wolf berries) Lycium Barbarum and Lycium Chinense, Wolf berries are antioxidant and aid in fighting free radicals. They help build your blood chi (according to Chinese medicine is your energy force). By helping to build your blood they help with anemia. Also, the stronger your blood chi is the more efficient your body is in governing your hormones and balancing them.

Cayenne - Capsicum Annuum -From the Greek Kapto, meaning to bite. It is in the nightshade family which Belladonna is also a member of. High in vitamins A, B6, C and E. It helps to heat and speed up the metabolism because of the capsaicin. The hotter the pepper is the more capsaicin it contains, increasing blood circulation throughout your body. I use it in my pain salve for heat.

Sage- Salvia which means to save or heal. It is said if a man has sage in his garden, he will never be ill.

Mullein Leaf - Verbascum-Mullein leaf is great for the lungs - from cough to lung cancer. (Post writing this I used it in my Covid Remedy it helped a lot of people but that is for another book)

Note: when harvesting herbs make sure you do not gather them near the road or in a place where they would absorb toxic fumes from vehicles or factories.

When you are preparing herbal preparations or meals for that matter, the energy should be peaceful, no anxiety, no arguments around. The energy will affect your remedy so be happy and calm. The more we learn to bond with the elements we are using the more peace we will discover through them.

I have a large shelf in my kitchen, in front of, floor to ceiling windows that surround the table where we eat. It overlooks the backyard and the alpacas and a small waterfall. It is beautiful and even more so with the large glass containers which are filled with wonderful roots and herbs. It is quite magical.

We also have a WITCH/WIZARDING ROOM, that has shelves filled with herbs, tinctures, flower essences and various prepared remedies and ingredients. One time when Nico was about 7, we took him to see the Harry Potter Exhibit at the Discovery Center in NYC. It was before he had read the book or seen the movie. I thought he would go crazy, especially when he got to the potions room. it was the actual set from the movie. As we entered the room, I waited to see his eyes light up, but they did not. He left the room pretty quickly with a shrug of his shoulders. I followed him and told him I thought he would have really liked that. He loved making "potions" with me at home. He loved going to Barrie's, Happy Rainbows and exploring the herbs and crystals. "Why don't you like it?" I asked. "You can't use any of those herbs," he said, "they are all fake. It's not like our house where we make real potions or like Barrie's where all the herbs are real herbs that you can use." He walked on as I thought, yes, we do live in a magical world.

CHAPTER 22

THE LOST GOSPELS

The Gnostic Gospels are sacred texts which were found near Nag Hammadi, Egypt, in a place called Jabal al-Tarif, which is a mountain that has well over one hundred caves in its cliffs. These caves are not easy to get to. You would either have to climb up a straight wall or down the rocks. One December day in 1945 Muhammad Ali (not the fighter) and his brothers found a huge clay jar, in one of the ground level caves. The jar was about 3 feet high. Muhammad was afraid to break the jar in that the Jinn or Jinni may come out and cause trouble for him as those spirits often do. Yes, they truly believe in Jinns and Genies in other parts of the world. He then wondered if the vessel might contain gold. His avarice overtook his fear, and he smashed the jar. Inside were twelve leather bound papyrus books that were very old. They were written in Coptic (a language spoken in Egypt from the 2nd century until the 1600's). The brothers did not know what they were and brought them home to their mother who tossed many of them into the fire because they did not have much else around to burn. Since the brothers were in a large feud with another family, they feared holding onto the documents for if the police came, they may think they were stolen so they sold them on the black market. These fifty-four texts were later found to be some of the most amazing documents in the world, *The Gnostic Gospels*. Gnostic means knowledge or enlightenment and in these books were The Gospel of Thomas, The Gospel of Mary, The Gospel of Judas, The Secret Book of John, The Gospel of Truth and many more. They were untouched through the centuries. Untouched is an important word here. No one had read them so there was no one to decide what should stay or go. Not one word had been changed. They were carbon dated and found to be authentic, going back to as early as around 120 AD. Sadly, though, there was much damage, and many sections were lost.

So, you may ask, why don't many people know of this? Well, if you read or saw THE DA VINCI CODE, you did, there were a few references there. Why were these gospels lost? Irenaeus was a Bishop in Gaul who later became a Saint. He was famous for deciding what was heresy and wrote a book called Adversus Haereses. He thought that the gnostic scriptures were a threat to the church and banned them. He felt that there were only four scriptures that were good enough to be read, or I should say were what he wanted to be read. These, obviously, were Matthew, Mark, Luke and some parts of John (but not much of what John wrote). He decided the others were heresy and should be destroyed. Who hid the books near Nag Hammadi? No one knows, but we can guess that it was someone who thought them important enough to save and not be destroyed. I am grateful for their effort. I recommend reading them yourself but here is some information from THE SECRET GOSPEL OF JOHN.

After Jesus was crucified John went to the temple and there met Arimanios, a Pharisee (a member of an ancient Jewish sect who believed in strict interpretation of the law of Moses). Arimanios asked John where Jesus was, and John said he has "returned from whence he came." Arimanios told John that the Nazarene had deceived him and filled his "ears with lies... turned you against the traditions of our ancestors." Which to me makes sense if you go back to what I said about John in the New Testament and Jesus saying that the god of the Old Testament was not GOD but the Devil. Of course, a Pharisee would be extremely angry with Jesus. Angry enough to put him to death. He was ripping apart their beliefs. So, I say, with my heart, that I respect the Jewish religion, which I grew up with, which my father was a part of, I respect their faith, as I respect all religions but if we do not "have eyes to see and ears to hear" (Jesus) then how can we truly see. I think it is very important to look at things as if you were an alien entering a new planet, like on Star Trek and learn all the details anew.

The Secret Gospel goes on to say that the sky opened and rumbled and Jesus, the Savior, appeared. John wanted to know who "The Father is, What is the Eternal Realm." Jesus said "*THE ONE* is a sovereign that has nothing over it. The parent of all that is incorruptible, that is pure light at which no eye can gaze...'*THE ONE*', is the Invisible Spirit." We should not think of THE ONE as a god or a figure, for *The One* is beyond that. It is all, "it is eternal, it is absolute, complete in the light. '*THE ONE*' is limitless, unfathomable, unmeasurable, eternal. It is incorporeal, no one can understand....... Not part of time."

"*The One* is a realm that gives a realm,

life that gives life,

a blessed one that gives blessedness,

knowledge that gives knowledge,

a good one that gives goodness,

mercy that gives mercy and redemption,

grace that gives grace.

THE ONE gives this and immeasurable light. There is peace and silence.

The Gospel continues with an account of the creation of man which is very different from Genesis. In my understanding it says that "*THE ONE*" is ALL, it is energy and is the origin of everything. From *THE ONE* came various energies. These thoughts became reality. From the thoughts came the first power who preceded all and came from the mind of Forethought of the All. Her light shone. She preceded everything. Then another Spirit, Foreknowledge appeared from She and She was given Incorruptibility which stood by Thought and Foreknowledge. There then came various realms of truth, insight, love and the fourth realm was Eleleth and with it was perfection and peace. Then came Sophia. Those 4 realms were and are the aeons (vital forces) that stand before the Child of the Great One, they belong to the Child, the self-Generated.

Now Sophia, who is Wisdom of Insight and who constitutes an aeon, wanted to bring forth a being like herself. She did this alone, without the spirits consent because she had invincible power within her. Her thought was not idle. Something came out that was imperfect, it did not resemble her. It changed into the figure of a snake with the face of a lion. She cast it away outside the realm and surrounded it with a bright colored cloud so that no one would see it, she named her offspring Yaldabaoth, who was the first RULER and that took great power from his mother. He then created his own aeons with luminous fire, who still exist. He produced from himself beings of jealousy and darkness. He stationed seven kings, one for each sphere of heaven, to reign over the seven heavens, and five to reign over the abyss. He is ignorant darkness, but he had light from his mother, so it made the darkness shine, but dimmed the light. Yaldabaoth had great power from his mother and called himself god, he said he was a 'Jealous god" and that no other gods should be put before him, which meant that he knew other gods existed but wanted them to be below him and not worshiped.

The text continues as Yaldabaoth decides to create his own being who will worship him, his own creation, MAN. He gathers 365 angels, each angel taking much effort to create various parts of this man, hands, feet etc. When the being was done it had no life, no vital force. Yaldabaoth breathed the power from his mother, which he inherited, into the being which then began to move and became powerful and enlightened due to the energy of Sophia, who had great power, for she was directly from THE ONE. When the other powers saw MAN, they became jealous. Adam was more intelligent than the creators, so they threw him to the lowest part of the material realm, Earth.

Sophia, filled with love and compassion, felt for Adam, he was enlightened now and needed help. She sent, Enlightened Insight, who is from the Mother-Father and is life. This being helped the creature by teaching it the way of the ascent, the way to THE ONE. Enlightened Insight was hidden within Adam. Yaldobaoth and the creators were upset with Adam's ability to think so they took fire, water, earth and the four fiery winds and made a great commotion. They made Adam mortal. They made Adam forget. Forget the light he came from. They brought him to "paradise" (which is from a Zoroastrian word which means a walled enclosure), near the Tree of Life and guarded it with their spirit. Then the Savior came and taught him to eat and showed him enlightened insight, (was this the serpent, you may think). Yaldabaoth did not like this, he was supposed to be the one worshiped, he was supposed to be the god and no others were put before him. He moved Adam to a sort of, deep sleep, the loss of sense and discernment. Yaldabaoth took part of Adam's power and created a female creature, not from his rib, and Adam connected to her for she was of him. Sophia then went to help her also and restore what she lacked, she was called Life, Sofia shone as perfect knowledge.

The Savior appeared in the form of an eagle upon the tree of knowledge to awaken humans from the depth of sleep. Insight appeared to them and awakened their minds. Then Yaldabaoth forced himself on Eve and she had Cain and Abel, Adam then mated with Eve and created Seth. Yaldabaoth made them drink from the water of forgetfulness, so they would forget again from whence they came.

The Savior later told John that, "you must find the pure light and remember, or you cannot be reunited with *THE ONE.*" The Savior said...

I am the abundance of light
I am the remembrance of Fullness.

So, as you may see, this is very different than the many texts we read that were edited. This is very different than the MALE oriented version of what we hear. This, to me, is mind blowing. What are we doing here on earth? Are we under a veil, do we not see or try to see? Did many stops seeking *THE ONE,* did we forget? I think this is VITAL. We think of Jesus coming at a certain place, a certain time but I believe he has always been. He manifested in human form for we were lost, and he wanted to help us. I think many of those beings, including Sophia have also come down, many times to help us, she was just given different names. There is "the Lady," in many religious texts, who is love and wisdom, who came for us, to help us find the Divine, THE ONE. There is a Supreme Being in many religions and a manifestation of this Divine One. Maybe if we see them as ALL, as DIVINE and as ONE we could find love with all beings.

CHAPTER 23

CRYSTALS AND HEALING STONES

One day I was thinking of our material body as one of those candle holders that are made from clay or metal and have the cutouts of stars and moons and various shapes. We are all part of the one fire. We take our little flames and surround them with material stuff. Hopefully we cut out shapes in the material to shine the light, but some keep putting more and more material on, so the light is barely visible or not visible at all. The more that we become seekers of knowledge, clearing our slate, the more openings we create. The more we see the light and shine it out. Seek. Open your heart. We work, we run, we rush, we have distractions, but we must stop. We must meditate. We must search our soul and go beyond so we can reconnect. We must not forget prayer and rituals. Consider setting up an altar, a place in your home that is sacred. A place that when you look at it you contemplate, you pray. Your altar can be simple or elaborate. Find a place that is calm and quiet, a table, a shelf, a corner. This should only be used as your altar and not for anything else. You can place a nice piece of cloth on it, if you like. On my altar I place various crystals and stones that have healing energy, a candle that I light (when I am in the room) and often a wisdom card that reminds me of something I need to work on. There are times when I need to activate an energy, to transmute something.

Transmutation is not a wish; it is an intention to be manifested. The intention can be personal, regarding healing, physical, spiritual, emotional or on a global or universal scale. It can encompass world peace and healing of the cosmos. This transmutation is something I do not take lightly. It is a somewhat long process with various steps. Every step needs to be performed with great care and intention. To begin have a special notebook that is used only for Transmutation and healing work. Do not write desires, write strong statements, remember the spoken word has power. If you are doing one to heal a sick animal you would not say, I want her to be better, I hope she will heal, but rather statements like:

I activate the energies in these crystals and stones to manifest health in my (dog/cat/alpaca).

I activate these energies to remove any and all illness and create vibrant health and happiness.

I activate these energies to shine healing and health into every cell of (insert name) body, mind and spirit. To restore the youthful energy through the Divine, the Mighty Sacred Christ I am.

Then see it as already done.

These are just a couple of examples. I usually have a list that is at least 6 statements or more. Before you begin, surround yourself in the white, violet, and silver lights. Next select crystals and/or rocks you have collected and place them in a pattern that you feel will best enhance the vibration. It could be a cross, a star, a circle, or some other shape. Place a candle, white for purity, violet for protection or any color that is calling out to you. Get some incense, I like Frankincense, Myrrh and Dragon's Blood (Dracaena- a red resin). The incense burner can be on the altar or next to it. After your altar is set up, light the incense and your candle, then read your statements ALOUD, 3 times each. Do this with good intentions, no negative thoughts, and feel the light pour through you. After you are done sit for a moment in peace and quiet. While your transmutation is active, light your candle (blow it out when you are not present in the room). Do not touch or change anything on your altar for either a set number of weeks or until your intention has manifested and even a little longer after that. When you wish to change your altar take the stones and cleanse them. You can do this by leaving them in the sun for a full day and moon by night, or you can swirl sage, frankincense, myrrh, or Dragon's Blood, around them or do both. After that put them away, let them rest for a while. You can then either set up a new Transmutation if you need one or just place a flower and other stones or intention cards on your altar with a new candle. You can add other things to this ceremony. For instance, this past Christmas Nico made me a beautiful music box in the blacksmith shop. It plays Fur Elise by Beethoven and Amazing Grace by John Newton. I light my candle and turn the tiny crank and breath. Everyone needs a place in their home that is devoted to breath, peace and light. A place to manifest your intentions and connect to something higher than yourself. In this crazy world that we live in we can get so very caught up in running from place to place and thing to thing that we forget our true purpose and our inner quest to find the light., THE ONE. We need rituals and aids to help us. Here are some healing stones that I love and value their great healing powers.

Fire Agate- Fire agates are a beautiful brown color with swirls of green, gold, orange and sometimes, blue and purple. They are a major stone of protection - physical, emotional, and spiritual. They send the energy back to who is sending so they may understand what they are doing. In other words, you never send negative energy to anyone, but if they are sending it to you, you can send it right back to them so they may be aware of what they are doing and hopefully, stop. Fire agates are a spiritual flame. The stones may even disappear after they have performed a great deed. I had a ring with 2 fire agate stones and 2 tiny diamonds. I was going through a very tough time in my life, and someone related to me was sending me horrible, negative vibrations. I was talking to a counselor, and we were working though how to remove myself from these people, how to deal with it. As I felt something break, I looked down and one of the agates was gone. We searched the room, but it was nowhere in sight (it was a tiny room). I had it when I entered the room. A week later I felt another break with someone else involved in the situation and I looked, and the other agate was gone, nowhere to be found. Following the disappearance, the people, somehow backed off, things changed. I felt the fire agates had protected me, saved me. I recommend wearing them for protection and keeping one on your altar.

Apache Tears - Obsidian - In the 1870's a group of Apache warriors were being targeted by the cavalry. The Apaches were driven to a cliff where there was no escape, and they knew they would be captured and killed. They decided to jump off the cliff, rather than meet this fate. These stones are said to be the tears of their wives and children. If you hold them up to the light you can see the tear inside. Due to this energy, they actually help you to recover from grief with ease. They are volcanic glass. One was given to Nico when he was born. They are a stone of peace for they bring insight to situations and help to remove barriers you set up that inhibit your growth. They help you choose, wisely, what to pursue and what to give up on, just as the Apache knew which road they should take, so will you when you use this stone. They help remove the poison of a snake bite. It is interesting that in Nico's life he indeed has great insight into plowing through any barrier that would inhibit his growth, he knows what he wants to pursue. Also, interesting that it is for snake bites, considering the past life experience he and I shared about me getting bit by a snake in a past life.

Carnelian - are a reddish, orange color. They help you open up to your talents and creativity and to
manifest inspiration and motivation. They also help you to dispel sorrow from your life, releasing fear and anger and can help in theatrical pursuits. They are great healers for your lower back and kidneys and

relieve depression.

Garnet- Garnets were worn on the breast plates of the high priest and priestesses. There is said to be a flash of lightening contained within them that, which, like a flash, expands your awareness, your energy, your realms. It helps you manifest what you need in your life. It lights your internal fire. They are a stone of health and help to balance your chakras and aid in moving your kundalini energy upwards. They are stones of love and devotion, devotion to yourself, to others and all beings in the universe. They help you see yourself and your emotions so you can balance them. Garnets are a deep red color and when you mine them, they can look black. They stick out of the surrounding rock in trapezohedron crystals. When I was young, I went to a garnet mine with my parents and thought it the coolest thing ever. When Nico was 4, I discovered there was a mine right near us. I brought him there and we were mining the stones. I turned and Nico had quickly climbed higher than was in my comfort zone. He tripped and it was as if time slowed. I saw him fly up, then back, where he landed safely. I ran to him, and he was fine, if he had fallen, he would have gotten really hurt. Nico told me that he saw my dad lift him and gently place him back to the ground. All was magic that day. We came home with a bowl of beautiful raw garnets.

Lapis Lazuli - Crystalizes into cubes and dodecahedral shapes. It is a deep blue and as I said earlier was used in the paintings of the Voynich Manuscript. It is a magical stone and was said to have existed before the beginning of time. It helps one to gain access to the unknown mysteries and the sacred texts, so you can see why it was used in the Voynich. It helps you understand information and aids in interpreting your dreams.

Moonstone - As its name states, it is a stone of the lunar energy. It helps you to balance and restructure your emotional, mental, physical, and spiritual energies and is wonderful for finding new beginnings. Moonstones shine the light to so you may, go with the flow, and rise to the higher energies of the universe. Using the stone heightens your perception and protects you in travel. This is a stone of finding Self, of taking the journey of the dark night of the soul and finding who you are. Letting yourself see all, all that is fun, all that is sad, all that is scary. When we take time to do this, we must do it with kindness to self. We must realize that we have made no miss-takes but have had lessons. It carries the energy of a new moon so we can discover that even in the darkness there is light, there is strength, there is still the light of the moon so we may see our SELF.

Quartz - comes in many colors but clear quartz is an amplifier, it has piezoelectric energy which is an electrical charge that accumulates in crystals, bones, and other matter. It can also be a reversible charge. The tip of the crystal is usually positive but when held and used for healing can reverse charge and send energy out. They amplify energy, healing energy and thoughts and help to unite one's earthly energies with the stars and the planets. They also aid in elevating the vibrations here on earth and raise your consciousness. It is a clear stone and is used for pure healing energy. You will understand their power even more when you get to the chapter on sacred places and the power of the stones.

Septarian Nodules - are from the Mississippi River Valley. They have a creamy yellow base of calcite with swirls of deep brown, which is the actual mud from the valley, argonite, which are crystal clusters and limestone, which is the grey. If you think about the composition and how it was formed you can understand how this stone helps with giving you a strong connection to the Earth, grounding you to her energies. I feel this stone connects me to my dad.

There are many other stones you can use. I recommend a book called LOVE IS IN THE EARTH by Melody

CHAPTER 24

NICO MANIFESTS

When Nico was four years old, we decided we would attend the BIG E ALPACA SHOW and let him train and enter his alpaca, Bella Sofia, in the event. There was a part of the show dedicated to children, in which they could show their alpacas in the areas of costume, showmanship and obstacle course. When Bella Sofia was a baby, her mom had mastitis and could not feed her until she healed, so Nico would bottle feed her with goat's milk. Bella Sofia and Nico were very bonded to each other, and Bella Sofia loved the practice times. She also liked wearing her costume. Nico decided he would be a pirate and Bella Sofia would be his treasure. He had a pirate shirt, bandana and sword and he made her a cloth for her back with gold coins, glitter, and an X. For the obstacle course the human had to guide the alpaca up and down stairs, which they do not usually do, go over ramps, jump, walk through fringe and other things that an alpaca would not choose to do on their own. Nico and Bella Sofia worked hard all summer preparing and having a great time. Nico would guide her under hanging willow trees, jump her over benches and walk her up and down stairs. One afternoon Nico was not feeling well and had to stay in bed. I went up to Bella Sofia and she was looking for Nico and ready for their training. I told her Nico was not coming out and she did not seem happy about it. Finally, I took her down to the house and brought her in the bedroom where she stood next to Nico's bed, staring at him as he smiled and stared at her. They were very happy.

When we got to the Big E they got blue ribbons, first place, in every event and were both prancing about happily. Nico ran to me with the blue ribbon attached to his front shirt pocket, where the judge had placed it. When he got to me, he said "look what we won!" Just to confirm the WE, Bella Sofia plucked the ribbon from his pocket with her mouth and dangled it from her lips with pride. When it was time for her to have dinner and rest, we took Nico to Storrow Town, a part of the Big E fair. It is a replica of an 1800's village with old houses, wood cutting tools and a blacksmith shop. We entered the blacksmith shop and Nico's eyes grew wide and he got very intense. He stared at the blacksmith working the forge and found a place to sit. People came and went every 3-5 minutes, but Nico did not budge. After about 20 minutes I told him we should head out. He shook his head no and just stared at the smith. Salvatore and I waited patiently as he watched. Finally, after about 30 minutes we said we had to get back to Bella Sofia.

Four years later I was looking for a place to go to Easter Mass. I love the Easter celebration and felt a need to find a peaceful and spiritual celebration that would vibrate with my beliefs. Barrie had told me about a local abbey called THE ABBEY OF REGINA LAUDIS and we looked up the website. As Nico and I were going through the pages we came upon a picture of Elvis Presley with a beautiful young woman. Nico loved Elvis and asked why he was on an abbey website. I did not know, so we read. Mother Dolores Hart who was then Prioress of the abbey had once been a famous movie and Broadway star. She was the first actress to kiss Elvis on screen and appeared in another film with him after. Nico thought this was so cool, so did I. We continued looking at the website and saw another picture, this one of a blacksmith shop. Nico told me to pause there. He said "They have a blacksmith shop!? Oh, Mommy, we need to go there. Do you think I could be a part of that? That is my dream to be a blacksmith!" Your dream? I pondered, then I remembered the Big E four years earlier. He had not said one word since that time, but obviously it was in his heart.

On Easter morning we attended mass at a beautiful church that was a large barn like structure with a huge, vaulted ceiling. In front were large metal sculptures of sheep made by Mother Praxedes who is a very talented sculptress. She also helped design the church which was built from wood harvested from their land on a road that the nuns built themselves. Yes, built themselves, pulling large rocks out of the way, clearing trees and all. After mass we went to the back of the church and there were jars of holy water. Nico was staring at them and this angelic looking nun, who we found out was Mother Angele, came over to him and said he could take one if he liked. Nico put his hands in prayer, as we do at the end of yoga class, bowed, and said "Namaste." She did the same to him with a Namaste response. I smiled and told her I was a yoga teacher. She told me she liked yoga and had done it at the Abbey. Nico then went on to tell her his dream of being a blacksmith and asked what he needed to do. She told him that he should write to Mother Anastasia, for she runs the Blacksmith shop. We went home and my little 8-year-old boy, who did not like to write, unless it was in Sanskrit or Hieroglyphics, sat down to compose his letter. He asked Mother Anastasia if he could be her apprentice. We sent the letter off and a few days later got a phone call from Mother Anastasia. She said that he was too young to be an apprentice, but he could come and have an experience. He was so excited.

When we got to the little shop Nico's mouth dropped open. There was a large forge, anvils and tools and he was standing in the middle of it all. Mother Anastasia said that beginners must learn how to make hooks and to become an apprentice, you had to first make 100 hooks. She began to make one as Nico watched, intently. When she was done, she noticed how excited he was and said he could try one. He did indeed, it took him over an hour and a half (now he can make one in 5 minutes). When he was done, he asked if he could be her apprentice since he had made a hook. She laughed and said he could come once a month. He then worked his way into twice a month and then every week. He became a full apprentice, on his 13th birthday for which he had to complete a big project. He made a beautiful 6-foot-long table with benches to match. The top is made of knotty pine. Salvatore helped him with the woodwork, and the bottom is all metal, for which Nico had to weld, cut, and shape. He has made many hooks, fire pokers, knives, candle holders and my personal favorite, my music box. He is now working on armor and knives and wishes to make swords one day. I am very proud of him.

He had to do a presentation which included the story of his Blacksmithing path for Mother Abbess Lucia, Mother Abbess David, Mother Dolores, and Mother Olivia Francis. Nico guided us to the Abbey to become a blacksmith, but we received much more. Mother Anastasia has become more than a dear friend, she is a part of our family. She is an amazing woman who has so much love in her heart that you feel it through her words and especially through her hugs. She loves Nico like her own child, she loves me, and I love her. Salvatore loves her too. We all have great talks and share laughs. She is a great blessing to Nico but also one to our whole family, a family that she is now a part of, and we are part of hers.

We have also become close with many of the nuns, all of whom are amazing. The Abbey also has a theatre where they do wonderful shows in a beautiful outdoor setting. It is open on all sides and was a gift from the actress Patricia Neal and the roof a gift from Paul Newman. About a month after Nico made his first hook I got a call from Mother Anastasia, she said the theatre company was doing SOUTH PACIFIC and needed a young boy for the part of Jerome, who sang a song called Dites-Moi in French. Nico and I were sitting on the back porch, and I asked her to hold on while I passed along the question to Nico. In Nico fashion, the man of few words, he calmly said "ok". We then looked up the song and he sang it over and over. The next day when we arrived for the audition Tom and Sally, who run the theatre asked Nico if he could sing a song for them. He said "yes." They asked what song he would like to sing, and that Happy Birthday would be fine if he did not know any others. He told them he would sing the song he was supposed to sing. They asked what song was he supposed to sing. "Dites-Moi" he said casually and sang in French for them. They were thrilled and he got the part and a part in one of the shows every year after that. It was the beginning of Nico's great acting career and at the young age of 13, I can actually call it that. After he did South Pacific, he was asked to star in a movie at the Institute for American Indian Studies. The movie was about an Indian boy whose grandfather is helping him to learn the importance of the sacred plants and animals that surrounded them. He was later asked to be in some college/student films where they loved him so much that they later created a starring role for him in another movie.

I attended most of the abbey rehearsals with him and sat while he rehearsed, usually knitting. One night Salvatore took him, and I stayed home to get some rest. I was sitting in bed with the bedroom door open to the yard. It was a quiet summer night and I glanced up and jumped. There was a light moving straight toward the door. It looked like one of those mini flashlights. "Who would come to my back door like this." I thought, quite startled. The light moved all the way up to the screen then moved straight to the left. I ran to the door, but it was not a flashlight, it was just a big light. It was surely not a firefly. It moved up and down and then stayed still. I suddenly smiled and realized it was a fairy. I had never seen a fairy before, although I believed they existed. She was beautiful. She stayed a couple of minutes then zipped away. I later told Salvatore about it, thinking he may not believe me, but he nodded and said he sees them in the crab apple tree, early some mornings.

The Easter Vigil Mass that next year was a dedication to the blacksmith shop so Mother Anastasia asked Nico to do one of the readings. He was excited. He was to read from Isaiah, and it started with "Ho, says the Lord." Well Nico let out this big booming "HOOOOOOOOOOO, says the lord." and I almost fell on the floor laughing. Mother Dolores coached him and loved his energy. The night of the Vigil was amazing. I had never been to one before. We entered the church, and it was dark. We were handed candles, but they were not lit. When everyone arrived, we were led out into the parking lot where the dry Christmas Tree, from months prior, was wrapped up and sitting on a large metal can. We all circled it and lit our candles from one main candle. The tree was then lit, and the flames burst into the air. It was magical. We gazed at the fire, and I felt such energy and strength. We prayed and returned to the church and Nico and his fellow Black

Smithers did a great job presenting.

Nico's love of blacksmithing grew and grew and so did his love for acting. He loved Shakespeare ever since he saw Romeo and Juliet, at the ballet, when he was little. Sir Kenneth MacMillan's Romeo and Juliet is one of my favorite ballets in the whole world. The score is by Prokofiev which is some of the most amazing music ever written. I watched that ballet hundreds of times when I was with ABT, and it got better and better each time. When Nico was 3 years old, I showed him a little bit of the ballet in a video. He was fascinated, especially with the big sword fighting scene. I decided to take Nico and Salvatore to see it performed live, at the Metropolitan Opera House. When we arrived at the theatre Nico was in awe of the beautiful surroundings. He sat and stared taking everything in. There was a woman sitting next to us that looked at Nico with an expression that clearly said, "oh no, a little boy at a three-hour ballet," but she kindly nodded. The first act began, and Nico barely moved the whole time. When the first intermission came, after one hour, I asked him if he liked it. "YES!" he said. The woman turned to him in amazement and then began a wonderful conversation with my three-year-old about the ballet. She then turned to me and told me it was certainly not what she expected. But Nico is not what most people expect. He is definitely the young man who at three was outside in the rain with nothing but red boots on singing "what a glorious feeling I'm happy again", without a care in the world. His love of Shakespeare blossomed from that day on. He loved it so much that when he was 8, I started a class at our homeschool co-op on acting Shakespeare and Nico blew me away. He got it all immediately and acted it beautifully. We would attend Shakespearean theatre and I would ask if he understood what was going on, in that Shakespeare can be difficult for some to understand. He looked at me like I was crazy. "They are speaking English, mom," he said, "of course I understand it." I sent Mother Anastasia a clip of him doing Hamlet. She was thrilled.

The next year I was asked to read at the Easter Vigil from Baruch about Sophia. I was so glad that was my reading because that was the one, I related to, Sophia from the Gnostic texts. Wisdom. I don't think I could have read about Abraham and the sacrifice (which was another reading for Easter). Mother Dolores was there to coach the readers and help us perform it better. At that point I did not know her very well. I had been intensely reading John all week and was talking about what I thought the gospel meant with Nico and Salvatore. It occupied a lot of my ruminations. When Mother Dolores finished helping me, she came over and Mother Anastasia showed her the clip of Nico doing Hamlet. She told him he was wonderful. She asked if he would like to do Shakespeare with her and that she would love to coach him. I was floored. The world was still writing her fan mail, asking if they could meet her, work with her, anything. She did not work with anyone but here she was asking Nico. I told him he was very blessed. She then turned to me and out of nowhere said "I know the Bible well but John baffles me and I fear he will until the end of my days." She then smiled and walked away. I thought, why did she say that? Why, when I was so absorbed in the meaning of John and taking steps towards understanding did, she bring up John out of nowhere or out of Hamlet, really. It had to be a sign. Later that week, I was contemplating this again and I opened my email to find a daily gospel reading. I had not ordered a daily gospel reading but decided to read it. It was the chapter from John that I was contemplating.

Nico has since been working with Mother Dolores on his Shakespeare. She is an amazing teacher and coach and most importantly an amazing and beautiful woman. Beautiful inside and out. Her understanding of the art of acting is like nothing I have experienced. The way she helps Nico create his character is filled with rich thoughts and insight. She told him not to use a gesture unless he meant it and use it fully. She brings a passion and life to acting, I am in awe to see how she works. It made me want to see more of her films. We decided to watch LISA, the story of a women who had been in the Nazi Concentration Camps where she was experimented on and was dealing with her pain after she was released. It is a wonderful movie, and she was brilliant as Lisa. After the movie ended Nico and I discussed how we felt that she was not Dolores Hart, she was Lisa, truly. That is a great actress, acting from her heart, but she gave it all up to be part of a community that shines God's love and light. Hollywood thought it was a publicity stunt, but it was not, it was where she was lead. She wrote a book called *Ear of the Heart* about her journey. I recommend it. We love her so and bless our moments with her.

At one point she decided that Nico should learn how to dance. Her friend June Christian is the Ballet Mistress for the Royal Academy of Ballet in London. She decides who will be in the Royal Ballet. The Abbey calls her Maria Salome. Mother Dolores set up Nico's first dance lesson on a lovely sunny day. The Abbey was doing construction and

Mother Dolores loved watching the hug backhoes and large trucks doing all the work. We found her in the middle of the site with Maria Salome, a beautiful lady who is 80 years old and proudly stands and moves like a young ballerina. She began to teach Nico how to dance and my thought was, good luck, I had tried many times and it just did not happen. Well, in 10 minutes she had him gliding and swooshing beautifully. She held his arm and kept telling him he was a "lovely chap" and was doing "splendidly" Nico loved being called a lovely chap and did whatever she said and was dancing around the construction site in no time. Mother Dolores was beaming. We went a few times after that, before she returned to London. Diana came once and got a dance lesson too. Nico called her "Granny London" and became very fond of her. Nico surely found a special home at the Abbey and has been blessed with Great Teachers.

CHAPTER 25

BLACKSMITHING

After four years of knitting while Nico did his blacksmithing it occurred to me that I would love to try myself. I asked Mother Anastasia if I could make a hook. She said yes and had Nico teach me. I loved it. She said I could begin working at the shop also. I was so happy. She thought it would be nice to incorporate my love of herbs into my work and suggested that I make a leaf out of metal. She sent me a You Tube video to watch, and it looked so wonderful and so easy, although I was not fooled because I had watched Nico make hooks. It looks so easy when he does but I remembered his first hook and I did indeed, find it difficult. It was a wonderful challenge to spread the metal out like it was play dough. I worked and worked, heating the metal then hammering it in a certain way to open it out, heating and hammering again and again. It took over an hour, but I finally got it to look like a leaf, a very, thin, long leaf, but a leaf, non-the-less. I put it back in the fire so it could heat it up for some finishing touches. I was feeling proud of my leaf, and I placed it in the piping hot coals. When I pulled it out, it was gone. I held the rod in my hand, but the leaf was not there. It had melted off and fell into the fire. I learned how to work with thin metal after that, but it was a great lesson in letting go. I was reminded of the monks from Tibet who make beautiful mandalas and then blow them to the wind. The idea is that nothing is permanent, my leaf surely was not. Mother Anastasia says there are many divine lessons that we learn through Blacksmithing. That was one.

A few months later. Mother Anastasia invited Nico and I to attend a weekend workshop with Simon, a master Blacksmith from Europe who was a dear friend of the Abbey. He made a sculpture of the Archangel Michael which is on the Abbey property. It is a favorite of mine. I feel so much energy from it. When we got to the workshop, we were told we would make a metal, park style bench. This was big, heavy metal, I had been working with little rods. I picked up a giant sledgehammer and there I was hammering away, pounding out a hot, giant piece of iron. It felt wonderful, powerful, strengthening, healing. When you pump the bellows for the forge, you turn a crank which sends air into the fire to add oxygen which keeps the fire going. As I cranked, I began to get lost in the flames. Fire, as always for me, had a life force, an energy that put my mind at ease. I just stared and stared at the flames as they jumped about, sparking and flickering. Then the color seemed to turn a greenish hue. I had never seen that green in a fire before. It was so beautiful. It made me think of the early study of thermodynamics and light done in 1860 by the physicist, Gustav Robert Kirchoff. Thermodynamics is the study of heat and motion, and the way heat can be generated and how it moves from one object to another. I was seeing this right before my eyes as the metal heated. When metal heats the intensity of the light shifts from a long wave, which is the red part of the spectrum, to shorter wave lengths in the orange then yellow end of the spectrum. It is so beautifully clear with the metal. Now when metal gets too hot it turns white, which is actually in the middle of the spectrum. That is the hottest I have seen metal, but now, in the fire, I was experiencing intensity of heat that was even shorter wavelengths, the green, then the blue which we see in some stars. Really fast and short waves. It was magical. Simon's wife Betsy gave us an exercise to do. What kind of metal would YOU be? I had to think about that one, but Nico knew immediately and said he would be Vibranium, which is a fictional metal from Captain America's shield, who by the way, is the superhero Nico thinks he is most like. Nico stated

"As the alloy I would need a strong hot fire to help me be forged and I would need a well-trained master smith to forge me, and I would be forged into a Shield to help fight alongside justice like Captain America."

Here is what I wrote after many weeks of contemplation.

As a metal I first crashed into, what is now Egypt, long, long ago, as a Fiery meteor. All the metals I was mixed with, tumbled across the desert and vitrified the sand, leaving behind glass formations. As I lay there I felt the earth, the warmth of the sun, the wind, and the powerful energies that were surrounding me. I was later formed into a tool to help build the monuments for the Pharaohs in Ancient Egypt and then was heated with a fiery flame and turned into part of a ship that crossed the seas. I seemed to go from place to place and time to time, observing and feeling the energies of the planet. I wound up in Peru at a sacred site where they were burying an ancient text with insights to help the world. I watched and observed. I was then melted down and traveled many places and united with fire, water, and air over and over. From my early existence I opened to the higher energies to see, to grow, to learn. I have grown stronger with each incarnation and when I reunite with the fire I feel the energy of the early times, of my existence, of the earth, the universe and life itself. When I see the sparks fly around me, I feel a thrill, I feel life and energy vibrating everywhere. I feel we all vibrate as one. I cannot be molded easily; I have to take my time to observe and trust. I, one day, wound up at an abbey where I was part of an ink pen that was writing the gospel of John, the energy of Jesus filled me with fire, love, and light. I believe that with love we can vibrate the fire in our soul and become whatever we want, growing, shaping, transforming, and uniting with the eternal light, the eternal loving energy of THE ONE.

Try this question for yourself. What kind of metal would you be? Explore your mind. Take time to think.

Months later the Blacksmith shop was gifted a metal cutting machine. Mother Anastasia taught me how to use it. At first, we thought I might make jewelry but as we let things flow other designs manifested. It was almost Christmas, and the Abbey has an art shop where they sell things that they make or are made by their apprentices, to the public. It is filled with Mother Praxedes artwork, honey, rose water, and hooks from the blacksmith shop as well as many other wonders. When Salvatore was sick, I wondered how we would make up, financially, for all the lost farmers markets that we attend, selling our socks and my remedies. The nuns came to our rescue and asked to sell our socks, my Dragon Cider, healing salve and some of my other remedies there. I will never forget the morning Nico and I stopped by the shop, before blacksmithing, to bring boxes of Dragon Cider and baskets of socks. Mother Angele and Sister John Mary were thrilled. It was Black Friday and they said they hoped that we would sell most of the goods by Christmas, it was a large order. Nico and I decided to stop back when we finished with Mother Anastasia. When we entered the shop both of the nuns threw up their arms with a smile and said, "It's all gone.' "What's all gone?" I asked. "Everything you brought." was the reply. I could not believe it, they said there had been a long line out the door. They asked if I could bring more next day, which I did. That night I got a call saying they had sold out again. It was a true Christmas blessing for us and for them.

This year I decided to make something for the shop with this new machine and scraps of shining copper that Mother Anastasia gave me. She suggested crosses. I decided to incorporate my love of stones into the mix. It was not easy cutting with this machine but as I practiced, I got better. Mother Anastasia says to become a master at something you must do it 100 times, like the hooks. When I felt ready, I made a cross that flowed from my energy and wrapped a stone in the center. I brought them to the shop and was thrilled when, they too, sold out the first morning.

The Art Shop also sells Mother Dolores' book THE EAR OF THE HEART, as well as, a book written by the founder of the Abbey, Mother Benedict Duss, titled in her name. Her story is a truly amazing journey. She was an American doctor and joined the Abbey of Jouarre in France just before World War II broke out. The Nazi's then invaded France and were taking over. She often had to hide in an isolated place when the soldiers would invade. They were seeking food and respite and they did not like Americans. One day one of the nuns was talking to a young Nazi soldier about his life and trying to get him to see the love in all beings. He told her he had a girlfriend that he loved very much and showed her a picture. The nun told him that she was lovely and felt his love. She then told him that European and American soldiers also had girlfriends they loved and maybe he could remove some of the bad feelings he had for them. He turned hard and cold and told her that if the Fuhrer asked him to kill his girlfriend he would. She felt the horror of the Nazis and Hitler go deeper than she had imagined.

Sister Benedict Duss decided to open an Abbey in America and had to go to Rome to get permission. This was not an easy task; she had to sneak around and hide out at times to remain safe on her journey but being a strong soul she accomplished her task and returned to Jouarre unharmed. Months later she heard a cheering sound and looked out the window to see a big green tank with a white star rolling up. She later found out that it was General George Patton's tank. She said he had saved them. Years later she did indeed open the Abbey of Regina Laudis in Bethlehem, Ct. She did not really have any funding, but gifts presented themselves along the way. She and the few nuns that were at the abbey with her lived off the land, which at that time was primarily nettle from which they made nettle soup. Many years after Mother Abbess came to America, she was introduced to a young woman who wished to become a nun, she was the granddaughter of General Patton himself. She remembered the tank and blessed him. This made me think of Mother Dolores' movie *LISA.* When the war ends Lisa is broken and leaving the camp, she falls and a tank rolls by, it has a white star and is her guiding light though out the film.

At the shop, Nico had started using the power hammer to make knives, he was also working hard at making chain maille, link by link. The power hammer can press hundreds of pounds of metal with ease and made Nico's work easier. For me, I decided to make myself a staff worthy of a witch. I had found some thick bittersweet vine in our woods and Nico brought up a saw and cut it for me. I then cut pieces of the copper into fiery shapes and attached them to the wood with a glass ball in the center. So, yes, the witch began making magical staffs at the Abbey. Mother Anastasia loved it. I wanted to thank her for all she had done for us. We were not using my dad's old car much and her truck broke. I felt the car still held my dad's energy and wanted her to have it. As I was thinking this Salvatore told me he was thinking the same thing.

There is not another person in the world I would have given it too for it still held much of my dad's energy. I had put a bumper sticker on the back that read MY OTHER CAR IS A BROOM. Mother Anastasia would later laugh and tell me that she got many a look when she pulled up somewhere and got out of the car in her habit after someone was staring at the quote. The nuns blessed the car and Mother Anastasia, named it the 7090 (Seven Oh Ninety) after my dad's computer. My journey at the shop is blossoming and I will open my heart to what will follow. I feel very blessed that I can experience Nico's beautiful journey, one that he manifested.

CHAPTER 26

THINK!

My dad had a sign on his desk that read THINK. I took it to heart, as did he and give thinking priority in my life. One time I was watching an episode of THE BIG BANG THEORY and Amy Farrah Fowler was sitting in the living room while Leonard worked, he turned to see her staring into space, and she had a slight smile. He asked if she was alright, she said yes, she had been reading and now she was THINKING about what she read. She smiled again, nodded, and returned to her thoughts. I turned to look at Salvatore and Nico who were staring at me laughing because that is what I do. But how can you read and not stop and think about it? Now stop and think about that.

I think the thinking that people fear the most is that which comes in the middle of the night. They don't want to face what is there in the darkness, but if you do face it and embrace it, it is transforming. When people tell me they are stressed because they can't sleep and that they wake up in the middle of the night I tell them, if they keep thinking, OH NO, I am not sleeping, I am going to be tired tomorrow, I need to get back to sleep, then I doubt they will ever get back to sleep. I have had quote "insomnia" on and off throughout my whole life, although now I think of it differently, as a "time for self-contemplation." One time, when I was much younger, I remember that I had barely slept for over a month, I was not enjoying the time awake, like now. I saw Stephen King's book INSOMNIA in the bookstore and bought it. When I got to the last page, I fell asleep. Insomnia is a novel about seeing other dimensional being's, auras (one's energetic life force that surrounds them like an electromagnetic field). I realize now that my "insomnia" through my life was guiding me to other realms of being and to other places. At times, not good places because I did not know how to open but at times to higher places. Now I feel I am at the point where I only open to the highest and the best, so when I wake at night, I embrace it. I feel that if we take the pressure off of ourselves and change our perspective this can be a very peaceful and meditative time. It is said that 10 minutes of savasana -meditation, after a yoga class, is the equivalent of 3 great hours of sleep for your body. If we can find the meditation in our waking hours, we can get more rest and wake-up refreshed in the morning. Try thinking or get one of those silly headlights and read a good book, something you enjoy. When you are done reading lay back and think about what you have read. This shift in how we view Insomnia or Time for Self can be life changing.

If you cannot sleep, don't work yourself into a state of anxiety. Change your PERCEPTION! Try thinking and say to yourself, WOW, this is so quiet, so peaceful. I do not fear the dark, or the darkness. I do not fear being alone with myself, and I do not fear thinking. Then you might really enjoy this time of solitude and peace and you might even find the light within, which you usually must go through the darkness to get to. There is a beautiful verse by Henry Beston in *Night On The Beach*:

"Our fantastic civilization has fallen out of touch with many aspects of nature, and with none more completely than night. Primitive folk, gathered at a cave mouth round a fire, do not fear night...Yet to live thus, to know only artificial night, is as absurd and evil as to know only artificial day."

This is the spiritual side but there is also the physical side. If you are not sleeping once in a while that is ok but if it is a pattern in your life, it could be a signal that something is wrong. I recommend finding a great nutritionist who knows BIOCHEMISTRY and takes a full Hepatic Blood Panel to tell you what nutrients you may be missing that may be throwing your biochemistry off.

The other thing to THINK about is what people say. Which means you have to really listen. I can't tell you how many times I have been talking to people and they interrupt. Many people do and don't even realize it. The other thing many do is to not listen. You start to say something, and it triggers something about them and off they go, often not letting you finish your thought, which they have now transformed to theirs. I also find many people don't really want to hear what someone else is thinking, they often have their own idea of what the situation is and talk about it but don't ask what the other person thinks. I THINK if we could all be better listeners it would help heal many situations. Ask what others think, then LISTEN, give them time to talk, LISTEN to what they are saying and try to stop your own CHITTA VRITTI (mind chatter) and see where the road leads. THINK and try to do it often, then when it is time to clear the mind and NOT THINK, it will be easier.

CHAPTER 27

SPELLS and WILLOW BARK

Before I rise in the morning I do my protection, prayers, rituals, spells, if you will. I first surround myself with white fire light, this is to cleanse my energies, to purify. Then I fill myself with it. Next, I surround myself in a Violet Flame light that has golden stardust speckles in it. The Violet Light helps to elevate your spiritual awareness and has protective energies. The golden stardust speckles destroy whatever you don't want, zapping them away. Imagine the speckles going through your body, zapping away pain, stress, fear, then moving through your spiritual body removing obstacles. I fill myself with this glorious violet flame light and see the golden stardust speckles move through me. Finally, I surround myself in a silver light, like a shield of protection. This light allows the energies that are good and of the ONE to enter but, as a shield it reflects all negativity away. I say the statements as follows 3 times each.

I Surround Myself in White Fire
I fill myself with White Fire
I Surround Myself in Violet Flame Light with Golden Stardust Speckles
I fill myself with Violet Flame Light with Golden Stardust Speckles
I Surround Myself in a Silver Shield of Protection

Then I do the same for my family, my animals, my farm, as I picture all surrounded in the healing lights. I don't get out of bed without doing so. It is a wonderful way to start the day. Protecting your energies and those who you love. You can also do it with the country, the earth, the universe and so on. After that I can arise and go outside. There is a giant rock outside my bedroom door which I stand on with outstretched arms and I tell the animals of the wild that we live in peace and harmony with each other, I send them blessings and healings and tell them we must live without harming each other. I send them love. It makes me feel strong and happy. I never feel like I want to "get through" my day, I embrace my moments and enjoy them. I take the dogs for a walk and enjoy the trees, the smell of the air, the heat, the snow, the rain, the plants, and the birds. I walk back to the place where the deer gather in the mornings to graze and send them blessings. Then I go to take care of my alpacas. After that we do our homeschooling lessons. Some of the lessons are Nico and I working together and then there is time for him to write his fantasy novel while I plan my homeschool classes or make remedies and potions. He often makes remedies and potions with me.

Homeschooling is something that I chose because I believe that children, and adults have their own way of learning. I don't think everyone learns the same, nor should they. We need to embrace how each individual learns and what they want to learn and work with them. If Nico was not homeschooled, he would not have as much time for blacksmithing, Shakespeare, herbs, and healing. The challenge though can be the regular academic subjects which you don't want them to just "get through." I have been working with Nico on trying to embrace History and not just get through it. This has been a challenge. When we found the mini-series Sons of Liberty, all of a sudden history became more exciting, because now, it was really cool. Hamilton on Broadway is also "really cool" so learning about Hamilton through Hamilton works. We also talk about what he is learning, just talk. At our homeschool co-op group my friend Diane was teaching History, she loves history and her passion passed to the students. She gave them great historical fiction books to read as well as textbooks and they talked about it. I think that kind of caring and teaching makes a difference.

We would incorporate our herbal studies into his history. For instance, did you know that when the early settlers arrived in North America from England, they were quite lost, in many ways. Most of them had lived in the city yet there they were, in a new land with few supplies and no knowledge of how to live with the land. Many got scurvy, a disease that causes gum problems, fatigue and more, due to lack of Vitamin C. Many died. These settlers feared the Indians and felt they were their enemies. Other settlers united with the Native American Indians, whose land they were settling on, (uninvited of course) and learned from them. Those who did so wondered how the Indians looked so healthy throughout the winter when scurvy was overtaking their settlement due to lack of nutrition. The Indians pointed to the Pine Trees and told them to make a tea from the needles. Pine needle tea has as much vitamin C as 4-5 oranges or lemons. It also has a lot of Vitamin A an antioxidant which is great for eyes (vision), skin, hair, and red blood cell regeneration. Pine can also act an anti-bacterial, anti-viral, anti-tumor, anti-inflammatory and has immune system-boosting powers due to the Proanthocyanins, which are polyphenols. It is great for colds, as a decongestant and an expectorant, and is good for cleaning wounds. There are over 100 different varieties of pine, a few are toxic, don't use those, they are the Yew, the Norfolk Island Pine and the Ponderosa Pine (mostly found out west). One of the safest and easiest to identify is the White Pine, Pinus Strobus, which has a clump of 5 long needles. Many people do not like the taste of Pine Needle Tea, but I do. I also like to add Willow Bark to mine.

Willow Bark- Salix Alba is an analgesic (pain killer) which was used in Ancient Egypt and Ancient Greece. In 1829 it was found to have salicin which is like acetylsalicylic acid (aspirin). It is anti-inflammatory and said to work better than aspirin. It lasts longer and does not affect the stomach because the salicin is converted to Salicylic acid, after it is absorbed, which does not irritate the stomach. It also helps to reduce fever. It is great for headaches, toothaches (add some myrrh for that one), and most aches and pains. (Do not use if you are allergic to aspirin). You can also just chew on the young sprouts. You could chew on the bark too if you want but it is pretty hard. (Tea recipe at end of book) Let's talk a little about pain and remedies. If I am in pain from Lyme Disease or inflammation or pain from a flu, I want to take my Lyme Be Gone Remedy, now called Phoenix Rising.

CHAPTER 28

DIANA

Years before I met Salvatore, Lilith held an event with a friend of hers who was also a Psychic. I thought I would attend but not ask any questions, just observe. In the middle of the event, she said she saw someone who was in a car accident that was close to someone in the room. I did not respond even though a friend of mine had been in a car accident earlier in the month. She then went on to describe the red car and details. I had to tell her it was my friend. I decided to talk to her after. She touched my hand and smiled. She said she saw my daughter, age 6, holding my hand and dancing around my foot. She said she looked like me, but her skin was darker, and her hair was very long and black. I told her I did not have a daughter. She said, "not yet."

A few months later a woman named Marli came to apply for a job at The Coffee Pot. She seemed like a nice person, and I hired her. One day, her daughter, Diana, came into the shop after school. Diana was 6 at the time. She had beautiful long black, wavy hair. I fell in love with her from the moment I saw her. She was adorable. She sat at a table and read while Marli worked. I brought her some goodies and juice. After that Diana came in often and got closer and closer to the counter. I finally asked her if she wanted to come behind the counter and help, it was a slow time. She smiled and did so. I showed her how to serve a small cup of coffee. Diana was very smart and observant, and she saw that we would ask customers if they wanted anything else. She asked why. I said this is a business and in business you are trying to make money so if you ask and even suggest some of the goodies, we have it is a good business practice. She said she understood.

When the next customer, a regular, came to the counter, I motioned for Diana to go greet him and ask what he wanted. He told her a small coffee, she went and got it and served it to him. Then I heard her say "would you like anything else with that?" He gave her a big smile and asked what she recommended. I made vegan oat cookies and she told him that is what she recommended. He said, "they look good, how much are they?" Diana paused for a moment then said "$45 dollars." He laughed "$45 dollars?! That's a lot for a cookie." She starred him straight in the face and said, "we're trying to make money here."

One day Diana invited me to her school to hear her read her story about "Baby Ducks." It was wonderful. Diana and I had a bond and I felt very close to her and protective of her. As I said before, prior to 9/11 I was having visions and had the opportunity to sell The Coffee Pot. I still saw Diana and one day she told me that she was starving because she had no money to get her breakfast in the morning before school. I asked her if her mom was making breakfast? Were they struggling? Did they have enough money for food? She said her mom was working nights as a security guard and Diana would sleep by herself and get herself up in the morning and off to school. My heart broke. How could her mother let this wonderful 8-year-old stay overnight by herself and get herself off to school? I contemplated what to do, how to handle this. I did not want to report her because I did not think it would be good for Diana if they took her away from her mother. I spoke to Marli and told her this was not ok. I asked if she could change her shifts to the day and she told me that she would have her sister take care of Diana when she was not home.

The next thing I knew Marli called and said Social Services was coming to her apartment and could I come to help. When I arrived, I told Marli that I was upset, why wasn't her sister caring for Diana or why didn't she call me? She knew how much I loved Diana. Social Services came and explained to Marli that Diana was too young to be home alone and needed to be cared for. They asked why I was there. I said I loved Diana and was trying to help and asked if Diana could live with me when Marli was out and come to Marli the couple of nights she did not work. They said that seemed like a good solution and they, of course, would be back. I then thought about how much I loved Diana and did not take my next statement lightly. "Marli, can I adopt Diana? I will still let you see her. You will still be her mother, but I will give her a great home and care for her." Marli got very upset and said NO. I took Diana home with me and I went in the bathroom and cried.

After that Diana stayed with often. We had a wonderful life and were very happy. I would miss her when she went home to Marli. Diana came with me to my dad's house every time I went, which was often, and he became like her grandfather. We went on vacations together, one of my favorites was a family trip to a beach in Maryland with my dad and stepsister. She attended all of our family outings. Diana a part of our family.

When I made the movie THE DOVE, Diana played my mom, when she was young, a starring role. She was to be my flower girl at our wedding, and I bought her a beautiful purple dress. On the day of our wedding, as I told you earlier, Diana was not there. We waited but finally had to proceed. Marli arrived with Diana, 2 hours late and said she was at the hairdresser getting Diana's hair done. Salvatore and I were very upset with Marli and we knew we could not formally adopt her but wished we could. When Nico was born, Diana had a brother and as Nico grew, he had a sister. All was well until one day we decided to move to Connecticut. I went to talk to Marli about Diana staying with us and she told me that she had not paid the rent in her apartment and had to move out and was moving to Long Island, near her sister. This was too far, I thought. Marli also started to get jealous of my relationship with Diana and did not let her see me as much. I was devastated. Diana finally had to move in with her aunt in Long Island because Marli, again, was not taking care of her. At that point Diana wanted to stay with her aunt because she had friends and wanted to go to the high school her friends were attending. This was all hard for me, but I stayed strong. Her High School Graduation was strange because her aunt and her mom were talking to me like I was a family friend but finally her aunt Luiza thanked me for helping to raise Diana and said we were both her mom. I agreed.

Diana worked hard and got herself an, almost, full scholarship to Pace University. I was so proud of her. She told me that she only needed $600 for her first year. That was amazing. I had planned to pay it, but she told me that Luiza and her mom had said they would, so I waited. Marli decided to take Diana to Disney world, which was very nice, except she spent the money that was to go for Diana's tuition, so she did not have it. Then Luiza said she could not chip in either so Salvatore and I gave Diana the money she needed. I felt her other family, once again, backing off. Diana also wanted to take a trip to India that was with a school program. No one would chip in from her family so Salvatore and I paid for that too. We were happy to do so for our beautiful daughter.

Diana worked as a Resident Assistant while she was going to Pace, for which she received free housing. I learned how difficult this job was in this day and age. Diana was dealing with kids who were drinking, doing drugs, and threatening suicide. I don't know how she did it. She was with her peers but had to act above them. She grew a lot and learned a lot. She ceased to amaze me. She got her masters as is teaching special education in high school, she is an AMAZING teacher and gives her students her all. She bought herself her own apartment. That is my strong, smart girl. When she visits now, we talk a lot and she now has great advice for me, when I need it. Nico loves it when "his sister" comes as do Salvatore and I. I have been blessed to have Diana, my daughter, in my life. I often think of the Psychic and that image of the little girl dancing at my feet.

CHAPTER 29

FOOD GLORIOUS FOOD

What we put into our bodies is so very important and the spoken word comes into play here also. Bless your food! Bless it when you harvest it, when you buy it, when you prepare it, and surely bless it before you eat it, for that energy will be part of what feeds your body. Many have lost this tradition, many don't even sit at a family table in peace, without cell phones. Put the cell phones away, light a candle, talk about happy and interesting things, and give thanks for your food. Whatever faith you are, you can thank, some energy, the Divine, the earth, the water, the land. When you begin to do this, you begin to see food for what it is or what it should be, nourishment. If it is not nourishing your body, then why are you putting it in there? I know - it tastes good. Well, once in a while that is ok but as a practice - no.

For much of my life I was vegetarian and even vegan. Salvatore grew up in Italy and for a long time he was not onboard with being a vegetarian, let alone vegan. How could I give up meatballs and pancetta? he asked. When I first met his family in Italy, I felt like I was in *My Big Fat Greek Wedding.* He told his 89-year-old grandmother that I was a vegetarian (in Italian of course), she wrinkled her face like she did not understand, he then told her I did not eat meat. Her eyes widened like "WHAT!?" then she looked at me and smiled and moved the Pancetta (an Italian type of bacon) towards me and said, "that's ok, she can have some pancetta." I smiled and thanked her and instead, partook of the wonderful roasted potatoes with olive oil and rosemary which were baked to perfection, homemade bread, a freshly picked salad and broccoli rabe with oil and garlic. At the end of the meal, I was full and happy. I think the best Vegan Cookbook I know is written by my yoga teacher and dear friend Sharon Gannon called *Simple Recipes for Joy.* Sharon's recipe for vegan meatballs is one of the best ever. (I did add a little ketchup to the ingredients she has listed). One day Salvatore's dad came over for dinner. He owned restaurants in Italy for many years and now owns them in NYC. He was a chef and is picky about his food. I placed spaghetti and vegan balls on the table and did not say a word. He began to eat and turned to me and said that, for a vegan I actually made very good meatballs. Then he realized I was eating them and knew they were not meat. He said I really fooled him, which was hard to do.

Einstein said the following:

A human being is a part of the whole, called by us the 'Universe', a part limited in time and space. He experiences himself, his thoughts, and feelings, as something separate from the rest - a kind of optical delusion of his consciousness. This delusion is a kind of prison for us, restricting us to our personal desires and to affection for a few persons nearest to us. Our task must be to free ourselves from this prison by widening our circle of compassion to embrace all living creatures and the whole of nature in its beauty. Nobody is able to achieve this completely, but the striving for such achievement is in itself a part of the liberation and a foundation for inner security. -

I recommend that you get Sharon's cookbook, make some healthy meals, even if it is only two times/week. The more we can strengthen our physical body and purify it the easier it is to open spiritually, so let's go a lot deeper here. In this country, many people drink way too much alcohol and coffee. Why? What are they running from or to? Alcohol removes you from seeing yourself through yourself and coffee gives you a false energy so you cannot find your own. In a wonderful book called QUICK REFERENCE QUIDE FOR USING ESSENTIAL OILS there is an amazing bit of information about how coffee affects your body. First let's get to simple science that everything has a vibration, everything has a frequency. Around 1811, James Clerk Maxwell and Hermann von Helmholtz believed that atoms and molecules where bouncing all around even though we could not see this movement. All things were moving and vibrating. Maxwell later stated that there must be some other form of electromagnetic waves or radio waves. In 1888 Heinrich Hertz expanded on Maxwell's work and proved the existence of electromagnetic waves based on light acting as a wave, which we now know can act as both a wave and a particle, but they did not know this at the time. Hertz built machines to measure the electromagnetic wave and the measurement was later named Hertz. Megahertz (MHz) is a million cycles of electromagnetic currency alternation per second. Frequency is an electrical energy that you can measure by counting how many waves there are between two points. In your body higher frequency is good, lower frequency is illness and finally death. The book states that Bruce Tainio of Tainio Technology made a piece of equipment that could measure this frequency. He then got together with Dr. D. Gary Young, an essential oil expert and the studies were amazing. Basically, they found that the human body's average frequency in megahertz is between 62-68, during the flu it dropped to 57, cancer 42 and death begins at 25. They then added various foods to the mix and found that processed/canned food did not increase the MHz, while fresh produce did raise it by about 15 MHz, Dry Herbs 12-22 MHz, Fresh Herbs 20-27 MHz and Essential Oils 52-320 MHz (Frankincense and Myrrh being on the higher end of the spectrum). Energy healing raised it 30. They then added coffee, just one sip and the frequency dropped about 16 Megahertz, it then took 3 days to recover. That's a lot of megahertz to drop. Coffee has other affects also. Too much caffeine inhibits collagen production, collagen is a protein in the body that gives skin it's structure and its strength. It is also in your muscles and bones, giving them structure. A Mayo Clinic study found that drinking more than 4 cups a day caused a 21% increase in a variety of causes of death. Caffeine raises your blood pressure, can cause gout, cystic breast tissue in women, infertility, headaches, hormonal imbalance and more. It is a fake start for your body. When and if you can cut out coffee and caffeine your body will eventually (give it a little time) adjust and instead of waking up cranky and "out of it", thinking COFFFFFEEEEEE, your body will wake with joy so you can clearly do your protections and start your day off right.

When Salvatore finally stopped drinking coffee, he got so much healthier. Prior to that he was always getting sick and had a tough time healing. I used to drink a lot of coffee too, when I got out of college and was working for American Ballet Theatre. As I said, it was a rigorous tour, and I was tired an decided lots of coffee was what would get me through. Well, it got me very sick and very run down. When I took one of the first big steps toward health after I left ABT, I stopped drinking coffee, I went cold turkey. I just stopped. I went from about 6 or more cups a day to nothing. I would literally walk into walls. I just didn't see them. My head pounded like crazy for 2 days straight. Now, I know, this is not the way to convince you to stop drinking coffee, so I would recommend doing it little by little instead of full swing like that, but when I finally detoxed my body, I realized the damage I had done. I was a mess. I could not fall asleep, (now when I talked about Insomnia before I could usually fall asleep, I would just wake up in the middle of the night). I realized that coffee was a drug and the drug had run my life. I began to eat healthier and drink lots of water and within a couple of months my life started to change. I started feeling better and better, happier and happier and healthier and healthier.

Alcohol is also abused in this country. In my opinion, it is not okay to drink every night and not okay to have 2 or more glasses of wine, beer, or alcohol. Although I must add that in Italy it is different, many do drink wine daily, but they have a half glass or a small glass and that is it. Just look at yourself and see if you are doing it because there is something deeper that you don't want to face or an underlying medical issue like your adrenals. Think about trying to skip the alcohol and coffee and see how you feel.

CHAPTER 30

HORMONES

As healthy as I thought I had been in my younger years, I realized that we can have a false sense of health. If all we know is imbalance, we cannot even image life without it. I thought I was a healthy kid, and I was, compared with many, but not compared to what I could have been. For one, my hormones were a mess. In high school, I had terrible PMS and cramps. When I got my period, it was so heavy that I would often get a cold clammy feeling and pass out for a moment or two. I thought it was normal and never even told my mom. It took me most of my life to figure out how to get my hormones into balance. Signs of hormonal imbalance are sleep problems, acne, before or during your period or acne that won't go away, memory fog, mood swings, depression, adrenal fatigue, headaches, and hot flashes. A hormone is a chemical made by your body that passes into your bloodstream and has many effects on the rest of your body. Cortisol is a hormone secreted by your Adrenal Glands, which are above your kidneys. Cortisol helps control stress, regulate blood pressure, your immune system, and your insulin levels. Too much cortisol can create depression, skin problems and general imbalance. Helpful things for Cortisol are reducing stress in your life, yoga, meditation, cutting out coffee and caffeine, drinking lots of water and avoiding sugar.

Estrogen is the hormone that helps transforms a girl's body into a woman's, it helps with bone formation, and menstrual cycles. It aids in keeping cholesterol levels in check, protects bone health in men and women, affects your mood, your brain, your skin, and your heart. Estrogen is produced in the ovaries, but a small amount is produced in your adrenal glands, adipose tissue and in the testes in men, so men have some estrogen too, although not as much. Your estrogen levels can be out of balance, and this will definitely change at times of menstruation, pregnancy and menopause. Testosterone is higher in men than in women and affects bone and muscle mass. Symptoms of low estrogen are infrequent periods, hot flashes, night sweats, dry skin, and mood swings. Symptoms of high estrogen are heavy periods, fibrocystic breasts, fatigue, depression, anxiety, weight gain from the waist down and in men increase in breast size and body fat. When I teach herbal classes to young women, I find that many of them have hormonal imbalances and they don't even know it, they just think they are depressed, or anxiety ridden or have bad skin. We need more health education in this country. Why are we living with things that we don't need to and don't need medication for, that healthy food and herbs would heal. (A note prior to publishing - I myself realized after completion of this book and a long illness that I too needed more education about Adrenal Glands and nutrition.

My hormones got better through time, but I found it to be a long road. First came the diet which, as I told you earlier, was vegetarian and later vegan, and only ate organic food, no processed foods, lots of veggies. Then I found out about goji berries, and they helped a great deal. Goji berries (organic only or they are sprayed) are great antioxidants, but the real story here is that they build your blood chi. Chi, according to Traditional Chinese Medicine (TCM) is the life force that flows through everything. This life force moves through channels in your body called Meridians which connect to your organs. It is not really about the organs and anatomy but rather the functions of your body, like digestion, breathing etc. Your blood energy is really important because blood flows through your whole body, if it is weak so are your organs, affecting everything from digestion to your heart. lungs and more. If it is strong many things come into balance including your hormones. In my opinion, without a strong blood chi you cannot be healthy. As I was saying earlier, my hormones got a little better after the goji berries, but I definitely needed more help. I tried the traditional herbs like American Ginseng and Black Cohosh, and they helped a little but not enough. I then formulated my own remedy. Once I began taking that I felt all came into balance and I was feeling great. I gave it to some friends who were experiencing hot flashes and other symptoms and about a month on my remedy they all felt much better.

Anemia is also important to be on the watch for. Here is how to check for anemia besides getting a blood test. I do this monthly with my alpacas and myself. First pull down the bottom of your eye so you can see the inside. Look at the color of the fleshy part of the inner eye, is it whitish, pink-white, pink or red pink? It should be pink or red pink. Then pull down your bottom lip and look at the color there. Again, you want pink, really pink or red pink. Press your finger on the skin and it will turn white, wait to see how long it takes for the color to come back. It should be about one second, longer means you are probably anemic and a light color that is whitish definitely means anemia. If you are anemic you need to balance your hormones first. Anemia is dangerous so don't let it slide. Eat a large handful of organic goji berries every day. I put them in a shake in the morning with a tsp of flax seeds (use only 1 tsp of flax, too much can be TOXIC). Make sure you are eating great sources of iron, besides the goji berries, like spinach, kale, swiss chard and adzuki beans. Drink Nettle Infusions which are FILLED with iron and cook in an iron pan. Try not to eat sugar and try to cut out or at least cut down on alcohol, a glass of wine a week is plenty but even that will screw you up when you are trying to balance your hormones. Drink dandelion root tea, not coffee. This is a great first step. (Post writing this I note that in my second book I talk extensively about anemia, macrocytic and microcytic).

I think everything has a place and time; I will not tell you that western doctors have no value for they surely do. I have a doctor named Mullein who is an orthopedic surgeon. Not only do I love his name, for obvious reasons, but when I go to him, he respects my way of life and originally called me "Nuts and Berries." When I tell him my symptoms, he asks if I want an x-ray, I tell him I do not because of the harmful radiation but mostly because I know he knows what is wrong, which he always does, the x-ray will just confirm it. I have a naturopathic nurse practitioner who I love and a naturopathic doctor. That said, I trust them, and they trust me. I don't go to them often but when I do, I know I am in good hands. I state this because I will now tell you another side of this coin. I often talk to people who tell me there is something wrong with them from Lyme Disease to Eczema to whatever. They say that they have been going to their allopathic or naturopathic doctor for years and feel a little better or not any better at all. They then tell me the list of either medicines or remedies that they are on. I ask them if this cost them a lot of money and the answer is often yes. I then ask them why they are continuing with this process if they only feel a little better or not better at all after much time. Some people say because they have tried everything, and this is the only thing that helped at all. Some people say they do the remedies because they don't want to do allopathic medicine. Some say they just do as they are told. I ask you to open your mind and heart here. If something is not working WELL and it has been six months or more, consider finding another avenue. I make a remedy for Lyme Disease. I cured myself, Salvatore, many friends and animals including my pug Sofia when she was paralyzed. Many people heard about my remedy and asked for it and they were cured too. Find what and who works for you and make sure it is working.

CHAPTER 31

PRACTICE and ESSENTIAL OILS

I was interviewed for a blog by my friend Mira at Terra Love. She asked me if I found it difficult to find a community that I felt was loving, giving, helpful and yogic. I think this depends on where you are. When I was in NYC my community was large and it is easier to find like-minded people when there are so many people in one place, but when I moved to Connecticut my community was very small, especially at first when I only knew my friend Beth and her daughter Sydney. As I found people who entered my life, I began to realize many things. One, it does not matter how large your community is, what matters is the quality of those who are in it. My community grew with quality people of like mind. I wanted to teach yoga, but I was taking care of Nico and he was very young, I was trying to figure out what would fit in. One day I thought of the prep school down the road and how I would love to bring yoga to those students. I thought it would be a steady job and a good income. I approached Kent School to ask if I could teach yoga there. I was answered by Todd Marble, the head of the Athletics Department. He was very open to the idea and grew to love yoga and do it himself. I wanted to give tools to my students to help them through life. I also thought about my ever-present desire to bring as much healing to those around me as I could. We all want to change the world, but we forget that each little step will do so. Changing the world does not have to be a grand matter. I thought about Gandhi and Martin Luther King Jr., I always wanted to be like them but then I thought, wait Gandhi had teachers, and someone who guided and inspired him. Martin Luther King Jr. had people who opened his mind. As I contemplated this, I thought, I need to change the world in small way, it does not have to be grand and maybe one of my students will do that. I realized my path was to gather the best information I possibly could and share it with my yoga students and whomever would listen. Maybe one of my students will be the next Gandhi or King or maybe they will teach love and light to just a few who will pass it on. As Gandhi said, we must be "the change we wish to see in the world". We must start this through our daily practice, be it yoga, meditation, chant, herbalism, or all of them but PRACTICE, and I do mean practice. Practice is something we do over and over and over and in so doing, we remove the layers. We strip down, bit by bit so we can find what is at our core. The more we do this, the more of those cut outs we are making in our candle holder so we can shine, be positive, and share that energy with others.

Little things we do and say can create positive energy around us and change the vibration in a room. The more supportive we are of ourselves and others, the more supportive they will be. The more loving we are, the more we get love back. This helps make it possible to leave behind negative emotions. If we put others down, we are putting the energy down and hurting all because we are all connected. Think happy thoughts. I saw this amazing young boy on a video. He said "if you practice fear, YOU WILL BECOME VERY GOOD AT IT. If you practice stress, YOU WILL BECOME VERY GOOD AT IT. If you practice anger, YOU WILL BE VERY GOOD AT IT. He continued on with is wisdom which we should all heed.

Our brain is hard wired to remember the negative things. Our amygdala governs fight or flight, our emotions - sad, happy, our memory and decision making. The amygdala uses about 2/3s of its neurons for negative emotions and once they are found they are stored in long-term memory. Positive emotions need to be held for over 10 seconds before they are moved to long term memory. So, we hold the bad much better than the good. We can overcome this with practice. The practice of yoga, meditation, mantra and simply changing our perspective can bring us past the negativity of the brain. A great daily practice to start with, is to stop complaining about the weather. It seems to be a great conversation starter, but a bad one. "Oh, it is so hot today", "It gets dark so early now!" It is so cold today; it is going to snow tomorrow and on and on. These are things that we definitely cannot change so why whine? We need to connect to Mother Earth, find the positive and change our perspective. What is really funny, is that we have removed ourselves so much from nature that nature is difficult for us. In the winter we like our house to be a nice toasty 72 degrees even 74 would be good. Don't get me wrong, I do like a warm house too, but then we go outside, and our bodies have been at 72 and if we don't dress warm enough and embrace Mother Nature, we will be freezing. Now, in the summer, when it is 80 degrees out, which, in reality, is only 6-8 degrees more than our toasty winter house, many complain, "oh it is too hot," and put an air conditioner on in their house. They set the temperature to around 67-68 degrees. Now if we step outside where it is 80 degrees we shift our body temperatures a good 12 degrees, which is much harder to adjust to.

Balance! We need balance and time with nature and time to step away from the material world for a bit and embrace the elements. The next time it rains, instead of thinking, oh no rain, try saying, I love the rain. I love the sound of rain. Take a walk in the rain and feel it on your body. We need rain for our plants to grow. Water, especially in Native American culture, is sacred. Feel blessed by this sacred liquid that is nourishing the earth because if there is not enough of it, which there is not, by the way, we won't be around for long. Maybe even do a Gene Kelly, Singing in the Rain dance and feel it on your face, enjoy it. Believe me it feels wonderful. When it snows, dress warm and walk in the snow, make a snow angel, enjoy its beauty and how it makes you pause. You will reap what you sow. Sow good and happy thoughts. Then incorporate some nice warming herbs into your diet in the winter and cooling in the summer. Fire Cider, of course and maybe some nice warming brews (Recipe at end)

Cinnamon (Cinnamomum cassia) which is great for your circulation and helps to dry dampness in your body. It also aids in digestion.

Cayenne (Capsicum Futescens), also great for circulation, helps to warm the body and is good for your respiratory system.

Ginger (Zingiberaceae), garlic (Allium sativum), horseradish (Rmoracia Lapathifolia), cardamom, and black pepper (Piper Nigrum) will help you feel warm and cozy inside. In the summer try a cooling Iced Tea.

We can overcome the negative thoughts in the brain through yoga, meditation, flower essences and love. When we do deep breathing in yoga we actually calm down the nervous system. Yoga also helps to reduce cortisol levels and therefore stress. Yoga, meditation and chanting all help us to rewire our brain so we do not fall into the pit of negativity. We learn how to overcome and be happy. I think that many women and some men too, do, do, do and go, go, go but we also have to do for ourselves and love ourselves, we need to stop for a while and let the world go as it will. It is okay to stop at the end of the day, especially if you are overloaded, even if it is dinner time and say, "I need to stop and go in the other room for 10 minutes, ALONE," and then GO! Go sit with self, peel off some layers of your being, try not to think at all, just rejuvenate and be. Chant, breath, light a candle, then the night will go differently. Try to stop running from project to project, thing to do, to thing to do. Then figure out your priorities and warp time, create magic. Believe you can accomplish it in half the time you thought and see what happens.

When Nico was born my priority was obviously him, all else

that was so important before did not seem to matter as much. Things that used to take me hours were either not important enough to do or took 1/2 hour because it had to be that way. We often forget, as Einstein said, that time is relative. Now this may sound contradictory to what I said about taking longer than others to care for my animals and enjoying it, but it is not. If you are doing something and have the time to do it and are happy about it and loving it, by all means, take all the time in the world and you will warp time and find all the time in the world to do it. But if it is something you truly cannot wrap yourself around loving and finding a way to love it, then warp time. I think a good example of this is a student doing homework on a subject they don't like. They often spend a lot of time complaining and just opening the book, then their mind is stuck on the fact that they really don't want to do this, and it is hard to grasp things, their minds are blocked in places. Now think about if they just let go and opened their mind and heart fully and only had a small amount of time to accomplish this task, all the extra stuff and mental blocks melt away.

A good aid to this is essential oils. There have been studies that prove certain essential oils help with focus and attention. One I found fascinating, showed that if you use a certain essential oil during study then the same one during a test it will help you remember what you studied. In other words, if you study History with the scent of vanilla, then use vanilla prior to your history test, it will actually help you to remember what you studied. The same if you studied Science with Myrrh Oil, then used the myrrh before the test and so on. You can do it at night before bed and then in the morning to remember your dreams.

Our sense of smell is connected with our memory. I remember my great Aunt Palma's Garden, as if I were there, every time I smell fresh basil. I remember picking it and just taking a deep inhale. This all relates to the limbic system in the brain, which is the name for a bunch of different parts of your brain on either side of the Thalamus (which processes sensory information and relays it) and includes the Hippocampus (short- and long-term memory) and the Hypothalamus, (metabolic processes, sleep and circadian rhythms). The limbic system helps with memory, motivation, behavior, long term memory and olfaction which is responsible for categorizing smells.

Some properties of Essential Oils are listed below:

Basil Essential Oil helps aid with memory, focus and helps you to not get distracted if you are tired (do not use if you have Epilepsy)

Bergamot - depression, stimulates dopamine and serotonin production, keeps skin young and heals scars and skin,

Clary Sage - is good for your hormones, helps balance moods and helps you dream.

Cypress- helps with your circulation.

Eucalyptus- is good for colds and congestion but never use it around animals, tea tree oil either. JUST THE SMELL CAN KILL A CAT.

Jasmine - gives you positive energy and a great outlook on life.

Lavender - Helps to calm you down and is great for helping you sleep.

Melissa (Lemon Balm) - makes you happy and balances your emotions.

Oregano - Great for killing germs, put it on your feet if you are sick but make sure to dilute it in a light carrier oil. (Test first for it can burn your skin. Then make sure to wash your hands really well before touching ANYTHING, especially your eyes)

Peppermint - Digestion - smell it, put it on your feet and your belly (again you may want to dilute this for it can also burn)

Rose - Helps to take away all of those emotional blocks.

Spikenard - Is the oil Mary used for Jesus. It elevates our spiritual energy.

Vanilla is an antidepressant, helps you relax, lowers blood pressure, makes you feel better and is an anti-inflammatory.

Vetiver - good for your nerves and is very calming and grounding, it helps you focus and recover from shock.

Wintergreen - good for sore muscles and injuries.

There are some companies that push people to sell essential oils and in one way this can be nice, spreading healing, but it can also have a downside. I see many people "experimenting" with oils. Using a lot of them in large quantities and not knowing what they are doing. Many did not even know that Eucalyptus can kill cats and they used it like crazy and had a cat. Thank goodness the cat knew better and hid. Herbs, oils, and flower essences are MEDICINE you should use them with caution and with the advice of someone who knows. I can't stress this enough; they are only safe when used properly and in proper amounts.

Essential oils and herbs are great in your bath, which should be another ritual. If it is spring gather some violets and lilacs, summer, some yarrow flowers, and calendula, fall artemisia and winter some pine needles and throw them in your bath. You can also make some fizzy bath bombs with essential oils. (Recipe at end) The bath bombs contain Epsom Salt, which is great for sore and inflamed muscles and nerves. Epsom salt is not table salt but rather a combination of magnesium and sulphate both of which are soothing and help you to relax and expel toxins. Run your bath and throw your flowers in with a little prayer or chant. "I open to your aiding me in healing, relaxation and peace." Then throw in your bath bomb and essential oils and relax.

CHAPTER 32

LIVER DETOX and LYME

I often hear the word detox. People love to detox but many do it in strange ways. Often, they take a new-fangled product for a week and think they have detoxified their entire body, but what actually is a detox and will it work. You cannot even begin to detoxify your body unless your liver is functioning properly, so it is important to cleanse it in the spring and fall. Your liver gets rid of toxins. It produces bile to break down food so you can digest it. It stores glucose for energy in the form of glycogen and it metabolizes fats and proteins and filters the blood in your body coming from your heart and from your intestines. The liver gets blood from our major organs, our spleen, pancreas, stomach, and small intestines, which it filters and processes, detoxifies it and sends it back to the heart. It metabolizes carbohydrates and converts them to sugar to use as energy. If there is some leftover, it is stored in the liver, but there are some toxins (ammonia) left and by-products that the body can't use. It then converts it to something that can't hurt the body (urea), which goes into the blood, then to the kidneys and out through our urine. All this must run smoothly, or our body will be overwhelmed with toxins and will not work efficiently. There are some great herbs for the liver. My favorites are yellow dock root, dandelion root, burdock root and milk thistle, which all present themselves in abundance at our sanctuary. I make a tincture out of these for a wonderful liver cleanse. (Recipe at end) The herbs are listed below.

Yellow Dock Root (Rumex Crispus)-
Docks come from the Lapathum Family, the Greek word lapazein means to cleanse. Yellow Dock is a great cleanse indeed. It is astringent, a mild laxative and helps with jaundice. It contains Anthraquinones which stimulate bile flow and triggers the excretion of toxins, therefore, cleansing the liver. Do not eat the raw leaves of the Yellow Dock, they contain oxalic acid, which Native Americans used as a poultice for cuts and skin eruptions.

Dandelion Root- Taraxacum Officinale (explained earlier) is great for your liver, helps build your blood chi, and is great for arthritis and skin problems.

Burdock Root - Arctium -supports liver and gall bladder function and cleanses the blood.

Milk Thistle (Silybum Marianum) - Blessed Thistle or Holy Thistle of Saint Benedict. It was said to be a cure that was a gift from God. It helps to increase circulation, balance hormones, aids in bringing oxygen to the brain and is good for painful menstruation. Blessed Thistle contains silymarin, a chemical compound which helps to protect the liver. It actually aids in altering the membranes of the liver too, so toxins cannot get inside. It is being studied for anti-cancer properties. The Milk Thistle plant is somewhat invasive, and its leaves are very sharp and hurt if you touch them. As it grows it gets taller and a flower forms, which is beautiful. It is a purple/pink color with a giant tear drop shaped base of green. I love these flowers but after their time they turn into those fun looking puffs of white that are each attached to a seed and they fly all over, spreading their seeds to spread the milk thistle. You don't want Milk Thistle everywhere, so after the flowers bloom, I harvest the seeds and leaves and cut the rest down. I crush the seeds and leaves and add it to my tincture. I also dry some of the leaves (This I do in August).

Celendine Root - Cheliodonium Majus - Is good for your liver and your blood. Celendine Root (externally) is also great for warts, skin viruses, fungi and hemorrhoids. Warts are a viral infection as is HPV- human papilloma virus. White spots that appear on the skin are often due to a virus, Celendine heals the virus and removes the spots. It dries up plantar warts because of the biological compounds and enzymes in the plant and the enzymes stop the cellular development. I make a Fungal Healing Salve from Celendine.

Lyme Disease is a very interesting disease, to say the least. I think there is so much more to this than we know. First let's talk about the journey of the tick. The tick adheres itself to many animals before it reaches a human. If you think about the various animals and the blood, they share with the tick it could contribute to the disease itself. For instance, a deer can live with something called the meningeal worm, whereas if an alpaca gets meningeal worm, it hits their nervous system, and they can die in a week. If some of the blood from the deer is shared with the tick isn't any bacteria or virus they have also shared? The tick could then attach to a rat and maybe that rat's blood can handle things that humans can't and so on. This needs to be studied and be a part of the treatment. I also find, in myself, in Sofia, and many others who have had Lyme Disease and have been well for a long time, that symptoms crop up in the spring when the ticks are awakening from their hibernation. At first, I thought it was just me and maybe I had gotten bit by a tick and did not know it, then I saw Sofia's symptoms occur around the same time. I began to ask others and it was affirmed to me that many experience this. Again, I ask, is there something dormant in the tick and the virus that awakens after winter. If so, another thing to study. It also makes it all the more important to do your spring and fall herbal cleaning and strengthening.

One day I pulled a tick out of my pig Ciccio, a long, clear string like a fishing line came out with it. I looked it up online to see what it was but found nothing. We are working with only partial information here and have a long way to go. The Lyme remedy I made has healed my family and our animals and many people I know. Healings have also helped. (Post writing this book I did a study on Lyme Disease and my herbal remedy, more in the next book on that.)

CHAPTER 33

HOBBITS, DOGON AND SAINTS

Darwin told us of the evolution of man, originating from the Ape, natural selection, but if you look at the evolution of a fish, cow, cat, or other beings, there is a steady and very slow progression but no extreme jump but when we look at man, there was a huge leap about 50,000 years ago, not the normal slow and steady progression and since then mankind is evolving at a rate of 7%, which is not slow and steady at all. If you consider Darwin to be correct, then all animals would have taken a large leap, due to the modification of species, but they did not, so what happened? I refer back to Ancient Aliens. In one episode entitled THE PROTOTYPE, they compare the origins of mankind to more of a LORD OF THE RINGS type world then the linear progression of ancient man. Scientists and archeologist have discovered very distinct beings in isolated parts of the world and are now trying to fit the puzzle pieces together. Two million years ago there was Homo Habilis, one million years ago branches on the tree of man sprouted off to Homo Erectus and Homo Rudofersis and then some interesting ones. About 60,000 to 100,000 years ago, in a hole in the ground, there lived the "Hobbits." That's right, I said the Hobbits. They were 3 and a half feet tall and lived on Flores Island, near Indonesia. Specimens of a skull were discovered which had a particularly small brain the size of a chimpanzee. They found tools there that would not coincide with this type of being. How did they get to the island? They found a Neanderthal grave that had bodies buried with their arms crossed in a ceremonial style, suggesting a belief in the afterlife, which we did not think the Neanderthal had. In addition to Hobbits, there were giants. The Smithsonian Museum led an excavation of a burial mound. Inside, one body was surround by eleven others, circling the central figure. These beings were over 7 feet tall, one about 7 feet 6 inches, one over 8 feet. A skeleton was discovered by Spanish Jesuits in 1765 that was 11 feet. In the religious texts it tells that some men were 11 cubits (1 cubit =18 inches) tall, that is about 16.5 feet, definitely a giant.

In the Pyrenees Mountains a large percentage of the population is blood type RH negative. This blood type does not mix with all the others, that is why a blood test was required before getting a marriage license because if the mother was RH negative and the father a different blood type the mother could reject the fetus. So, our Lord of the Rings world consisted of Hobbits, giants and other species that lived separately but at the same time. How did this happen? This does not seem like a slow adaptation of the species to me, especially since they lived in separate areas. We must go beyond what we are told over and over and explore. We must open our minds and see.

Gunung Padang has also blown the whole timeline. Although they are still working at the sight, so far, they have dated parts of the site back 26,000 years. It is an engineered site, there is a pyramid, large andesite stones and a well that is called *The Water of Life.* Many archeologists are fighting this find because they cannot disprove the dates and they are afraid that this blows their theories but those that are investigating like Graham Hancock and Dr Danny Hillman are changing our thoughts of our past.

Explore deeper and you will find the Dogon. A tribe whose abode is in Mali, Africa. They have a mysterious culture that has many similarities to that of Ancient Egypt. The Dogon do not allow many people inside of their circle and do not often share their history. They did with French anthropologists Marcel Griaule and Germaine Dieterlen, whose research began in the 1930's and continued until Griaule's death in 1956. Germaine was shown a 400-year-old document of the Dogon that depicted the star system of Sirius. They knew of Sirius A and B. Sirius A is massive, about 2 times the size of our sun and is the brightest star in the night sky. You can find it if you look down from where Orion's belt points. Sirius B is a white dwarf star, that collapsed in on itself, so it is extremely dense. It is very faint, and you need a very powerful telescope to view it. It was not photographed until 1970 by a large telescope and is moving closer to the Earth. Sirius is linked with the Egyptian goddess, Isis. The Dogon performed ceremonies celebrating the cycle of these stars and knew the density of Sirius B. So how did they know all this in the 30's when it was not seen until the 70's? The Dogon say that their knowledge came from "the star people" whose home was a planet that circles Sirius C. Evidence of this planet has not yet been proven. The Dogon Myths and symbols describe the correct cosmology of the universe. They showed Marcel and Germaine their hieroglyphics and told them that they had the meanings correct but the symbol for water also meant energy. They described atoms, spiral galaxies, sound traveling as waves, the correct configuration of DNA and much, much more. They said that matter behaved both as a particle and a wave. How could they have known these things, if not from "the star people." Check out Ancient Aliens and you will find an abundance of great facts and discoveries around the world.

Now, of course, our Lord of the Rings world needs seers, those who have visions. One day while at the abbey listening to Mother Dolores do a reading from her book Ear of the Heart, I was struck by one particular sentence. She was saying something about the monastic women mystics. My mind stopped right there…. monastic women mystics, I thought, who were they? I asked Mother Anastasia who said I should look up Saint Hildegard von Bingen, so I did. When Hildegard was young, she had visions. She would see things that others did not, including a light that surrounded her entire visual field with a luminosity that she called "the reflection of the living light." In this light she heard a voice which others did not. She was sent to an abbey as a young girl. I often wonder if she was in a different place and time if she would have been burned at the stake (she was born in 1098). She was eventually guided to start her own abbey in Bingen where she heard music, beautiful, heavenly, peaceful music. She created a secret language to form a community of solidarity with her fellow nuns. This reminded me of the VOYNICH MANUSCRIPT. She wrote books about stones, herbs and magical charms used for healing. She believed that her magical charms, or incantations, came from God.

When using mandrake root, the screaming root from Harry Potter she incanted - "God, who madest man from the dust of the earth without grief, I now place next me that earth which has never transgressed in order that my clay may feel that peace just as Thou didst create it." This, to me, is very similar to a transmutation. She also spoke of the Basilisk and the Dragon with no doubt that they existed. She herself, performed miraculous healings. She wrote against the Cathars, one place my thoughts differ from hers, I think the Cathars were great, they believed there was the one they called "HIGHEST BEING" who was spirit and created all that was of the spirit, the soul and all that was good. Then there was evil which created the material world. They believed that their soul was of the Divine and they had direct contact with the spirit of good. They came from Languedoc, near the Pyrenees.

Hildegard, as many medieval herbalists, believed the earth was made of the elements, fire, water, earth and air which presented themselves in the human body as hot, cold, moist or dry. This is the idea behind Chinese Medicine. Harmony of the elements was a healthy body, imbalance was illness. Hildegard recommended herbs, stones, and metals to help with this balancing process, to create a healthy body. She was credited with being the first to use Euphrasia, or Eyebright for eye problems. Hildegard spoke of cosmology from microcosm (the human body, the atom) to macrocosm (the universe, the human body).

She saw visions of light and was guided by the light. When I do healings, I feel a light and am guided by a higher force. I relate to Hildegard in many ways. I too, often have visions. When I was little, I used to see an image of Jesus standing at the foot of my bed. I would talk to him and hear him talk to me. I cannot remember what he said but I remember the wonderful feeling. My mom said that I would freak her out sometimes, especially if we went for some quiet time in church, when no one else was there. She said I would stare at a spot and start having a conversation. She said she really felt like I was hearing someone and responding to them. She asked who I was talking to and I would say, Jesus. I think we can all talk to Jesus or the Divine Energy we connect with if we try. I think we need to practice, just like they said in Dr. Strange, you don't become a great surgeon overnight, it takes practice and study and so does reconnecting to the Divine. Reconnecting because when we were young, we had it. Once we reconnect, we see those of the other realm. They are there to help us, we just have to listen.

In her book Physica, Hildegard commences with a section on Plants. I can't say that I agree with everything she says but I find it interesting. I think J.K. Rowling may have gotten many ideas for Harry Potter from her for Hildegard writes:

Mandrake (mandragora) is hot and a little bit watery... When mandrake is dug from the earth, it should be placed in a spring immediately, ... so that every evil and contrary humor is expelled from it, ...

She then goes on to poetically discuss the elements:

Air (aer) ...situated near the moon and the stars wet the heavenly bodies, just as terrestrial air enlivens and sets in motion the earth.

The Sea (mare) sends forth rivers ... Some rivers go out from the sea with a rapid motion, some with a gentle motion, and others by storms.

Earth (terra) is naturally cold and has many powers in it.

She discusses trees then Stones and follows with fish, animals, and metals.

CHAPTER 34

COUSIN TONY

Before my mom knew she was sick she told me that she had a dream. She was walking on the beach with Jesus, and she was carrying a lot of wood. Jesus told her to give it to him and he would carry it for her. He said the load was too heavy for her. When I look back now, I think that the wood was the burden of the stress she was having in dealing with the "stuff" my sister was going through. It was too much, and he was telling her she could pass to another realm and leave her body. My mom then said that she went into a stone cave and there were long shelves which held, what seemed like, bodies covered in white cloth. She decided to lay down and rest, it looked very comforting. Just as she was about to proceed, her cousin Tony appeared. Cousin Tony

Sofia

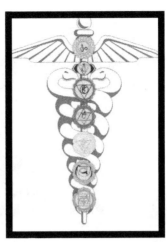

Chakras

Nico and Diana

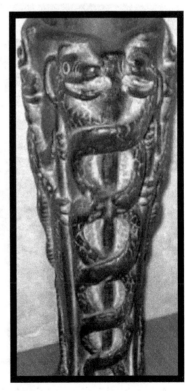

Dragon?

Bella Sofia and Nico

Nico and I at the Blacksmith Shop

had died a few years before and it was a huge blow to the Di Marco family. He was a kind and loving man, a strong force in the family and his loss was very difficult for all. Tony asked my mom if she was going to stay, she said she was thinking about it. She then said there were guests at the house, and she had to get back. Tony told her it was okay but to remember that when she was ready, he would be there for her. When my mom finished telling me her dream, I did not know she was sick, but I knew after that dream that something was happening. I remember, all I could say was, why didn't you give Jesus your load and why didn't you want to be with Tony. She smiled and we sat in silence.

I had never told anyone the story. Years later, my Uncle Hank was in the hospital, and I went to visit him. He told me that he had been in really bad shape, and he had a vision of his cousin Tony. He said that he saw a long tunnel that was dark and at the end was a beautiful light, as he got closer to the light, he saw that Tony was there. Tony smiled and greeted him and asked if he was staying. Hank said, "not now" and came back to his body. He said he felt that Tony had really been there and felt comforted from what he saw. He told me he believed Tony would be there for him and for the family.

Years after that my crazy and wonderful cousin Scott was fighting addiction and got into a car accident. I went to visit him in the hospital, and he told me that he had been pronounced dead but was back. He laughed and said, "and guess who was there to greet me?" "Who?" I asked, though I already knew. Uncle Tony, he said. I told Scott about my mom and Uncle Hank, and he said that Uncle Tony must be the Gate Keeper for the family. I think he was right.

I believe that we can see the other realms whenever we choose, if we practice, but I also believe that when something big happens in our lives, like illness and near death, we just open and see. We see and touch the other realms. We see past the physical body to the wonder beyond, or the wonder that is right here.

CHAPTER 35

THE ELDER FAIRY and DRAGONS

One night we watched the movie Heaven is for Real. It is a wonderful movie about a young boy who was near death, but not pronounced dead and went to heaven, saw Jesus, and returned. It is based on a true story. What struck me as amazing is how close minded we are as a species. The father of the young boy was a preacher who talked about heaven but did not believe his son, at first, and questioned him. Many others got angry that this was even being discussed. It was "crazy," they stated but the young child kept his faith and finally made some others see. In the book Proof of Heaven by Dr Eben Alexander, a neurosurgeon who did not believe in anything spiritual, especially heaven, tells his story. He became ill and went into a coma where he visited HEAVEN. He gives scientific evidence for the fact that in a coma the part of his brain that would create a dream state was not working so it had to be real. A skeptic, wishing to prove him wrong, said that some astronauts during training, when they were in the centrifuge, almost passed out and experienced a sort of near-death experience. Why do people fight this, why do they get angry and not want to listen and call people crazy, which you may call me after reading this book. Why did the skeptic not even consider that in this centrifuge the astronauts actually reached an altered state of reality or the other realm or heaven? Maybe it is a point where the mind opens and releases to .... something greater. Why are we so closed minded? We did it with Galileo, we did it with Newton and we are doing it again. As a species we get angry when something challenges us as opposed to seeking knowledge and coming to a logical conclusion.

I realized, in our culture, many people like stories but do not actually believe them. Why do we reject what people are sharing with us? Do we really believe in heaven? Do we really believe there is another place than this? A place where the star people came from? The Native Americans do, as do the Dogon and the Incas. If you go to other countries, you will find they believe in many different places and beings. In Iceland, over half of the population believes that elves live in the country and refuse to build roads in places that will disturb their homes. There are often elf sightings and according to Icelandic lore, these beings actually live in a parallel realm that is invisible to humans, though some with an open heart can see them, especially if "they" want to be seen.

In Iceland, Ireland, and Scotland they believe in fairies. Sir Arthur Conan Doyle (Sherlock Holmes author) even wrote a book on his belief in fairies, entitled, *The Coming of Fairies.* There is also the legend of the Elder Fairy who lives in the Elder Tree. She is said to be an old and wise woman. She represents beginnings and endings. She helps you remove, from your life, that which is unnecessary and draw into your life that which will benefit you. Do not take her branches, her fruit, or her flowers unless you ask permission first and only use that which is necessary or, it is said, she will curse you. So, ask first and only use what is necessary. She is not evil; she is just protective. She has a very strong union with Mother Earth and has powerful elemental magic. Many people love this "story" but do they actually believe it? If the Elder Fairy appeared to them, would they find an excuse for what she could be? The Elder Tree (Sambucus) has different varieties. The tree grows to about 13 feet in height and flowers in the spring with tiny white blossoms. In the late summer/early fall it has deep red berries. It is a magical tree. It is said that elves and fairies appear around the tree in the evening in the middle of summer. Use her energy for only the highest and the best healing purposes.

The Elder Fairy is a fairy of transformation, and her medicine is strong and will, indeed, transform. All parts are used, the leaves are used (externally only), as a poultice for inflammation and pain, the delicate flowers are used internally for sore throat and cough and externally for your skin. You can add them to a cleanser or a lotion. The berries are used to fight colds and flu. They decrease the chance of getting an illness and also shorten the time of the illness if you have it. (Recipe at end) The wood itself holds much magic. The Elder has the power to drive away evil. A wand made from the branches will send evil fleeing. You can make a flute from the appendages for they are hollow. Music played from them protects against spells, drives out evil and negativity. If you remember in Harry Potter the Elder wand was the most powerful wand that ever existed, J. K. Rowling did her research.

Now if you believe in Fairies, surely you believe in Dragons, I do. There is so much evidence that supports their existence. Prior to the 18th century Dragons were spoken of as fact, not fiction. Shakespeare wrote of Dragons; Hildegard wrote of Dragons. There are stories and images of Dragons around the world, Canada, US, Mexico, Iceland, Ireland, Italy, Egypt, China, Japan, and the list goes on. These are stories and images from long ago. Long ago when there was no mass communication. They were not copying each other. Do we really believe that all these people just thought up the same fantasy? It does not really make sense.

Years ago, we went to see an exhibit of the Terra Cotta Warriors and there was a small part of the exhibit that had a scene from their everyday village life, formed in little clay figures. As I looked at the scene, there was a woman cooking near a fire. I noticed that seated next to her was a tiny dragon. I did a double take at the description. It explained an "everyday scene in the life of the villagers". I thought, but there is a baby dragon there. Do people really believe that this whole exhibit is real, but they decided, just for fun, to throw in a bit of fantasy? Are we to believe that everything is real EXCEPT the baby dragon? There is also a dragon, at the same exhibit on top of a pottery bowl.

We find dragons in Norse Mythology, in Sumeria, in the Hindu

Rig Veda and even in the Bible. Look at this text from Job 41

Who can open the doors of his face? his teeth are terrible round about. His scales are his pride, shut up together as with a close seal. One is so near to another, that no air can come between them... Out of his mouth go burning lamps, and sparks of fire leap out. Out of his nostrils goeth smoke, as out of a seething pot or caldron. His breath kindleth coals, and a flame goeth out of his mouth. In his neck remaineth strength, and sorrow is turned into joy before him...When he raiseth up himself, the mighty are afraid: ...The arrow cannot make him flee: slingstones are turned with him into stubble. Darts are counted as stubble: he laugheth at the shaking of a spear....: he spreadeth sharp pointed things upon the mire.... Upon earth there is not his like, ...

What do you think? I think it sounds like a Dragon.

In May of 2017 in Alberta Canada a specimen of a preserved, mummified dinosaur went on exhibit. It was strange, there was only the outer shell and head preserved, they speculated on what could have happened to the rest but to me it made no sense. As I looked at it I saw a dragon. What if we open our minds, our thoughts? What if dragons existed, maybe this is one right here. Maybe their wings were more gelatinous in substance and dissolved so we don't find them. THINK.

CHAPTER 36

JEN JEN and CHAKRAS

Jen Jen is a wonderful young lady who came to us a few years back asking to work on our farm one or two mornings a week while she was in high school. She knew she wanted to be a VET and was seeking the experience of working with large animals. We were thrilled that someone wanted to help us and from the day she came to visit, with her mother, I knew I adored her. Once she started, it went from do you want to stay for breakfast, to do you want to stay for lunch, to do you want to stay for dinner, overnight, forever? In other words, she became our family, and we love her dearly. She is highly motivated, in every way, academics, farm work, but most of all in her heart. She is a wonderful loving soul. She has a way with animals and a peace about her that draws them to her. If an alpaca does not know you, they will not run up and greet you. They may stay away or sniff you, but it takes time. Jen Jen would stand near them and be still, her peace and her love for them drew them to her. I would turn around and they would be sniffing her and letting her touch them. One day we were sitting in the field and Maggie came up and sat next to us and put her head in Jen Jen's lap.

When we did the morning chores, Jen Jen worked hard and never complained. After our work was done, we would come down to the house and make a healthy shake and talk, often doing projects like needle felting and knitting. Jen Jen needle felted a fairy and a dragon and knit beautiful scarves. She became a vegetarian and embraced yoga and all the while we grew closer and closer. After she graduated from High School, she went to UVM in Vermont. We missed her very much, but she came to visit on her breaks and spent every Christmas eve and Christmas day with us. Diana would come on Christmas day. Our whole family was together. When Jen Jen graduated, we went to celebrate with her and I was so very proud of her for all of her honors. She worked so hard and was destined for wonderful things.

When it was time for her to choose a Veterinary School, she chose Glasgow in Scotland. I thought this was a perfect fit for her. It felt so, energetically, right. Every time she talked about Glasgow, I felt such good and positive energy, which I did not when she spoke of her other choices. I am so happy she wound up there. I know she will be a great Veterinarian and most of all I know she is an amazing young lady and I love her dearly.

Jen Jen shared a book with me, entitled, The Gene by Siddhartha Mukherjee. It is a very interesting book that discusses the scientists who hypothesized and researched the steps of revealing DNA. There is one part of the book where he describes how hemoglobin functions and how the "physical structure of the molecules enables the chemical nature, the chemical nature enables it's physiological function and it's physiology ultimately permits it's biological activity."(Mukherjee) He says this idea of the body being like a machine dates back to Aristotle, but it was actually much earlier than that for Aristotle's father was a physician who taught Aristotle. He then describes how medieval biology departed from the idea of the body as a machine-like organism and the belief that there was then the "conjuring up" of the idea of "vital forces and mystical fluids that were somehow unique to life......... invoking special forces or inventing mystical fluids to explain life was unnecessary." (Mukherjee)

Now on the one hand I love science and love to understand the workings of the body, the universe and all but if we do not also incorporate the vital force in us, then we are missing, well, the essence of life or really LIFE ITSELF. I thought of this as I was teaching my yoga and anatomy class. I was talking about the layers of muscles in the back and how each one functions in the various asanas. The human body is so amazing, when you think of all of the muscles and bones in our bodies and how they work. Then I thought, but if I were to only teach yoga like this, through anatomy, then my students would totally miss "yoga." It would be exercise, more like gym yoga, no deeper meaning. We must unite medicine, spirit, and yoga, we must never forget the vital forces. This brought me to describe nadis which carry life force energy, which is prana. These nadis are like tubes or channels that carry nutrients like blood and water around the body. Then there is the subtle body and the causal body and there we get into the "mystical" where the nadis are channels for cosmic energy, for vital life force energy.

The three most important nadis are the Ida, the Pingala and the Shushumna. The Shushumna runs up the center of the spine while the Ida and Pingala form a double helix structure around each chakra or energy center. Yes, double helix. Sound familiar? Like the structure of

DNA? The Ida starts and ends on the left and is the feminine energy, the moon energy. While the Pingala is the male energy and the sun. As I thought about this double helix I thought how perfectly science, yoga and our vital and mystical forces work together. To me it is impossible to leave out the magic of our vital force. It is funny to think that it took so very long for scientists to understand the double helix shape of DNA when it was right in front of them, well, if they were in India or studied yoga, it would have been.

Let's go a little further down the rabbit hole. The caduceus that was held by Mercury who was the messenger of the gods, It was two snakes in a double helix with a staff in the center. Now we traverse to one millennium prior where we see the Ningishzida (which means lord of the good tree). He was the Mesopotamian god of the underworld and is seen with the Ida-Pingala, Mercury and the Cadeuceus and DNA. (see above)

This energy of our chakras, our DNA, our Vital Force, is a central part of yoga, it is energy. Activating the Kundalini Energy, the sleeping serpent at the base of the spine, awakens you to who you were, who you really are, ONE WITH THE DIVINE. When it is activated, it moves from the Red Root Chakra at the base of the spine all the way out through the Crown Chakra which is above your head. Many human's chakras are blocked or stuck, especially in the higher chakras. We activate them through better living, through healthy living, through prayer and our connection to the divine and through meditation and yoga.

Here is a Chakra Balancing Meditation that may help you.

Lay on your back or sit comfortably as you picture each chakra. Place your hands just above your body and above that chakra and picture the light pulsing, then rotating clockwise. At first it may rotate the other way but give it time. When it moves clockwise and strengthens, wait until it is steady and strong and keep the motion with your hand. You will feel when it is time to move to the next chakra.

Start at the base of your spine, your coccyx bone area and picture a beautiful red light, as bright as the sun, radiating at the base of your spine. It is your Muladhara Chakra, your Red Root Chakra. It is your connection to Mother Earth. Picture this red sun shining with brilliance and energy. Now picture red roots of light coming out of the sun and going into Mother Earth, connecting you to that beautiful energy of the mountains, the oceans, the rivers, the trees, the animals, and the air. Feel that strength and power move up through the roots and into your Red Root Chakra.

When you feel it is time, move your hands an inch or two below your belly button and picture there an orange light, like the sun, vibrating and pulsing. This is your Swadisthana Chakra, your orange chakra. It is your reproductive system, and it is how you can help to balance your hormones. It is your creativity, in the arts and in life. Create your life with strength, healing, and Divine love.

When it is time to move up, go to your Solar Plexus. This is your Manipura Chakra, your Self chakra, your yellow chakra. It is how you see yourself and how the world sees you. See yourself as a being of light, as Divine. You have not made any MISS - TAKES, but rather, you have had lessons. Learn from them. Love yourself, not in a selfish, self-centered way but in a simple Divine way. Love yourself, that is when you can truly love others.

When you are ready, move up to the center of your chest, to your green, heart chakra, your Anahata. As you picture the green fiery sun in your chest, picture LOVE, pure LOVE and shine it in and out and all about. Flood yourself with love and let anger, fear, jealousy and doubt dissolve in the love.

Then move up to your Throat Chakra, it is a blue, fiery ball of light and is called your Vishuddha. Shine it strong. Remember your words have power so watch what you say. Speak through the highest and the best and ONLY ACCEPT speech that is of the highest and the best. Never let anyone speak to you unkindly. Tell them it is not acceptable.

When you feel it is time, move up to your third eye chakra, Your violet chakra, your Anahata. This relates to your pineal gland, your higher consciousness. Stay with this one for a while, it takes time.

Then move to your Crown Chakra, it is white (some see the white turn into gold, some see the gold above the white). It is above your head; it is called your Sahasrara. It is your connection to the Divine. Let the Divine flow through you, in you, with you. We must awaken the Serpent and let the energy flow from the root and earth to the crown, then to the Divine and back. Do this to find peace, prior to sleep and during meditation

CHAPTER 37

PERU

We just returned from a Pilgrimage to Peru. I say a Pilgrimage because we journeyed to places of great energy that, I believe, change you for life. The entire journey fell into place perfectly so one can only deduce that it was meant to be. My friend, Joyce had asked me, in March, if we could go to Peru before the end of this year. I thought that would not happen but could, perhaps, be a trip for the future but it remained on my mind. One day in May, I was walking out of my yoga class at Kent Prep School, I saw a sign on the notice board with alpacas, so of course, I read it. It was a service trip to Peru, in June, run by a friend and yoga student from the Kent Administration. I emailed and asked if she needed chaperones. No, she responded, but I could go with a Kent discount if I liked. I emailed back and told her, I had just really thrown it out there, for I could not go to Peru without Salvatore and Nico, Diana, and my friend Joyce. She said that, for some reason, there was not a lot of response this year and we could all attend. The next step was to find someone to stay with the dogs, especially Sofia, who was back to her normal self and doing great but still needed her daily herbs and care. My friend Sandee and her daughter Dolly came to my rescue and stayed at our house with their two pugs, Trixie and Pixie, a dog party for sure. Our other friends Peggy and Ron who help us with the alpacas, said they could take care of them. It was all happening so.... according to a Divine plan, except it wound up Joyce and Diana could not come.

As I began to research Peru on the internet I came upon a lecture by Freddy Silva. I was blown away and immediately got his book, *Common Wealth*, (a gift from Salvatore and Nico), which quickly became one of my favorites. I often ponder, as do many, what is Stonehenge? What were the pyramids used for? What are these sites all over the world and why are they so similar? Well, I found the answers in this book, so beautifully stated. They are places where the telluric energy is stronger, "navels of the earth," he calls them. Places we can go to "remember who we really are."

Stones, especially megalithic ones generate energy, they contain magnetite, which is found in veins where quartz formed. Magnetite is, of course magnetic so it will attract small amounts of iron. Silva uses the example of the iron shavings that you used to move around with a magnet underneath when you were a kid. Your body, your blood contains iron. Quartz, when struck, vibrates and the sound returns to the quartz and makes it continue to vibrate, like a singing bowl, sending healing sound and vibration to those surrounding it. When you are standing at a megalithic site you are surround by these stones. Surrounded by magnetite and quartz. You are in a small magnetic field, where electromagnetic energy is present. This affects the iron in your blood. It will also affect your brain which has magnetite in it. Birds, by the way, have magnetite in their beaks which is why they are so great with navigation and the magnetite in our brain helps us navigate to magnetic north. These stones that are now affecting our brains affect our pineal gland. The pineal gland is that little pinecone shaped gland in the center of our brain that is our third eye, our higher consciousness. It helps us to connect with the higher realms, the non-material. Silva says this actually raises the DMT count, so there is science behind this.

DMT is Dimethyltryptamine which occurs naturally in the brain in small amounts. It is also found in some animals and plants. It is a psychedelic, like the "green fairy." It opens you to experiences like being in a different reality or seeing beyond the normal physical realm. It was used in the 8th century in snuff and in ayahuasca ceremonies in Peru. It was later synthesized into hallucinogenic drugs that became popular in the 80's. But what was really happening here? Was the DMT actually bringing humans

beyond the physical to a different state? DMT is thought to be more present at the time of death or a near death experience. So, is the science just finding what is released in the physical to get us to the spirit realm?

In the 60's Ram Dass, the one who brought Krishna Das to his guru, partook in a study at Harvard with Timothy Leary to discover the effects of DMT. They were trying to view the TIBETAN BOOK OF THE DEAD as a psychedelic experience. At one point he even brought some LSD to his guru, Neem Karoli Baba. Baba could transport to any state he chose, for he was already "connected", but he decided to humor Ram Dass and take it. As Ram Dass looked on, he saw that there was no effect on Baba who smiled at him and said he knew what Ram Dass wanted him to experience but he could do that anytime he pleased because he was always connected to the higher realm, to the Divine. When Ram Dass completed his experiment he wrote:

"the thinking mechanism you have works with time- so time and space are the matrices against which you think. The predicament of dimensions which are not linear- not linear time or linear space- where here and now are both here, and now and then are both now- those are ones we can't think about."

Now the question is, can we reach those states as Neem Karoli Baba did by connecting to the Divine through meditation, yoga, and practice. Is it possible that those who partake of the drug are also opening themselves to realms which are not so good? I tend to think so. I have heard some friends who decided to try this talk about their experiences. Their "leader" told them all was great but to me they sounded quite scary and negative. If we use our tools, yoga, meditation, headstands, and sacred sites we get there, slower perhaps, but we do indeed get there. We get there through the highest and the best rather than just opening. This thought made me excited to do a headstand at all the sacred sites.

At the heart of every temple is water because water attracts the magnetism, this is why NASA looks for water when it is trying to find places of magnetism on the earth. This force holds the energy that will change you, open you, give you sacred knowledge and is therefore a sacred space. A space that connects the realms. The stones of these sacred spaces attract the energy, so it does not fluctuate, the stones anchor it. When we need to connect, we go to these sites where the essence of God comes into a mound or a perch where the falcon stands. Many temples in Egypt, including Edfu, Karnak and Luxor are presided over by Horus, the Falcon god, whose right eye represented the morning star, power and strength, and left eye was the moon, the evening star, healing. How were these energies able to be repeated in different areas of the world where there was no supposed connection? The same structures, the same presiding force? Why is it that images of dragons, snakes and serpents are often located at these sites where the telluric energy or key lines preside, like an X marking the location of the treasure? (Silva)

Before we left for Peru, I met with Mother Abbess David from the Abbey. Mother Abbess is a true light in the world. Her whole essence seems to smile and send warmth and deep love. When you are near her you feel it. She is connected to the earth like the mighty grandma oak tree with her deep roots. She has a quiet wisdom and strength about her that makes you feel safe when you are near her. Her father was born in Peru and was half Moche, which was pre-Inca and then the Moche tribe became the Inca. The Moche society was based on Agriculture, and they built canals and irrigation systems. They were outstanding metal workers who created beautiful headdresses and artwork. Their techniques were highly advanced and are still not understood. They created a copper alloy by hammering copper ingots into thin layers and then used some kind of electrochemical process to purify a very fine coating of gold or silver. They still do not know how the gold or silver was added to the copper, a theory is that they would dip the copper sheet into a boiling, aqueous solution of corrosive compounds which they found in the desert in the North. "Double, double toil and trouble," and we arrive at our alchemical result of a red colored gold alloy. Gold has an atomic number of 79 so there are 79 protons in the nucleus but the way the outer electrons are arranged gives gold its yellow color. The copper atom is smaller than the gold, so it changes the lattice structure of the gold and makes it stronger and gives it a reddish color. The art of the Moche is spectacular with a mystical quality to their work. As Mother Abbess spoke, I imagined her father's ancestors working as a community in the APU (mountains), taking a break to eat of the sacred coca plant. Feeling the energy and life of the land and all beings as one. She told me that he got the "opportunity" to come to America and did so. He wrote a little book about his life in the USA. I would have loved to have read a book about his life in Peru, a place where the material world is second to the magnificence of nature. Mother Abbess said that her father was "primitive" and expressed she did not mean it in a negative way. Primitive meaning, he was in touch with the animals, the earth, he could hear them speak, he could talk to them and would listen to them and the various forms of nature. I connected with that immediately for I am primitive. I hear the animals speak also, I hear the plants speak, I hear the wind speak. It made me think, what is our concept of happiness? Is it money, is it material? I don't mind hard work, but I don't do it to be rich and to me, it is more important to be one with all. The commandment of the Incas was DO NOT LIE, STEAL OR BE LAZY.

There is NO WRITTEN HISTORY of the Incas, so there is a lot that was handed down by word of mouth, some was written when the Spanish arrived and conquered them, and some is mere speculation. There were many tribes, that date back to before 10,000 B.C. They "guess" the Incas lived around 1400 AD and there were around 40,000 of them. They say they lived for around 100 years before they were conquered by the Spanish. They "guess" is a big statement because from there a lot does not make sense. They date the ruins of Machu Picchu and Sacsayhauman to this time and say they were built by the Emperor Pachacuti. Now that is a lot to construct in 100 years, but I will get to that shortly. The Inca's did not think of time as we do, it was more like Einstein's thoughts - Time was not linear to them, time was cyclical.

Inti, The Essence of the Sun, was their Spiritual Father, Pachacuti was his Demi-god, his executor on earth. Inti created the divine edict and Cuzco was the navel of the universe. Pachacuti and his son Topa were conquerors. The creator was Viracocha, he had caused the sun to emerge from Lake Titicaca, an area that had been inhabited by giants. Viracocha had created people and animals from clay and gave them customs. He then descended into the earth where they later emerged separately from caves, lakes and hills, with a magical golden staff that would tell them where to live. Manco Capa was Pachacuti's father and when he arrived in what is now Coricancha, in the center of Cuzco, he struck his golden staff into the earth and decided this was their place, their home and center. He later turned to stone and became a sacred object or Huacas. The leaders that followed had to resist the Chanca which were trying to invade Cuzco. Pachacuti, whose original name was Yupanqui, remained and stood his ground. At one point in the battle, he said that the stones themselves turned into men who helped him fight. Upon winning the battle he spread the stones around Cuzco as shrines. Yupanqui took the throne and was now called Pachacuti or "Earthshaker." He struck his brother's name from the dynastic kings list and probably other documents. It is important to note that in many other places around the world it is said that warriors turned to and from stone.

Although Pachacuti was considered a conqueror he did it in a most peaceful way, through the art of negotiation. It is said that he was visited by Inti, the sun god in a vision and shown what he would achieve. To honor Inti, he created Coricancha, which was laid out in the shape of a Puma, representing strength. Coricancha was the city of gold. The walls and doors were gold plated, there were golden statues and a golden garden with flowers made of gold and precious gems. The Spanish raided all the gold upon their arrival. Although Coricancha is dedicated to the sun god it has been thought that is was the temple of water due to signs that were discovered there. Coricancha, from above, looks like the sun with it's rays coming out from all around. Freddy Silva feels that Coricancha is the place of water. He tells of the large stone in the center, which is andesite, and is packed with quartz crystal and magnetite. The courtyard where the stone was the centerpiece would be flooded with water. The water would move towards the center stone and attract the magnetic energy to it for at the heart of every temple is water. In the Egyptian Building Texts, it states "the purified water that sanctifies the landing place of the god,' to create the sacred place to unite with the divine. Silva states that in the Temple of Edfu, in Egypt when you are leaving the main initiation chamber, it reads, in hieroglyphics, "we will continue building temples until people recognize they are the temple." Truly these places are divine gifts where humans can go to seek knowledge and, if open, can obtain it, bringing it back with him to be forever transformed.

When we went to visit Coricancha our tour guide brought us to a room which she told us was believed to be the place of sacrifice. There was a large stone table in the center and across the room was a sort of mouse hole. She said, the one to be sacrificed would be placed on the table and the blood would flow across the room and out the mouse hole. I thought of ABU GARAB, in Egypt, and felt this was incorrect. First due to the energy and feeling of the room, which was more healing than sacrificial, second because it did not make sense. There would have to be gallons of blood to be able to flow off of the table, move across a flat floor and go out the hole. As I was thinking this Nico asked the tour guide why they used "crappy stones" for the foundation and such perfect ones above. She did not understand the question. He said that the upper stones were perfect but the ones on the bottom and on the floor looked, well, "crappy".

She stated that she did not know. It suddenly occurred to me what Freddy Silva said about water. This was not a room of sacrifice; this was a room where an abundance of water flowed and had done damage to the bottom stones. Silva also states that the stones are much older that the "Incan Period" and that they probably date back to over 10,000 B.C. That brings me to another point, WATER. Cuzco's average yearly rainfall is about 22 inches. Connecticut receives about 50.3 inches of precipitation per year. We have a beautiful natural spring on the mountain where we live, which dries up in the summer. We also have a stream at the bottom of our hill that is flowing year-round but when the summer gets dry it reduces to about 1/4 of its usual size. Considering that Cuzco gets less than half of our rainfall and is at the top of a mountain and we are at the bottom of one, I found it quite mystical that water flows in abundance at all of the temples and sacred spaces. One of these sites is Tambo Machay, which is above Cuzco. It is a place where they worshiped water and used it to cleanse their being, to purify before expanding to reach the higher realms. It is said that if you drink the water there you will live forever. Live forever how, I asked. Live forever because you are spiritually opening so you know that the spirit is forever, so when you touch the divine realms, you KNOW what forever truly means?

At the top of the hill was a beautiful, small structure made with the usual "Incan stones" fit together perfectly and out of the center flowed a beautiful stream of water. I asked where the water came from. This was the highest spot at about 3,700 meters (over 11,000 feet) above sea level. No one knew, it just flowed, never stopping. I pondered the magic of these sites, the water, the energy. I asked Nico what he was feeling, and he told me he had been there in a past life. He was a guard of the temple. He told me there was a bridge that, long ago, crossed over the road right next to the fountain. We walked up the hill and saw where there seemed to be the remains of what was once a bridge exactly where Nico was describing.

We moved to the next site, which was Puca Pucaru, it was a small structure. Not much remained but the foundation. It was in eyesight of Tambu Machay. This was said to be a military site that was used to protect Cusco. It is next to the Inca Trail and legend states that relay runners would travel from there to Machu Picchu in one day to get a message to Pachacuti when he was there. It is about 112 km or 70 miles. Nico felt he had been there also as a guard and knew that if you were running you could make it, in a relay, to Machu Picchu, even though it took us 3 hours by train and was through steep mountain trails, but he felt it because he had done it, long ago in another time.

The next site had a tunnel like cave with a large, high, stone table. Of course, they said it was a sacrificial table, yes, another one. Nico felt that this was a courthouse. The water there was a stream that ran below. We also visited the salt mines, which were stunning, they looked like terraces of crystal. As we entered, Nico and I kept grabbing little chunks of salt and started popping them in our mouths, they were so yummy. Salvatore thought we were crazy. Near the entrance another guide showed us the stream coming out of the rocks which filled the salt mines making them harvestable. It was warm due to the salt and flowed ceaselessly. I asked where the water came from, they said that no one knows. For a dry area there was an amazing amount of unknown water magically appearing.

THE MAGIC OF MACHU PICCHU

The magic continued on the day we went to Machu Picchu. The ride is 3 hours from Cuzco, and it is spectacular. The roof of the train is glass so you can clearly see the living APU (mountains) and their various forms. They truly feel alive and fill you with an energy that is difficult to describe. I had brought *Common Wealth* to finish reading on the journey but the ride was so spectacular that I did not get any reading done. I did contemplate Silva's words in anticipation of the magic to come. Was this a country retreat for Pachacuti, as the tour guides state, or was it more? When Hiram Bingham III rediscovered it in 1911, it was overgrown, unknown to the outside world. Of course, no one knew how this place 2430 meters, (7970 feet) above sea level was built, so there was more speculation. Again, to me it made no sense. It seemed difficult for even the bus to make the journey up the mountain (I wanted to walk but due to our union with a school trip we had to move according to their plans). How could they carry these huge stones up and place them so carefully? Of course, the answer was, once again, that they probably used Llama skins and dragged them through the mud. Why? How? I tried to clear my mind of expectations for I did not know what to expect. When we got to the top and looked out over Machu Picchu, it felt as if I had stepped into another time and place. At first, I just took in the beauty of the site and let the feeling run over me.

We traversed farther up the mountain where there were two Llamas that they had brought up for the tourists. They were happily grazing, and I took this moment to execute my plan of doing a headstand on top of Machu Picchu to accentuate my already vibrating Pineal Gland and the Divine energy. I got into position and then heard a yell. It was a security guard telling me to stop. Are you kidding? I thought, but I laughed for it was done. It felt wonderful. As I got down from the headstand, I looked behind me as the guide described the area where the sun at the winter solstice moved between two pillars high above our site and shone into a round structure just below us. Near the pillars, above us, was a profile face. It was said that the tourists would not notice it, but those who knew it would not step on her head. I asked our guide about it, and she told me there was no face up there but one ahead. She showed us the profile of the face laying down but did not even look to see the face behind. I let it go. Here, again, water was in abundance, but the Urubamba River is far below. There were many canals and channels that were built, for the water to flow through so they could fill the site of Machu Picchu. We moved along to find a long bench or low table, I sat on it and the energy was very strong, I felt floaty.

The next area had two large stone bowls on the ground that were filled with water, called water mirrors. They were used to view the stars and the sun. When you walked around them the images of the sky were extraordinary. The clouds and the sun glistened in the water. It was beyond a normal reflection, it was magnificent. I could only image how beautiful it would be to stargaze here and see the night sky.

As we walked to the various areas which they called the "living quarters," all of the rock structures were placed together like a puzzle.

Some of the steps were made from one piece of stone that was carved. One temple was very different, it was smooth and could possibly be a natural formation. At the center of one temple was a smooth stone that was called the TEMPLE OF THE CONDOR. The natural giant stones were shaped like wings and on the ground were large rocks that made a triangular shape, headed by a tear drop and then a curved stone around the tip. They say it is a condor, the sacred bird which united earth and sky and showed them the ability to fly. To me I can see the wing idea with the large stones that are the wall behind, but the Condor did not really cut it for me. It seemed to be something else. Below the wings is a cave and tunnels, which you cannot go into. They say they found a mummy down there and bones.

Before we exited, we all sat to take our last look at Machu Picchu. My eyes fell upon the form of a giant dragon in the rocks. I wondered if it was just me. Was I wishing to find the Dragon that marked the telluric energy? I asked Salvatore if he saw it and he said he saw a dinosaur, Nico saw a horse. The curves in its spine pointed to the Temple of the Condor. I had never heard or read about this Dragon. Just in case you don't see it I did one with an outline with an arrow pointing to the Temple of the Condor. (See below) Since the tail was pointing to the Temple of the Condor, I went back to look at the photo I had taken from above (see below) to see if I could see the Dragon (we could not reenter from where we were). As I looked at the photo, I did not see the Dragon but rather above the wings of the supposed "Condor," was the head of a Falcon. As I looked closer, I saw the entire bird. Again, if you don't see it, I did one with an outline also.

Some call Machu Picchu THE FLYING CITY, perhaps these are two more reasons why. The story of the falcon appears in the legend of Manco Capac, Pachacuti's father. He was born of Viracocha, the creator. Manco Capac was said to have been accompanied by Inti, a falcon, who belonged to his ancestors. The falcon was his soul mate. The falcon was considered enchanted, an oracle and was sacred. As I stated earlier Sacsayhuaman is the "place of the satisfied falcon" or throne of the falcon, relating to Horus - The falcon god of Egypt. So, the Incas had a connection to the falcon as well. I realized there was much more to this temple than the tour guides were telling us or knew.

Once again, I was reminded of Abu Gorab, the perception of what it was thought to be and what it truly was. Was the Temple of the Condor really the Temple of the Falcon or the Temple of Horus and healing? Was it the site where there was the greatest electromagnetic energy? Had I found the X that marked the spot? Later in the week I looked up the references to the Dragon of Machu Picchu and the Falcon, but I found nothing. I kept searching, maybe it was a serpent or a Dinosaur. I found nothing. I finally sent an email to Freddy Silva, thinking he would not reply but, what the heck. To my surprise he replied right away and said he knew nothing of it. I sent him my photos. This all brought me back to Hatshepsut and the story of when she was given the royal title of "friend and consort of Horus" (the Falcon god) and here I was with the falcon image at Machu Picchu, sitting on a rock in the "place of the satisfied falcon," looking at the Dragon! Did I make a true discovery or rediscovery?

The other experience I had at Machu Picchu was an interesting

Falcon in the Rocks? plain and with my drawing on top.
Picture of actual Falcon below

Dragon at Machu
Picchu?
then with my drawing
over the picture

Jesus

Salvatore & I at Sacsayhuaman

Me doing a headstand at
Machu Picchu

Sacsayhuaman water damage at bottom

mystical vision in which I saw the upper peak Huayna Picchu and atop of the mountain stood a large being dressed in the native Incan manner. He had his hands uplifted and was looking down at Machu Picchu. I saw him as if he were right there, yet it was a different time, long ago. At this time the area upon which he looked was a jagged peak just as all the surrounding Apu were. With a wave of his hand or wand, the being lifted the top off of the Machu Picchu peak and broke the peak apart as it floated up in the air. I felt there were one or two more beings also present. The giant levitated stones were then gently floated down in perfect order to build the structures, all according to his command and plan. As I came out of this other realm, I looked around with "new eyes." This made sense, at least to me, but then a lot of strange things make sense to me. Every other mountain around Machu Picchu was a jagged, rough, mountain peak. As a matter of fact, every other mountain that we saw on our entire journey from Cusco and the surrounding area to Machu Picchu had been the same, but Machu Picchu was completely flat and not valley flat, uniquely flat. Think about it, how often do you see that? I thought about the city below, perhaps there had been an earthquake or something that knocked the top off but there were no signs of massive fallen debris. I expressed my vision to Salvatore, who looked around and said it really did look that way. You saw the picture in the beginning of this chapter. Now look at this photo with new eyes. Unless they had the biggest floating bulldozer you could image, that magically bulldozed the top and then carted the debris away, they could not level a mountain perfectly like this and have no debris leftover. What we have been told may not be so!

When we got down to the bottom of the mountain it felt like we had dropped into an entirely different world, and it was difficult to re-adjust. I don't think it was the altitude I think we were in two different realities that day.

SACSAYHUAMAN

Now regarding altitude sickness, Cuzco is higher that Machu Picchu so you would feel it more there. I was hoping to find some Uno de Gato (cat's claw) which is indigenous to Peru. It is a beautiful herb with a big yellow flower that has little spikes coming off the stem that look like cat's claws. The bark and root are great for altitude sickness, but I quickly discovered that the plant is found only in the jungles, which was not on our itinerary. In our area they used the coca plant for altitude sickness. I did not feel sick but did notice it when we walked up stairs or were hiking because we all got really winded. I had brought some Calc Carb 30c homeopathic and that helped a lot. I was afraid to try Coca because I know that it is a stimulant. Although it is what they make cocaine out of, it does not have that affect when drinking the tea. It is a sacred plant. The Incas used it to keep them going during a workday. I am very sensitive to any stimulants and cannot even drink a sip of coffee. Finally on the 5th day that we were there, Salvatore drank a cup of the tea and said it did not affect him at all, it was very mild, he does not drink coffee either, so I decided to try a cup. It was not anything like I thought, I barely felt any stimulus and it did help with the breathing while hiking around.

Finally, we made our trip to Sacsayhuaman, this was what I had been waiting for. We saw it the first day when we went to visit the large statue of Jesus that overlooks Cuzco but now, we were actually going there. Upon our arrival, I asked the tour guide if she would show us the upside-down staircase and she said "no." I asked why not, and she did not answer. She then proceeded to tell us that there were two ways to enter, either through the very dark cave that twists and turns (she stated like she was telling a ghost story) or up and over the top of the cave (she joyfully stated). We all decided to take the cave route, she walked over the top. As we walked through the cave there was no light whatsoever and you had no idea how long you would be in there. If you did not put your hand on your forehead, you would bump it on a rock. The walls were close around you. Part of the journey here is to face your fears before you get to the sacred space. To shed what should not be in your energy. I placed my hand on my forehead and took deep breaths and was feeling the darkness, letting it energetically take away what needed to go, when Salvatore suddenly turned on the light of his cell phone. All the students and Nico yelled at him, so he turned it off. It ruined the affect a bit, but we still had a way to go. When you came out into the full sunlight, it seemed brighter than before. I felt as if I had shed something. Nico wanted to run right back and do it again, but we told him to wait, there was plenty of time. He wound up doing it 7 times total which is very interesting considering the following. Silva explains in his book that THE FUNERARY TEXTS of Saqqara state, "Seven degrees of perfection enable passage from earth to heaven." He explains that the seven degrees are actual challenges the soul needs to encounter and move through before entering the other realm. The text states that there are many sacred temples in which you have to pass though, seven areas to "master oneself before crossing the threshold of each gate." Perhaps you also were to do it seven times like Nico did. This seemed to be the first threshold. Next, we walked across a huge courtyard, in the courtyard there was a man balancing his chakras, I felt a shift as I was crossing, was this another threshold?

We came to some rock thrones, which seemed to be the third threshold. We continued on a path and then the guide stopped and looked right at me and said, "ok, since you asked, here it is, the upside-down staircase." The explanation she gave for this was very different than all the other stories that were supposed to make sense. She said, "we cannot explain this, maybe it was built by aliens." Then she moved on. I stood there with my mouth hanging open. Had she really said that? Is this why it was not part of the tour? I stood underneath it and looked up at the perfection of the carving. Why upside down? Was this the fourth threshold? We caught up with the group after a while to encounter the biggest slide you ever saw, all natural, formed from the rocks. Perhaps the fifth. Then a smaller slide, the sixth.

There was yet another giant courtyard to cross (perhaps the seventh threshold before we arrived at the temple) and as we looked upon the lightning wall of the great temple we stopped. You could feel the energy, there was something else happening here. When the Conquistadors invaded Cuzco, a man named Pedro Cieza de Leon kept a chronicle of the events he observed. This was in 1549. He stated, "I asked the natives whether these edifices were built in the time of the

Inca. They laughed at the question affirming they were made a long time before the Inca...they heard from their forbearers that everything to be seen there appeared suddenly in the course of a single night." (Common Wealth). The same as the Codex Gigas. This one-night story is heard all around the world at various sites. On Easter Island the Moai Statues were said to have been built by an intention, word or thought. In Peru, Virachocha, used the spoken word, or a spell, if you will. Sacsayhuaman legends say it was constructed by sorcery. I thought of my vision.

As we got closer to the layers of lightning bolt stones, it became clearer than ever that this could not be man-made. The stones, (some 130 tons) fit together with such fine precision like a perfect jigsaw puzzle. I mentioned earlier when I worked for ABT that there was a scene in Romeo and Juliet for which we had 2 huge, two-ton angels, that hung from above. We needed special trucks for them, and they had to be lifted by crane, one at a time. That was just two tons. Now imagine 130. Not only the lifting and moving, let's say you could do that, but then how did you fit them together so perfectly without a space in between for a human hair? They were not just rectangles, they had various shapes and some of the stones even curved around corners. Salvatore said that even if you had a tool to scrape the stone you would have to take it out from the wall and shape it, then put it back in and see if you were getting closer to the right fit, then pull it out again and shape it, then repeat over and over. All this does not really seem possible.

The energy of these stones draws you to them. It is truly

amazing. At this point Nico decided to do his 7 rounds of running through the dark cave and many rounds of sliding down the rocks. The rest of the group went off and Salvatore and I were left alone with the magic stones of Sacsayhuaman. We just stared for the longest time. Then I did my headstands at various points near the lightning bolt shape. I was gently sliding into another realm. I wanted to do a healing for Sofia and my family, so Salvatore and I sat and began. I felt the strength of each being I was sending to, and I felt the healing fill them. It was very powerful. I felt like I was floating, and we continued to walk along the wall. We came to a flat stone that begged to be sat upon, so I did. I know that I can go "out there" easily but this was different, it was more like a DMT trip, that shoots you out of reality so fast you are scared that you will not return. I saw myself shooting away from the reality I knew and was not sure if I would come back. Everything was fuzzy, like I was in the clouds but then I was in the darkness of space with stars around me. It was very peaceful, very calm. Everything was beautiful. I remember saying, but I have my family there, I must return to them and after a bit of time I did. I felt that bit of time was maybe a minute or two, tops. I thought later, wow, why didn't you stay and experience more? Was it fear, I asked myself? I did not know.

I told Salvatore to sit on the rock and see what he felt, maybe it was just me. He sat down ready to cross his legs and then jumped off the rock saying "I can't! That thing is spinning so fast it's making me nauseous." Well, it wasn't just me. A few months later I was thinking about my experience, and I asked Salvatore how long I was out on the rock, or did I even seem out to him. He laughed and said, "over 20 minutes, for sure." 20 minutes? I could not believe it. He said he kept walking around and waiting for me. Until finally, the van to go back was leaving and he had to yell to snap me out of it. Apparently, that is when I said I had to go back to my family. I remember the feeling but not specifics. So where was I? I don't know. What was I doing? It was not until over a year later that I remembered, some of it.

Why do many insist that this was built by the Inca's when the Inca's laughed and said it was not? Why can't many accept that it may have been built in a single night? Why do they not tell you about the upside-down staircase? Because we like neat little answers that fit into our physical reality and anything that departs from that is pushed aside. Let's step into the light without preconceived ideas. I asked Salvatore for his take on it, and he said that he was feeling that this was not built by the Incas. He felt the Incas were afraid of it and that it was a place of the gods, akin to Mount Olympus. There are legends that are in accord with his sense. They say that Sacsayhuaman was the place where the heavenly deities dwelt in the physical world of matter. It felt like it. The energy there was truly incredible. I did not want to leave, but alas we finally had to.

We were staying at an albergue, which was a wonderful place, set up by an amazing woman named Roseo. Roseo had grown up in the Andes mountains about 2 hours outside of Cuzco. The town was very poor and there was no opportunity for an education. She knew that if these children lived in Cuzco, they could attend school because they were living in the city. They stayed with her during the week and traveled home to see their families on weekends. There were bedrooms, study rooms, playrooms and a dining area. It is a happy, healthy place and these kids are now getting a good education. She helps to motivate them in hopes that they will later attend a university. At one point she discovered GLOBAL AWARE, which is an organization that helps those in need. Global Aware sets up trips, like the one we did. The money you pay helps to finance the albergue and part of your trip is given in service.

Our service at the albergue was to paint the dining area which took two days and was fun. I grew close to Roseo, who was trying hard to continue her education, to grow and expand. I shared with her much of what I read in the book Mother Abbess David had let me read and a lot from *Common Wealth*. She shared many of her stories with me as well. I asked her about Shamans, since there seemed to be many self-proclaimed ones in America. Roseo said that they would not be considered real Shamans for to become a Shaman in Peru, you must be touched by "the light". It is not something YOU decide or only YOU know about. It chooses you and everyone knows it.

Roseo did many ceremonies with a local Shaman on a regular basis. These were ceremonies to connect the elements of Fire, Water, Air and Earth that did not entail drugs. I asked if the Shaman would come and do a ceremony for us at the albergue. She said yes and suggested the one which brought together the serpent and the condor through the strength of the Puma (the Shaman). It would help to nourish the earth making it fertile for plants to grow strong and animals to be healthy. I loved the idea. Being an herbalist, I asked if he could talk about the native herbs, many of which I was not familiar with. To my great delight, the day of the ceremony he had a table filled with herbs.

His wife was the herbalist and they described many of the local plants and their uses. He then asked if anyone wanted to come to see the herbs on the table. The kids from the albergue ran up and were so excited, they did not want to leave. He finally told them to be seated and went on to express that what he was showing them was being lost and forgotten, that they must carry on with these traditions. He said it was more important than their mathematical studies for they lived in the mountains far from a hospital or any doctors and this would be the only care that was available for them and their families. They must learn about this and keep it going, so it would never die. Roseo smiled and said he had done many ceremonies at the albergue but never brought or discussed herbs before. I knew now why I was guided to ask him to present this. It was not for me. It was for them.

He then took a cloth and started to add various treats to it and then let us all come up and pick 3 of the sacred coca leaves and place them inside the cloth. He said prayers and gave us some essential oils for our bodies while he burned the incense of Pal Santo. He then wrapped everything up in the cloth and we burned it to nourish Mother Earth, the smoke rising up to the sky. A truly wonderful experience. I also had the opportunity to share the herbal information that I did know with the Kent students. I found a nettle plant near the door of the dining area and each morning we would gather a bit and make tea while we discussed it's healing properties. At the end of our Peruvian journey, I felt like I had traveled beyond our realm, and we had all changed, TRANSFORMED. I came back different.

CHAPTER 38

FLEW BREW

On one of Diana's visits, we went to the liquor store to buy a bottle of wine to have with dinner. When we entered the store, they had a tasting of Yeigermeister -Jägermeister. "Yeigermeister," I asked, what is that? She laughed and said it was a hard liquor that years ago, was the drink of the guys who sleep on the streets in Manhattan but later became a hip drink for the Millennials. When we got home, I decided to look it up. Yeigermeister contains 56 herbs and spices and takes about a year to brew. It was originally used as a medicinal remedy. Only 16 of the ingredients are known, the others are secret. It contains –

Cinnamon bark which aids in digestion and helps with gas and bloating, is warming and a good source of Vitamin A, Calcium and Manganese. It helps to prevent osteoporosis, PMS and is good for your blood chi which relates to Anemia. It was considered to be precious and would be given to kings as a gift. The ancient Egyptians used it for embalming and witchcraft. It is great for your respiratory system. Cinnamon oil is antifungal and antibacterial.

Cloves are a wonderful anti-inflammatory and help with arthritic pain. They are also antiseptic and aid in getting rid of germs and helping to fight infection. If you have a tooth infection clove oil is an amazing healer.

Ginger root aids in digestion. It heals bloating, heartburn and nausea. It is a wonderful anti-inflammatory and is great for tendinitis, arthritis and rheumatoid arthritis. Ginger will keep your arteries clean. It works to heal colds and flu in that it is anti-viral.

Star Anise contains shikimic acid which is anti-viral, and the medication Tamiflu was produced from it. There is a big controversy now with Tamiflu, there are many deaths that were related to the medication which would, obviously not be present in the herb itself. Alone the shikimic acid did not do much but with quercetin added it did. This is something of importance. What our pharmaceutical community often does not note is that nature and natural things work in synergy. It is the whole plant not an element that heals. You may find what element is working in a certain way, but it needs the other elements of the plant to actually work well. It is the synergy that works to make the vitamins more potent. Star Anise is now being studied in relation to cancer, in that it reduces the cancer development of those exposed to carcinogens. It is also a wonderful antibiotic. We now have too many resistant bacterial strains due to the overuse of antibiotics and Star Anise is a great choice.

Chamomile is wonderful for your digestion and is very calming. It helps with cramps and IBS- irritable bowel syndrome.

Orange skins which are anti-fungal, anti-bacterial, help to fight cholesterol and are a wonderful source of Vitamin C, aiding in fighting colds and flu.

Licorice root is great for cough, it is also an anti-depressant, helps with hay fever, bronchitis, and heart health.

Saffron is for vascular health.

Lavender is for anxiety and inflammation. It helps to relax and calm you.

Rose hips are high in vitamin C, higher than 5 oranges and aid in it's absorption.

Poppy seeds are for cough and digestion.

The thought of a liquor that had been used as a remedy got me to investigating and I found that Chartreuse was brewed with over 100 herbs in abbeys as medicine and so was Benedictine Liquor. The Benedictine recipe is a big secret and is now a family-owned business. Supposedly only family members know the recipe. The Brandy contains 27 herbs and spices. Some of the ones known are:

Angelica - Angelica Archangelica - often called root of the Holy Ghost was an magical herb used by the pagans and was later said to be used as a connection to the Archangel Michael who appeared to a monk to inform him that angelica could help heal the plague. Now think of what I said about Von Daniken here. There are and have, indeed, been beings who helped humanity. The pagans wore angelica for protection against evil. Paracelsus (1493-1541) praised it as a "marvelous medicine." He was an alchemist and physician who brought chemistry into medicine. The whole plant was used. The roots, the stems, leaves and seeds were used for lung disorders, colds, flu and respiratory problems. It is useful for inflammation, nausea, cramps, gout and circulation. In studies it was found to contain calcium channel blockers in the heart which helps with angina, high blood pressure, arrhythmias and improves kidney function. It is a beautiful plant that grows to about 5 feet. I harvest it at our local farm where we get our summer vegetables. It grows near the river.

Hyssop-Hyssopus officinalis - is a holy herb used for cleansing sacred places, it's use was written about in the Old Testament, for cleansing rituals. It is a great expectorant and aids in pulmonary disease. It is antiviral, promotes sweating and is used as a poultice, externally, for inflammation.

Juniper-Juniper Communis - It is an evergreen conifer with grey/green needle like leaves. The berries are a blue/black and when dried look even more black. Juniper berries are the main ingredient in gin but it's medicinal use is probably the reason why it was preserved in alcohol. It is great for urinary infections, kidney and bladder disorders, joint pain and digestion. It was also important for protection against dark magic and spells. It was burned inside of the temples to remove bad spirits. It was bad luck to cut down a Juniper tree. It was planted near front doors, in ancient times, to keep witches away, obviously bad witches, but if the witch could correctly state the number of needles on the plant, then she could come through. The Native Americans used it in ceremonies to protect and bring good fortune.

Myrrh- Commiphora myrrha- The Myrrh trees, with its thorny branches and aromatic resin were brought by Hatshepsut, as I said earlier, to Egypt from the land of Punt. It was used to embalm the mummies and ensure that they would have a safe passage to the other world. It was also used as a powerful medicine in the Middle East to help calm a fever, ease stomach disorders and cure mouth and gum sores. It was given to the baby Jesus from The Magi because it was more valuable than gold and was also used to anoint the body of Jesus when he was alive and after he was crucified. It helps with thyroid function if you rub it on your thyroid. It is also anti-viral, anti-microbial and good for deep skin sores that are hard to heal.

Fir flower - Is from the Douglas Fir Tree. At the tip of the branch grows a spiky reddish flower. It is good for coughs and colds.

Lemon balm- Melissa Officinalis - This is the "make you happy" herb, just smell it and you will understand, it has a heart lifting lemony scent. Melissa comes from the Greek word for bee and bees love to hang around Lemon Balm. This is beautiful because we need bees, and we are losing them. If we don't have bees, we don't have us, for they are the ones who pollinate. Externally, it is used to sooth stings and bites. Internally it is used for depression, to help you sleep, to boost your memory and brain function. Thomas Jefferson grew it in his garden, and it was used to make jellies and jams.

Each bottle says D.O.M which stands for Deo Optimo Maximo - TO GOD, most good, most great.

I decided that I had to create my own, Judy Meister which later became known as Flew (FLU) Brew. A great remedy to take before bed when you are sick. It clears your sinuses, helps your digestion and aids in sleep. It is also yummy. (Recipe at end) Ironically, I share my Flew Brew with the Abbey and many of the nuns say it helps them. Ironic because brews were made in Abbeys and shared with the community, and this is the reverse. A note here about my sun brewing method. I brew my remedies in a glass jar in the sun. Many herbalists will tell you to make tinctures in a dark jar, heating it in the sun. I have always used glass jars and feel that the remedies get the energy of the sun this way. Every time I have contemplated this, I feel the energy of many past lifetimes and know I made it this way for many of those lives. In my brew I add other herbs listed below.

Mullein - Verbascum - is an amazing plant that not many people seem to know about. The huge leaves are fuzzy, and the Native American Indians used them to line their moccasins and keep their feet dry. They also used it for toilet paper. The leaves are one of the best things for your lungs, helping with cough, lung congestion and even lung cancer. The long stalk was dipped in lard and used as a torch and the pretty yellow flowers are used in oil for ear infections. For me personally I use my eczema spray for the ears, and it works for humans and animals, but just a drop around the outside edge of your ear, you don't want water in your ears and if there is a bad infection go to an ear doctor and never stick anything into your ear or you will stop the natural process of the removal of wax.

Spice Bush- Lindera Benzoin - Spice bush likes to grow near rivers and streams. I add the fruit (berries)
to my concoction. They are great for colds and internal parasites. The bark is used for coughs and colds and when added to your bath encourages sweating and helps ease body aches. It was used to treat Typhoid Fever.

Mugwart - Artemisia- Mugwart is easy to identify in that the front of the leaves are green and the back are a lovely silver. As they blow in the wind a wave of argent flows. There are over 200 species of Artemisia and Artemisia Vulgaris is Mugwart. Thujone is a component of this herb, which is also present in cypress, juniper, sage, oregano, and tansy. The homeopathic remedy Thuja is made from Thujone. Thuja homeopathically, is used to detox from vaccines and is great for warts. Artemisia Absinthium is the "green fairy," which is a spirit or liquor that was famous in the 18,19 and 20th centuries with artists like Pablo Picasso, Ernest Hemingway, and Edgar Allan Poe. Because of the thujone it was thought to be a dangerous hallucinogenic and psychedelic but later it was believed that this was not true. It was given to the troops to treat Malaria if they were in areas in which it was prevalent. It is anti-parasitic and is used in Ayurvedic Medicine for the heart and to boost energy. It is great externally as a poultice for insect bites, especially tick bites because it will actually clean the toxins out. It was one of the "NINE HERB CHARM," an Anglo-Saxon spell to treat poison and infection.

Wild Black Cherry Bark-Prunus Serotina - Has been used for centuries and the Native Americans made a syrup out of it to treat coughs. Prunus Serotina contains prunasin which soothes the muscles that line the bronchial tubes, calming the cough. It also calms the body as a sedative which also helps the cough. It is a great blood tonic and helps reduce headaches.

Schisandra Berry - Schisandra, as well as Ginseng, are both adaptogens - an herb that helps the body to ADAPT to stress, fighting stress and fatigue. Schisandra is great for your mental performance and your physical stamina. This herb is great for kidney and liver health, asthma, respiratory problems, bronchitis, and insomnia. It aids in calming the mind. Schisandra Berry use dates back 5,000 years in China, where legend states that the "divine farmer" Shen Nong who identified, catalogued, and tested hundreds of herbs was the first of his time, to make teas from the herbs.

Marshmallow Root - Althaea officinalis - This is not the same as the puffy white thing you put in hot chocolate, but rather a wonderful root that is sweet and grows near marshes. It is a mucilage, meaning, when you make a tea, it creates a slippery slime that is great to coat your throat, your stomach, and your urinary tract. A poultice can be used externally for inflammation.

Yarrow- Achillea millefolium (thousand leaves)- This beautiful flower was said to be used by Achilles to stop the bleeding in his soldiers during times of battle. It is great in accomplishing this task. There was one time when Sofia's toenail got pulled off and it was bleeding like crazy and would not stop with pressure. I thought we would have to get stitches but first I put my yarrow salve on it and wrapped it tightly. The bleeding stopped within ten minutes. Yarrow is a magical herb, and the stalks are used for prophecy in the I Ching and the Druids used them to foretell the weather. A tea made from the leaves is good for colds, lowers blood pressure, helps with hay fever, allergies, improves circulation and heals inflamed gums. The flowers are great in a poultice for your chest when you have a cough. I love these herbs and they are a great start if you are commencing an herbal journey.

CHAPTER 39

BELIEFS

I feel it is now the time and place to put together all the various parts and explain, fully, my beliefs and thoughts. I believe that one religion will look at another's religious history as myth but their own as fact. I do not. I think all of these texts are true. I think that Zeus and Thor existed but who and what they were is a lot to ponder. I can tell you that I believe that The Divine One, The Father, Our Father is a spiritual being, an energy so vast and beautiful that we are all part of and The Divine One is in us, and that we are all ONE. I believe that the father created different energies/beings that were also of spirit but one of them became arrogant and believed he was God. I believe that this being created matter and humans. I think other spiritual beings followed this being and they worked together. My theory is that they all got arrogant and self-centered, and they all wanted to be God, so they went off in different directions, some to Mars, some to other planets. From there they created their own species. Some got along with others, some did not. I think the stories in the Mahabharata and the

Ramayana tell us clearly that there were some serious weapons that were even beyond the technology we have now. There is even evidence of these weapons and their destructive remnants on earth. I think the gods thought they made a mistake and decided they would just wipe out mankind, they felt that they created them, and they were not supposed to be there anyway but, they did adore being worshipped, so did not fully complete the task. I do believe that Sophia and other energies of The Divine One helped man to remember from where and whence he came but many did not. Many humans got too attached to the matter. I think, this is why there is so much struggle and strife. Out true state of being is supposed to be spirit and the farther away from The Divine One and spirit we get the more we become like our creators.

I think at one point or more than one, the Divine One felt mankind was really heading in the wrong direction and manifested his form in the physical, as the Son, as Jesus. Out of the many gods and beings Jesus is one of the few who did not tell us to fight, to battle. He taught us to love one another. I know many of the other great beings were fighting monsters and demons that were bad and fighting for good, but Jesus did not fight. Jesus loved and taught healing and compassion. I think that many people get angry with Jesus because they don't like the ideas of the Old Testament and only certain people being chosen. They don't like the idea of the killing and fighting, neither do I, but I think Jesus was separate from that. I think that if we look at different religions we should see with new eyes. I think the Divine One came into form to many cultures and that is why there are different thoughts but are they different?

Most RELIGIOUS text were not written until years after they happened. They did not have the daily newspaper and the daily update. They passed these stories down by word of mouth and even through the Bards (story tellers). Then a scribe or scholar finally wrote them down. Many stories were passed down through poems and song. Stories about our families are told to us, not written, although it might be a good idea to write them.

Nico asked, how do we know that someone did not change them. I think that many of the stories are written, as is, and are not changed, but I do know that some major editing went on, especially with Constantine in Nicea. He threw out the texts that did not give HIM power, the ones that made mankind feel like they could directly be in contact with The Father. Those are the lost gospels that we found, that were not edited. There may even be more out there. I think so and these are surely unedited. Professor Velcheru Narayana Rao stated that, if we really look at stories from the past, it is only fiction that remains the same. True history, always, has many different versions because it was seen by many different people with their own perspective. There are said to be millions of versions of the Ramayana, the Epic Story of Sita and Ram. There are various versions of our news now. I think that if you truly want to KNOW you should read these texts for yourself, with an open mind so you can SEE. I think that if you were studying something that was of a scientific nature that you would, hopefully, try to get all of the evidence you could. I feel that we don't do this with religion, surely most do not even try to research a religion that is not their own, but most don't even research their own. This is why I love Eric Von Danikan. He thought for himself, from the time he was a boy. Then he read, he read the sacred texts from every religion, he visited the sacred sites. Now that is a study.

Nico asked me to explain Communion to him and I can only do so from MY THOUGHTS as "Other" as they may be. Jesus told us to remember him when we take bread and drink wine. He said, "This is my body, this is my blood." I think that Jesus meant that, to the ONE, The Father, all of the matter, the atoms, the molecules are indeed, matter. The spirit is the spirit. So, when Jesus became matter, he wanted us to remember that when you eat and drink, to remember matter, but the spirit is from where you came. As crazy as many may think these thoughts are, I did not come upon them lightly. I have spent a great deal of time studying religious text and I strive to be more like Von Daniken. I have meditated on this and contemplated much since I was young, and this is the only story that makes sense to me. If it does not to you that is your choice, I just hope you will take time to investigate various texts and see them with new sight. I recommend some great books to read at the end.

CHAPTER 40

A FAMILY OF WITCHES

Another time when Diana was here, she was talking about marking off on an application or document of what ethnicity you were, and she did not like that. "What does "other" even mean?", she asked. I smiled and told her that I always mark OTHER because I certainly feel that I am Other. She laughed and said she never thought about it that way. The reality is that I do feel OTHER, and I am happy about that. I am glad that I see the world in my "witchy way." I don't need to be accepted by all and fit in. As a matter of fact, I like to be different and alone, to an extent. I love being open to getting rid of the "shadows that are taller than our souls," and open to something daring and brave and "mystical."

As I wrote my story there was a lot I re-membered. I thought about my mom and her mom, who I never knew. Were they witches, was it in my family? I tried to recall things they said. I remember about a month after my grandma, on my dad's side, passed, I was thinking about her when the phone rang, and I went to pick it up. There was no caller ID in those days, just a phone on the wall with a dial. I heard a voice, and I handed the phone to my mom. She asked who it was. "Grandma," I said, matter of factly. She did not blink an eye, she just took the phone, listened, and then hung up after a minute.

Another time she was running around like crazy, doing, doing,

doing and I needed some of her attention. She often tried to remember the story of Lazarus' daughters in the New Testament. Mary was sitting with Jesus, enjoying his presence, while Martha was running around doing and going. Jesus told her to stop and enjoy the time she had with him. As my mom ran, the phone rang, she picked it up and it was someone who just kept repeating, Martha, Martha, Martha, in a way that reminded her of the story and so she stopped, and we spent the afternoon together. These things never seemed like a shock to her. After she passed, if things got hectic in the house all the lights would suddenly go out and we would all calm down, reset the breaker, and start anew. I knew it was her, so did my dad.

I then thought back to my grandma Marianna, was she a witch? I don't know but I remember one story my mom told me. Marianna was very ill and awoke to a vision of a lady, dressed in light blue and white robes. The lady was glowing and floating. She stared at my grandma who was then filled with light. The lady disappeared and my grandma coughed up a big black thing and was healed. When I was very young my grandpa died, my mom, her brother, my Uncle Freddy, and my Aunt Dee Dee decided to keep the house and rent it but after a while decided to sell it. I remember going up into the attic and opening a large, wooden chest. It was sitting right in the middle of the room. I don't remember what was in it, but I remember it was special and magical and I wanted it. I don't remember any more than that and I don't even know if it really happened or if it was a dream from that time, but it still fills me with a sense of strengthen and mystery when I recall it.

I remembered a time when our chicken had chicks and we went up and one was cold and dead. Nico told me to heal it. I told him it was dead, and I could not do that. He said I could, he knew I could, so I held that chick and gave it a healing for 15 minutes, I told Nico I was sorry, but the chick was gone. He said no, please, so I continued. Five minutes later that little chick chirped back to life. Nico knew.

I often thought of my mom's lineage as I thought of being a witch but then smiled as I remembered my dad's crystal ball, which he said was just for fun, and how her used to read us Edgar Allen Poe's, *The Raven*, especially, as a bedtime story. I think of how he knew how to get to the moon. I think all the weird scary stuff that happened when I was young was because there was negativity around me, not my parents for sure. Was there someone else in my family that was a bad witch and sent me negativity? I don't know, or actually I really do. Was it on purpose or through jealousy, anger? I don't know, or again, I do. What I do know is that I learned how to protect myself and not "OPEN" to all that is around. I know now that I am protected and how and when to "open" up. I know how to protect against evil and negativity. I feel safe now.

Am I descended from a line of witches? Is Nico a Wizard? That I know for sure. Am I a witch? Yes, I can truly say, yes and embrace it. No matter what part of my energy I am using or "which" Judy I am embracing, I am Witch Judy. So, as I close, I urge you to find time each day to shine your light and find yourself, to not fall into the earthly patterns and perhaps find your inner witch too.

Addendum

As I prepared this book for print, I had some important realizations. In a vision, a few years back, I was told that I was going to die 2 weeks after Nico's birthday obviously I did not. Following that I was guided to write this book, as I said in the beginning, so my family would know my thoughts. After completing the book, 2 weeks after Nico's birthday (but a few years after I was "told") I got hit with adrenal depletion, triggered by post-traumatic stress, from all I had been through. I went down for almost 8 months during which time many insights and visions came to me in one I was shown what happened on the rock in Peru. I was told that this state that I fell into would happen and I was given the choice to possibly live or not. I was told that this would be a difficult choice and that is why I did not remember it. I added a chapter at the end, after the recipes with this story and how it transformed me, once again.

RECIPES

DANDELION WINE

3 qtrs. dandelion flowers
1/2 cup elderberries
1/4 cup rosehips
1/2 cup violets
1 lb. raisins
1 gallon water
1 lbs. organic sugar
1 lemon
Champagne yeast

Boil water and put into a large glass container add the dandelions, cover and leave for 2 days. Stirring daily. Day 2 bring to a boil with the sugar and the lemon rinds and rose hips. Remove from flame and put it back in your container. Add the juice from the lemons and violets cool and add 1 packet champagne yeast. After cool cover and leave for 3 days. Day 3 strain and put into a fermentation bottle with a fermentation cork and let stand until all bubble are gone, may be weeks. Cork and store in a cool dry place for 6 months. Then enjoy.

See, so much from a so-called weed.

DANDELION SUMMER COOLER

In a blender put 3/4 cup of seltzer water
1/4 cup of grapefruit juice
1/8 cup chopped, fresh, dandelion leaves
2 tablespoons agave
1 tablespoon almond butter
1 handful goji berries
1 large ice cube
Blend and enjoy

NUTRITIONAL BOOST
1/4 tsp, crushed fresh dandelion root
1 pinch nutritional yeast
1/4 tsp master blaster pro biotics
1 pinch nettle
2 drops flower essence
1/4 tsp honey

PAIN SALVE

1.5 cups Castor Oil
1 cup Organic Safflower Oil
1/4 cup fresh chopped ginger
1/4 cup ground cayenne
1/4 cup chopped lavender, leaves and flowers
2 large, fresh burdock leaves
1/2 cup of beeswax balls

Bring to a low simmer for 10 minutes. Turn off heat and let sit for 10 more minutes
Pour into a strainer covered with cheese cloth over a funnel and funnel into jars to harden and store. If it is too thick reheat.

FLOWER ESSENCE RECIPE

*On a sunny day find a flower that is waving and saying "pick me," then
ask if you may and feel the
response. Get a large glass bowl and fill it with water. Place your flowers
face down in the water until the whole top of the bowl is filled with
flowers and you don't see much water. Sit the bowl outside, in direct
sunlight for 3 - 4 hours. Say a prayer of intention over the flowers and
ask them to send their healing energy force into the remedy to help
those in need.
I like the following,*

*Dear gift of the earth, I thank you for your energy and your healing, I
know your power will infuse this water with healing energy. Dear sun,
"I thank thee for shining now so bright, for by your your gracious,
golden, glittering gleams" (a little Shakespeare- Mid Summer Night's
dream tribute)*
*After 3- 4 hours strain, measure the amount of flower water you have
and add the same amount of brandy to it and put it in a dark, glass
container and label it with the name of the flower, date it was bottled
and the phase of the moon. Store. This is called the Mother. When you
want to make a bottle for personal use, get a 1 oz. dropper bottle, then
place a dropper full of the Mother that you need into the dosing bottle,
shake and take 1 dropper full of the dosage bottle as needed.*

NETTLE TEA INFUSION

*In a 1-quart jar
place 1 oz of fresh nettle, you can use dry, if you don't have fresh
As I said before you don't boil leaves, pour boiled water over them.
Fill the jar and let it sit for 5 hours (you can add honey and lemon to taste)
After 5 hours, strain, refrigerate and drink.*

NETTLE PESTO
*in food processor place
1 cup of fresh nettle packed tight in the measuring cup (harvest with gloves)
1/4 cup extra virgin olive oil
1 handful pistachio nuts
2 cloves garlic
1/8 cup vegan parmesano or vegetarian parmesano cheese
blend until pureed, keep refrigerated*

MYRRH TOOTHPASTE
*1/4 cup baking soda
1/8 cup ground myrrh powder
1 tablespoon apple cider vinegar*

When adding the vinegar keep in mind that it will make the baking soda bubble up, like when you were little and did volcano experiments but just stir, wait a minute. Let it settle then put it into a glass jar.

PINE-WILLOW TEA

Look on your Willow Tree for those small shoots growing out of the lower trunk of the tree. Peel a few off and then peel the bark off and chop or cut with scissors. Boil 1 quart of water then turn down the heat to a simmer, add your chopped shoots and leave for 15 minutes. Gather your pine needles, the ones that said it was ok to use them, thank them and, cut off a small branch and place the whole branch (about 5 inches long) into the water with the Willow Bark that is now turned off. Let steep for 10 minutes, you can drink straight or add a honey.

FLEW BREW

This remedy should be brewed in the sun for at least 6 months.
Fill a gallon glass jar with a wide mouth with Brandy and add
1/2 cup of fresh chopped ginger
4 cinnamon sticks
1/4 cup cloves
1/2 cup nettle
1/8 cup sage
1/8 cup of each of the following herbs
angelica, star anise ,juniper, rosehip, lavender
and schisandra berry
add a pinch of spice bush
peel of one lemon
peel of 1/2 orange
1 heaping tablespoon elderberry powder
1/4 cup chopped wild cherry bark
1/4 cup chopped mullein
1 tsp star of Bethlehem essence
1 1/2 cups organic raw sugar

Stir well daily and set it sunlight, then stir daily for 2 weeks, then 2 times a week for two months than once a month until use. I don't strain this until I drink it because it will just get stronger and stronger.

WARMING WINTER BREW
bring 1 cup of almond, coconut, or hemp milk to a simmer
add 1 tiny pinch of black pepper
1/2 tsp cardamom
1 slice of fresh ginger
1 tsp cinnamon
1 tablespoon honey or agave
turn to a low heat for 5 minutes, then enjoy

SUMMER ICED TEA
Boil 1 quart of water and turn off heat
Add one ounce of fresh lemon balm
one ounce of fresh mint
one ounce of nettle
Honey or agave, lemon to taste

LIVER CLEANSE TONIC
In a 32 oz glass jar place
1/2 cup chopped Yellow Dock Root
1/2 cup chopped Dandelion Root
1/2 cup chopped Burdock Root
1 tsp flower essence of Star of Bethlehem and any other essences you need.
Cover up to 1/2 of the jar with grain alcohol and the rest with water.
Shake vigorously and place in the sun. Shake daily for at least 2 months before straining and use.

FIZZY BATH BOMBS
3/4 cup Baking Soda
1/4 cup Arrow Root Powder
2 Tablespoons Himalayan or Peruvian Salt
1/2 cup Epsom Salt
115 grams melted coconut oil
mix well
add 3/4 cup citric acid and essential oils to your liking
Mix well and form into balls
Stir and then press tightly with hands into balls, if they don't stick well
add a little more coconut oil, lay on wax paper and dry for about 1 hour,
store in a glass jar.

ELDER SYRUP

1/2 cup dried elder berries
1 1/2 cup water
Bring to a boil and then turn down to a high simmer for 30 minutes.
Stir and mash the berries as much as possible, they are really hard so
they
don't mash too much. Add 1/2 cup of organic sugar and stir.
Turn heat off and keep stirring then let sit for 5 minutes.
Strain berries and add 1/2 cup of brandy.
Store in Fridge.

After completing this book, I had a fall, a big fall. My adrenals were so low that I was on the ground for months and later rolled around on a skateboard to get from room to room in my house. For the first few months I did not know what was wrong with me and got misdiagnosed, my heart raced out of my chest for weeks with no respite, my blood pressure went up and down. I was weak and very ill. I did not know if I was dying or if I would be able to walk again. Then I found the right person, or I should say, Salvatore reminded me of the right person, and I healed. I decided to leave my book as is and add this chapter on with additional information about my journey. As I re-read my book during this time, I saw the trauma I had been through, and I saw how it got to me. I saw my love for herbs and how it had helped me but I also discovered the importance of studying the body through biochemistry and the functions of the adrenals, adrenaline, noradrenaline and more. I realized that many doctors, often, have no clue what is really wrong with us. I had doctors read my blood work and tell me I was fine only to have one doctor read it and give me a thorough diagnosis and cure me. That was Dr. Dulin, a great nutritionist that I had been to years earlier. He for-saw this but at that time I stuck to part of his diet and the supplements for a year then went off of it. My journey and Dr. Dulin inspired me to get my Masters in nutrition, which changed my life. I had to change my diet and what I had thought was healthy and embrace a whole new world of my biochemistry. It was hard but with his guidance I got through and was healed. I am now writing a book about eating and living healthy and my Lyme study in detail. I hope you enjoyed Witch Judy and will continue with me on my next adventure.

Recommended reading: Erich Von Daniken, Freddy Silva, Vrinda Sheth

CPSIA information can be obtained
at www.ICGtesting.com
Printed in the USA
LVHW010938160921
697948LV00007B/177

9 781006 597336